I purchased this book while staying at "Above Tide" - the

June 7/8 2004

Deep Currents

Roderick and Ann Haig-Brown

VALERIE HAIG-BROWN

Foreword by Steve Raymond

ORCA BOOK PUBLISHERS

Canadian Cataloguing in Publication Data
Haig-Brown, Valerie.
Deep currents

Includes bibliographical references and index.
ISBN 1-55143-108-4

1. Haig-Brown, Roderick L., 1908–1976–Biography. 2. Haig-Brown, Ann. 3. Authors, Canadian (English)—20th century—Biography. 4. Conservationists—Canada—Biography. I. Title.

PS8515.A3Z7 1997 C818'.5203 C97-910425-4 PR9199.3.H29H29 1997

Library of Congress Catalog Card Number: 97-68868

Orca Book Publishers gratefully acknowledges the support of our publishing programs provided by the following agencies: the Department of Canadian Heritage, The Canada Council for the Arts, and the British Columbia Ministry of Small Business, Tourism and Culture.

Cover design by Christine Toller
Interior photographs from the Haig-Brown family collection, except where noted.
Printed and bound in Canada

Orca Book Publishers	Orca Book Publishers
PO Box 5626, Station B	PO Box 468
Victoria, BC Canada	Custer, WA USA
V8R 6S4	98240-0468

97 98 99 5 4 3 2 1

Contents

Acknowledgements

To my father for the diaries and notebooks he kept, mainly between 1925 and 1935. To my mother and father for writing so frequently and well to each other, and for keeping the letters over the years of their engagement and marriage. To my grandmothers for keeping the letters my mother and father wrote them; to my brother Alan for keeping his; to Thor Peterson for keeping mine to him; and to Edward Dunn and the Dunn family, with Mary Anne Ryan, who gave me access to my parents' letters in the E.B. Dunn Historic Garden Trust's files.

To Robert Cave, for his masterful bibliography which helped me keep a complicated body of work in order and properly dated. To George Brandak, who sees to the Haig-Brown papers in Special Collections at the University of British Columbia and always makes me welcome there.

To my partner John Russell, who got me started and stayed with me all the way; to my brother, Alan, my sisters, Mary and Celia, and daughters, Ann and Charlotte, who plodded through early versions and urged me to keep going; to the good friends who also encouraged me; and to Bruce Morrison who made me think some more when I thought I was done. To Frank Amato who had faith from the beginning. And finally to Bob Tyrrell and the people at Orca who made this book real.

Foreword

Most biographies have only a single subject; this one has two. Yet for Roderick and Ann Haig-Brown, the subjects here, it could not have been otherwise. Their devotion to one another was complete and they functioned always as a team, with the accomplishments of one due to the understanding and support of the other. And what marvelous things they accomplished!

Roderick, or "Roddy" as he was known to his friends (and is called here), was born in England, Ann in the United States, and together they made British Columbia their home. Few immigrant couples ever did more for their adopted land. Roddy eventually won fame as one of Canada's greatest authors, but his literary efforts were only the most visible of many achievements by this extraordinary pair. And now we have this candid portrait of their lives, skillfully and lovingly crafted by their eldest daughter, Valerie.

"If ever there was a romance made from books ... this was it," Valerie writes of her parents. "The lovers were introduced in a bookstore, their early letters are mainly about books ... and books, writing and reading them, were the constant theme of their lives."

Roddy is best remembered for his books about fish (*Silver*, *Return to the River*) and fishing (*The Western Angler*, *A River Never Sleeps*, *Fisherman's Winter*, *Fisherman's Spring*, *Fisherman's Summer*, *Fisherman's Fall*, *A Primer of Fly Fishing*), which made him perhaps the most revered angling writer since Izaak Walton. But he also wrote adult fiction (*Timber*, *On the Highest Hill*), juvenile fiction (*Starbuck Valley Winter*, *Saltwater Summer*), and non-fiction books on a wide range of subjects, including his family's life on their Vancouver Island farm (*Measure of the Year*) and British Columbia's great wealth of natural resources (*The Living Land*). His writing was notable both for its logic and its lyricism, qualities that helped establish his reputation as one of North America's most distinguished men of letters.

Yet writing was only one of many endeavors for Roddy. At various times he was also a carpenter, gardener, magistrate, army officer, radio broadcaster, conservationist and university chancellor.

Such a wide range of accomplishments shows evidence of a superior intellect, but Ann was every bit his intellectual equal. In addition to her traditional role as homemaker and mother, she was an activist and leader in community and church affairs, a teacher, and a librarian. She raised four children of her own and yet still somehow managed to find the time and energy to care for other children and provide shelter for abused women. Deeply interested in Renaissance art and architecture, she took on the study of Italian late in life and became fluent in the language. And because Roddy wrote in longhand and Ann was an excellent typist, she typed the manuscripts for most of his books — sometimes twice, because there were no copy machines in those days!

Roddy and Ann settled in Campbell River, B.C., during the 1930s, on the edge of what was then still a wilderness. At first, they cut their own firewood, grew their own vegetables, relied on a shaky "Rube Goldberg" water system, augmented their diet with fish and game, and sold farm-raised produce to supplement Roddy's unpredictable income as a writer.

In the process they developed a deep love and respect for nature that is an inevitable by-product from living close to it and being largely self-reliant. It was a type of life that has almost vanished from the modern scene, and although it undoubtedly had hard moments — some are detailed in this book — it seems in retrospect to have been an enviable way to live. Surely it accounts for much of the feeling of reverence toward nature expressed so vividly in all of Roddy's books.

Roddy and Ann worked hard to help the young community in which they lived, raising funds for a host of public projects and serving repeatedly on various local boards and commissions. As their stature grew in the eyes of their fellow citizens they were called to serve in posts of even greater importance, finally culminating in Roddy's election as university chancellor and his appointment to the Pacific Salmon Fisheries Commission.

For the most part, Valerie wisely lets her parents tell this story in their own words. Both are prolific letter writers, and their thoughts and feelings are well expressed in these missives, which also provide an amazingly detailed record of their daily lives. The letters reveal a man and woman who not only loved each other deeply but also relied on one another for emotional support and intellectual stimulation. Theirs indeed was a relationship with many deep currents, as so aptly indicated by the title of this book.

Yet not all the words here are Roddy's and Ann's. Valerie also weighs in with many small things remembered, such as "the whispering sound of my father's corduroy trousers as he strode along the trail" or the scent of blooming honeysuckle on the porch of the Campbell River house in June. These touches add a warmth and immediacy lacking in most biographies.

Since books were "the constant theme of their lives," it seems only fitting that the lives of Roddy and Ann Haig-Brown are now preserved and celebrated in the pages of this one. Surely there could be no higher tribute to these remarkable people who led such full, interesting and productive lives.

It was my privilege to have known them; I only wish I had known them better. But now, after reading this book, I feel that I do. And so will you.

Steve Raymond

Introduction

When they married in 1934, Roderick and Ann Haig-Brown settled on the east coast of British Columbia's Vancouver Island for what they thought might be a few years. They were typical of many Canadians in that they were immigrants. Roderick had come from England and Ann from Seattle, Washington. Soon the tiny village of Campbell River began to grow on them and they grew with it. So they stayed, raising their four children on the twenty acres they bought shortly after their arrival.

In many ways the Haig-Browns were also typical of any couple living on a small farm on the green and fertile coast of B.C. in those years. They worried over money, the weather, cows, chickens and children, not necessarily in that order. In many other ways, however, they were not at all typical. Roderick became an internationally respected writer, best known in fly-fishing circles because many of his books were ostensibly about that subject. He was appointed magistrate and, later, judge of the provincial court. Very much before it was common, Roderick was an avid conservationist. Ann was always heavily involved in church and community, both on a personal basis and through organizations. Later she became a teacher and a librarian. But perhaps the real story of this book is in the life they lived together, for theirs was a true partnership and a great and lasting romance.

It is Roderick's reputation as a writer and conservationist that keeps their memories alive and will no doubt continue to do so for many years. Above Tide, their house beside the Campbell River, where they lived almost the whole of their lives together, is now a British Columbia Heritage Property, mainly because of Roderick's reputation, but will serve to remind people of both their individual and collective contributions to their community for generations to come. Noted literary critic, and Haig-Brown friend and admirer, George Woodcock, writing in 1977, just after Roderick's death, said:

> *... he has been for thirty years one of our best essayists, yet his widest repute has developed not among writers, who should have responded naturally to his mastery of a difficult prose form, but among outdoorsmen. Yet I am sure many readers sensed the artistry of Haig-Brown's prose, and that his success among them was due very largely to his literary quality, to his extraordinary power of making one experience not only the feel and smell and look of the natural*

> *environment but also the sheer excitement the angler feels when he has made a catch with proper skill, using his wits against an adversary he respects and, in a strange, oblique way, loves.*

Woodcock's essay on Haig-Brown concludes: "... he was not only a good writer; he was also that much rarer kind of being, a man made wise by the patient observation of nature and of life."

A lot of Roderick's observation of life occurred in his capacity as magistrate for the town he lived in. If patience is a virtue for a writer or a fly-fisherman, it is even more so for a judge. The job is to sit and listen carefully and patiently, and it is as a wise and patient judge that many people in Campbell River knew him best. In judicial circles, his reputation for wisdom went well beyond Campbell River.

In contrast, and this may have had something to do with the success of their union, Ann was intellectually brilliant, lively, and outgoing. She also understood Roderick's needs as a person and a writer, and met them and more. At the same time, as a woman somewhat ahead of her time, she made her own life in the community and as a librarian.

As their eldest daughter and Roderick's literary executor, I have spent a couple of decades on the receiving end of a lot of questions about, and perceptions of, my parents. Over this time I have gradually grown to feel that I have a story to tell – one that can give readers a greater understanding of my parents.

Deep Currents is obviously and of necessity a very personal biography; it is my story of my parents and our family life. But it must be remembered that I have three siblings, and each would tell a story different from my own. For much of this story I have relied on diaries and a great many letters that we have kept in the family – when your father's papers, your family house and quite a bit of your childhood are already available to the public, it is nice to keep something for yourselves. Those diaries and letters are very much the heart of this book; they provide a sound basis for the chronology and many of the facts of my parents lives. They also provide an insight not generally allowed a child into her parents' thoughts and emotions. My own experience of life in our family is part of this book, too, because it was a lot of fun, in spite of the hard places of growing up, and because it sheds further light on the lives of two people who were interesting any way you look at them.

I did not set out to write a romance, although we always knew our mother and father were very much in love. It was only in the course of moving from the basic facts I set out to convey to the feelings expressed in their letters that it became obvious to me that I was writing a love story. This is a tale of a great writer, a great teacher and a great romance.

.1. Roddy (1908 – 1932)

My father, Roderick Langmere Haig-Brown, was born on February 21, 1908, in Lancing, Sussex, England. His parents were Alan Roderick Haig-Brown and Violet Mary Pope. They had met when Alan was tutor to Violet's younger brothers (she had eleven, and three sisters). When his son was born, Alan was a master at Lancing College and a prolific writer. He had published a book of sonnets and was writing articles on various aspects of sport. He was one of the last great amateur rugby football players and had played for Tottenham Hotspur. He was also a fine shot and fly fisherman. The family lived at Stratton Cottage, Shoreham-by-Sea. Roderick was baptized on March 25, in Lancing College Chapel; his godfathers were General Robert Baden-Powell, founder of the Boy Scout movement, and his uncle, Harold Haig-Brown.

The family spent the summer with Roddy's maternal grandparents, Alfred and Elizabeth Pope at Wrackleford, their country house near Dorchester, as Roddy would almost every summer of his life in England. His grandfather Alfred, with his father and brothers, had bought into a brewery founded by Sarah Eldridge, and eventually gained control of the firm known still as Eldridge, Pope & Co. There are pubs all over Dorset with the EP insignia carved into the facade. Christmas at South Court, Alfred's house in Dorchester (now a school), was also an annual custom, although Roddy's father often went to shoot with friends in Norfolk instead. The journeys from Shoreham to Dorchester were usually punctuated with a stop at 19 Tite Street in London to see his paternal grandmother Annie Marion (Roswell) Haig-Brown.

His mother notes, in a brief paragraph she wrote about each of his first five years, that when he was a year and a half old, he "fell into the river at Wrackleford and was rescued by Mummie and Auntie Hilda (none the worse)." Is this evidence of an early fascination with flowing water? On December 14, 1910, Roddy's sister Joan Marion was born, and on May 31, 1913, Valerie Violet followed. In that same year Alan published *My Game Book*, which is dedicated to his young son.

In 1914, when the First World War began, Alan stayed on at Lancing College, where he was commander of the Officers' Training Corps and lectured, chiefly on musketry, to the men of the infantry brigades training at Shoreham Camp. He also wrote *The O.T.C. and the Great War*, which was published the following year. In December of 1915, Alan went on active service as second in command of a service battalion of the Middlesex Regiment and was sent to France. The commander of the battalion was killed in September 1916 and Alan took over. He was awarded the companionship of the Distinguished Service Order in June of 1917. That fall he spent a few weeks on leave in England and then returned to the front. In March of 1918, he was killed in action in France near Bapaume.

Alan's death would have been devastating to Violet, a gentle, quiet woman who adored her handsome husband, but she was one among many who were widowed in that tragic war that cost so very many lives, and she had to cope. The little family went to live in Oxford at 15 Banbury Road. Years later, Roddy recalled, "Things weren't going along too badly when my grandmother died [1920]. Well, the family — that is, my mother's father's — was an organizing family ... and they decided that the only possibility was for my mother to go down and live with my grandfather, and look after him, and this would be a nice break — free lodging, and the kids would be there, and so on, and this is exactly what happened." It was here that Roddy's hunting and fishing days really got started because his grandfather's country estate, Wrackleford, had "about 3000 acres of woods, meadows and farmland and about ten miles of pretty good trout stream" along the Frome in Dorset.

Roddy's formal education began at day school in Shoreham in 1914 and continued at Southey Hall School in Worthing. In 1918, he entered Twyford Grammar School near Winchester, where some of his uncles had also been, as a boarder — the norm for many little English boys of his class even now. The headmaster of Twyford at the time was known to be a particularly severe disciplinarian — boys might be caned for not having the right answer to a question. This atmosphere may have started Roddy on his somewhat defiant course vis-à-vis school authorities. He had probably already begun to develop the sense of fairness for which he was noted in later life, and would have had a hard time accepting the harsh, not-to-be-questioned discipline. Roddy's stay at Twyford ended in the summer of 1921.

That fall he entered Charterhouse, one of the great English public schools, where his paternal grandfather, William Haig-Brown, had been headmaster. William is credited with being the second founder of Charterhouse because he moved the school from cramped quarters in London to a country setting near Godalming in Surrey and revitalized it. William was headmaster from 1863 to 1897 and had died the year before Roddy was born. And, continuing the family educational traditions, his sisters were sent to Oxford High School, where their aunt, Rosalind Haig-Brown, was headmistress.

In 1925, Roddy began keeping diaries on a daily basis. This habit he kept up faithfully until mid-1933, although there were many writer's notebooks and a few occasionally kept diaries after that. There were even a few pocket diaries prior to 1925, but these are devoted to the young sportsman's records of fishing and shooting, kept perhaps partly because the management of an estate such as his grandfather's required such information. It certainly was commonly done in the family.

The daily diaries begin in this same sporting tradition, since they record the remaining three weeks of his 1925 Christmas vacation which were spent hunting and fishing with Major Greenhill, a family friend who had taken his sporting education in hand. There were also dances, movies and shopping excursions, often with his mother, whom he adored. On January 20 he went back to Charterhouse: "BACK TO SCHOOL!!! How absolutely too damn awful for words." The diary entries described days that are either "utterly foul" or "not bad." He set himself a regimen of cold showers which lasted for a couple of weeks, though he had earlier complained bitterly about the water always being cold. On January 24 Roddy wrote: "O God, this place is boring ... Jack and I are planning a show at the end of the quarter. Roger Frankland is taking us up to the 43 [a notorious London drinking club] on the last night in his car & then heigho for the delights of London town. Women & drink for one night and then back to the more healthy pursuits of the country."

On his seventeenth birthday in February, Roddy and his mother went by car to Lancing and visited friends from the days when they lived there. "We went to evening chapel and walked all over the school ... damn funny seeing all the old things. It's 10 years since I was there."

He dreamt about his ideal girl, had crushes on his mother's friend

Kitty, his friend Roger Frankland's sister, Bardie, and Bubbles, a dancing girl at the 43 Club in London, among others. "You will notice, dear reader, that the writer of this scrawl is *not* very constant in love." He seems to spend as much or more time on athletics as studying – the marks he mentions are not very respectable, though he is often commended for his writing, if not for his knowledge of the subject. Still he passed exams in Latin, French, English and Greek that qualified him for university. By late March he and his friends Roger Frankland and Jack Munroe were planning the best escape route for their London "show" on the last night of the term. They succeeded in their endeavor, but at some point, a still-inebriated Jack managed to escape the custody of his two friends. They caught up with him just as he carried out his threat to meet the school train arriving at Waterloo station next morning. Unfortunately there were masters on board escorting the younger boys who had to change trains to go home for the holidays and no escape was possible. We never asked why they didn't just abandon Jack, but I think we knew that the answer lay in loyalty to friends.

In the holidays Roddy fished for salmon on the Frome near Wareham with Major Greenhill. He caught his first Frome salmon on April 28 on a prawn – ten pounds. He returned to school on May 1 to discover that he and Jack were to be "shot out" or expelled. (Roger's participation had not been discovered, but he later owned up and was not sent down because he was younger and it was his first offence, although he did get "swished" or caned.) The official reason for Roddy's dismissal was that he was "not amenable to discipline" – that discipline undoubtedly having consisted, in part at least, of getting swished. Roddy was most upset at the sorrow and trouble he would cause his mother. "Oh Hell, I was an ass, a damned bloody fool." The story of this episode eventually became part of family lore, told in an amused tone. Perhaps the occasional retelling was cathartic. It is certainly the sort of pivotal experience that a person can ponder for a lifetime, though I never heard my father speculate about what might have happened if he had behaved himself better.

The Haig-Brown family gathered in London to discuss Roddy's fate and scold until May 10, when he and his mother returned to Dorchester. While they may not have admitted it to Roddy at the time, his cousin Hilda reported many years later that it was generally thought among the Haig-Browns that the punishment had been excessive. A week later he and his mother went to Winchester to talk with "Dr. Davies, a coach [tutor]. He thinks he can have me." On May 25 he went to Headbourne Worthy to live with the Davies family at the rectory, where, except for holidays, he was to spend almost a year studying history with hopes of qualifying for a university scholarship. He liked the family, which included a son and daughter, both at Oxford. Roddy settled into a routine of studying and exploring the local countryside with his ferret in his pocket, quickly finding what local fishing and hunting were available to him. In June he bought a Sealyham pup. Summer social life consisted of lots of tennis parties, where he regularly fell in love. Then it was home to Wrackleford for August and most of September.

On October 2 he wrote, "Heard from Major Partridge about joining the Terriers [the Territorial Army]. Also from Hope to say that I have been elected a member of the Dorset Rangers." During a visit to Cambridge at the end of October he found he would have to take maths as well to get in and was generally not impressed. Perhaps this was mainly because he was also told that his Charterhouse record would be held against him if there was any trouble. He liked the look of Oxford better on a visit a few days later and decided to go there instead, with a view to ultimately joining the Colonial Civil Service.

Roddy (and all that huge family) were obviously considering all the possibilities open to a young man of his class who had to support himself – as the son of a daughter Roddy had no claim on his grandfather's money. Britain ran her huge empire with an army of civil servants and a military force which together formed the government of her multitude of colonies. By putting in enough time in the army to be a commissioned officer and qualifying for the civil service, Roddy would have a sure way of earning a living.

During the Christmas holidays at South Court in Dorchester his favorite uncle, Decimus (the tenth son of the family), and his wife, Elspeth, who was from Seattle, Washington, visited. He also paid a visit to Roger Frankland and fell rather seriously in love with Bardie, but he was interested, too, in Eve Foster of Warmwell in Dorset, a daughter of family friends.

On January 21, 1926, Major Greenhill shot himself and Roddy was devastated. "I have cried like a baby ... Major Greenhill was a perfect gentleman, a perfect sportsman and a perfect friend." The cause was said to be financial worries. Roddy went back to Headbourne Worthy after Major Greenhill's funeral on January 26. The plan was to attack the maths, for which he engaged another tutor. Two days later, he developed the mumps, but work continued. He also did a lot of reading and letter-writing, often to *The Fishing Gazette*, which printed some of the letters. On February 19 he wrote, "I received joyful news this morning ... I am through without taking Maths again! ... Now I have only got to pass the entrance exam and I am a member of Lincoln College, Oxford."

His mother took him to the Crown Hotel at Ringwood for a fishing weekend to celebrate his eighteenth birthday. He fished for pike with some success and then on the last morning caught a twenty-four-pound salmon. "I played him right out and then let him go because we had no right to keep him." (They would have had to pay to fish for salmon.) As soon as they returned to Dorchester he went off to Buckfastleigh to fish for salmon with his Uncle Cyril. In the bar of their hotel he "spotted a pretty girl in a green hat. I sent a note to her and she rose and was hooked ... went home to her flat. She was awfully nice to me, and I liked her very much indeed, *but* it is an over rated game." Did his uncle arrange for the girl in the green hat to be in the bar? They also caught some nice salmon.

Rod went back to Dr. Davies on March 1. He wrote to Bardie to ask if he might write her once a week, and received no reply, but dreamt of her endlessly, often imagining her accompanying him on fishing expeditions. Bardie was visiting friends in Egypt. But on March 30, "Well, it happened. I saw in this morning's *Times* that Bardie is engaged. I took it far better than I had hoped ... I wrote and congratulated her, but life seems empty." The 1926 diary ends in mid-sentence on April 18 after many entries bemoaning the loss of Bardie, who never knew of his grand passion. Roddy was to write his entrance exam for Oxford the next day. He must have done not too badly because he asked Dr. Davies some years later for a recommendation for the Colonial Civil Service. This would hardly have been worth doing if he had failed.

But university did not appeal in the end and Roddy tried the army. He was already qualified as a 2nd lieutenant from his time in the Officers' Training Corps at school. He was stationed at the Dorchester Barracks of the 4th Battalion, Dorset Regiment, from May until November, training for a regular commission in the Indian Army. By late fall he knew that the army was not what he wanted and went on reserve. He went up to London and saw the Colonial Civil Service people. They told him they would be just as glad to have people with practical experience as with university degrees, so he took up the invitation of his Uncle Decie's father-in-law, Alex McEwan, whom he had met at South Court the previous Christmas, to work in one of his logging camps in Washington.

Roddy arrived in Seattle in late December after travelling from England by boat and train. He stayed with the McEwans, who lived in the Olympic Hotel. Marian Fisken, the McEwans' other daughter, took his social life in hand and gave a party in his honor. He went skiing on Mt. Rainier and fishing for steelhead on the Pilchuck and Stillaguamish rivers near Seattle with Edward Dunn, who would become a lifelong friend. In some ways Edward was rather like Roddy. He was a quiet man, dark and very neat, who enjoyed fishing and grouse hunting, good food and good talk, and had a gentle sense of humor and a warmth about him that charmed both family and friends.

In early February Roddy started work in a logging camp at Lake Cavanaugh north of Seattle as a scaler, measuring logs to determine their size and value. In a note on accents much later Roddy wrote: "I arrived in the Pacific Northwest many years ago with what I have no doubt must have seemed a highly improbable accent. It was I suppose a respectable middle-class English accent ... drawling, painfully artificial to Northwest ears, effete no doubt and often incomprehensible. It caused a certain amount of healthy laughter, infrequent protests and, in the logging camps where I first worked, the conviction that I must be a remittance man. I was often questioned directly on this point, and even my admission that I received no remittances [money from family, often provided to get a problem brother or son out of sight in the colonies] did little to dilute this."

In April, after some time off due to an injury caused by tripping over a saw while running from a falling tree, he was given a job on a survey crew. This meant "a lot of walking through green woods and camping out a good bit," which suited him no end. The greenhorn was told plenty of fearful stories about bears and cougars, but he was not too much taken in and soon started a regular habit of spending days off fishing, as well as camping out when he could to make the most of time off. The plummy-voiced English kid was beginning to fit in.

In late June the cut on Roddy's leg opened up again when he caught it on a broken branch, and he returned to Seattle. He was delighted to find his Uncle Decie there. On July 4, he and Decie came down to breakfast with black arm bands on to show mourning over the loss of the British colonies as their American hosts celebrated their victory over the British.

In late July 1927, because his U.S. visa had expired and he did not need one for Canada, he went to work at Wood & English Logging on the Nimpkish River on the east coast of Vancouver Island. In those days the Island, which lies off the south coast of British Columbia, was sparsely populated. Roads were few and ended well south of the Nimpkish. Access was by steamer from Vancouver and the majority of people who lived beyond the road existed on a combination of fishing, logging and subsistence farming. Roddy spent the first few days in the new camp working around the sawmill at Englewood and cursing his fate. But on his first day off he set out to find the fishing, and a few days later he was assigned to a survey crew, which two things made his new world look much better.

For the next couple of years Roddy worked in the Nimpkish logging camps and learned the fishing in the rivers and lakes of the area. He came to know the Lansdowne family, particularly sons Buster and Ed, who lived on a farm near the mouth of the Nimpkish River, which drained the fifteen-mile-long Nimpkish Lake in a wild six-mile rush to Johnstone Strait. All the time he was writing articles and taking photographs and sending them to publishers. Some were rejected, and some were published, usually in English magazines, the market he knew best. He kept up a steady correspondence, mostly with family, but also with various fishing experts and editors. He read *The Fishing Gazette*, the weekly edition of the London *Times*, *Punch*, and books he bought in Seattle or ordered from England. Much of his life in these years is to be found in *A River Never Sleeps* written in the early 1940s.

When the logging camp shut down for the 1927–28 Christmas holiday, Roddy went back to Seattle, stayed with Keith and Marian Fisken, and picked up the social round. He also spent an hour each morning boxing and even fought an occasional bout for a little money at smokers – men-only gatherings, usually at private clubs.

In the fall of 1928, Roddy decided he had had enough of the logging camps and arranged to spend a few weeks as a paying guest of the Lansdownes. He caught his first salmon in the river, a twenty-pounder, did a little hunting, and made plans to make his fortune with a trap line on the Kilipi River (Kilpala). The food and the company were a pleasant change from that of the logging camp. In early December, he and Buster Lansdowne set out for the trap line. They returned in time for Christmas with little fur, but the trip was the inspiration for *Starbuck Valley Winter*, which appeared twenty years later.

The story of 1929 is a saga of unsuccessful money-making schemes with the Lansdownes, designed to raise the fare to keep his promise to his mother to return to England. Mrs. Lansdowne went to Vancouver for the winter and Roderick, Ed and Buster were left to take care of themselves. In early March they put Buster's boat *Kathleen* on a railroad flatcar and took it up to Nimpkish Lake to spend the summer beachcombing for logs that had escaped when being floated to the railhead for loading. There were good days and bad, but in early August it became apparent that they were going to do no better than break even, so they gave it up. Ed and Buster went to work in the camps and Roddy settled back at the Lansdowne farm. A fractured elbow limited activity somewhat, but he still fished most successfully and cut winter wood for the household. He had to accept the money his mother offered for his fare back to England in order to keep his promise to her to return.

On October 1, Roddy bade a very sad farewell to the Nimpkish and headed for Seattle via steamer to Vancouver and bus from there. He again stayed with Marian and Keith Fisken. One afternoon in Harry Hartman's bookstore Marian introduced him to "a really charming girl called Ann Elmore who is working there." After that he found almost daily excuses to drop into the store and the two saw each other occasionally at social events. He met Ann's parents, Dr. and Mrs. Bruce Elmore. He wrote, "She is a most interesting talker and really amazingly attractive. Very widely read for her age [the same as his]; I shall be sorry to say goodbye to her."

And on November 2, 1929, aboard the Furness Line steamship *Pacific Ranger* off the California coast, the diary says, "I wrote a letter to Buster this afternoon – not a good one; my heart is too full when I write to anyone at Nimpkish. How long will it be before I go back there?" He had clearly found a place for his spirit in the green forests and tumbling rivers of eastern Vancouver Island.

He enjoyed the cities during stops on the California coast and was very enthusiastic about the Panama Canal. He also read a great deal (*Madame Bovary*, *The Brothers Karamazov*, *The Egoist* and *The Forsyte Saga* – this last almost certainly from Hartman's; Ann and Roddy credited it with being the catalyst for their introduction) and wrote letters. Some of the letters were concerning "testimonials for Africa" – asking for letters of recommendation – the idea of joining the Colonial Civil Service to serve in Africa was still in the picture.

Roddy arrived back in England on December 6, and was met on board ship by his mother and his uncle, Bertie Leas. They stayed with the Leas in their house on the edge of Regent's Park. He and his mother went to the zoo in the Park after lunch and, as he mentioned on a previous visit, it was the aquarium that interested him most. The next evening the Haig-Browns, including his sisters Joan and Val, gathered at Tite Street. The theater followed dinner, as it had the evening before. A couple more days of shopping and theater-going and it was home to Dorchester, South Court and the Guv'nor (Grandfather Pope) who "met me with open arms (more or less)." Grandfather, always a bit capricious about giving permission to shoot at Wrackleford, was as difficult as ever – which must have seemed more frustrating than ever to a man of almost twenty-two who had been on his own in North America for three years. But all seemed to be soothed over dinner, most days, with a bottle of good wine from his grandfather's fine cellar. Dinner in his grandfather's house would routinely have been served with linen tablecloth and fine silver and lingered over for some time. On formal occasions the men would remain at the table after dinner over brandy and cigars. Roddy spent the Christmas season settling in and reconnecting with old friends, including the Partridges at Higher Kingston and the Fosters at Warmwell, both near Dorchester.

After a month in which he led the good life and managed to get quite a lot of shooting – even some at Wrackleford – Roddy travelled to Bordeaux with the Partridges for a couple of weeks. In spite of a busy social life, the question of his future remained – a job as a head forester was vetoed by the family – with the possibility of earning his living by writing still the most acceptable to Roddy himself.

By the end of February Uncle Decie had returned to Dorchester (he was in the army and had served in India and Egypt, as did several of the Pope uncles) to recuperate from an operation on his back. Decie read and criticized Roddy's articles and they talked of fishing – "he is the only man I have ever met who is as keen on fishing as I am. He is really a wonderful fellow, quite the best of all the eleven uncles."

In March, Roddy visited several London editors and had a consultation with his uncle, Harold Haig-Brown, who was his guardian and controlled the fund that had been set up for his education. Harold thought he might read law. He returned to Dorchester and tried to discipline himself to get on with writing, but social life kept interfering – especially Eve Foster. Still, several articles went out to publishers. But on March 18 his mother "came up from breakfast to say that the Guv'nor has decided that he's had about enough of my being in the house ... He can go to hell a dozen times for all I care, but I'll probably speak a few words to him on the subject of his treatment of Mother before I set out." Violet, whom I remember as a very gentle person, was theoretically in charge of the household, but seems to have spent most of her time just trying to keep the peace. Now approaching ninety, Alfred was as autocratic as ever, still grudgingly giving permissions, and likely to withdraw them at the last moment. My father's sister Valerie told me of being allowed to invite a school friend for a few days and then being told to send her home after lunch on the first day. More than sixty years later she was still fuming.

On March 29, Roddy "had tea at Delcombe with the Partridges. Good to see them again and Dicky too. I told him salmon stories without number after tea." This was the beginning of *Silver, The Life Story of an Atlantic Salmon*, which is dedicated to Dicky. The next day Roddy's Aunt Hilda, who was visiting, summoned him and delivered the word from his grandfather that he was definitely to clear out. Yet there was not a mention of the subject over dinner that night and Roddy continued to work on an article on logging. A measles quarantine on the household delayed his departure and on April 12 he wrote: "I've started a book, and it promises to be a most successful work. The life story of a salmon, written for children with a view to collecting a fair number of adult readers. The notes are made up and the first chapter has been written."

On April 24, Roderick left for the Haig-Brown household in Tite Street where he "had tea and then took a walk round with Uncle Willie to look at some lodgings (from the outside)." The Haig-Brown relatives were now encouraging him to try for a Parliamentary secretaryship. He began a course in typing and shorthand at Pitman's, found lodgings in Chelsea and continued writing *Silver*. His Uncle Harold had agreed to pay four pounds a week from money put aside by the family for the fatherless boy's education to keep him going. The Fosters had taken a house in Carlyle Square for the London party season when Eve and her sister would be "introduced to society" or, simply, declared eligible for marriage. Roddy's social life was as busy as ever, and he was falling seriously in love with Eve.

As the weeks progressed he continued at Pitman's, mostly hating it, and searched for a job through connections on both sides of the family and newspaper advertisements. He and Eve and her sister Joan had an interview with Basil Dean, a noted film producer of the day, from which the girls got some work in a film. There was talk of marriage with Eve, but his prospects were so limited that there was no hope, much as her family liked him, so they broke it off. By July he was revising *Silver* and reconnected with his old friend Jack Munroe from Charterhouse, who provided him with yet another unsuccessful newspaper connection. His mother was again urging him to take the Colonial Civil Service examination.

Then Roddy, too, got called to work for a few days as an extra in the Basil Dean film. There he met Christine Eliot, an "older woman" of twenty-six with an eight-year-old son. He enjoyed the company of Christine and her friends during the few days he worked on the film. He continued to write articles and some were published. Late August was so hot in London that he asked his mother if he could go down to Wrackleford. She replied, yes, but he must stay at an inn because his grandfather would still not welcome him. He finished *Silver*, sent it off to publishers Adam and Charles Black and began making notes for a book of philosophical essays, while spending his days enjoying the summer with family and friends, including the Fosters. In mid-September he made a second trip to France for a few days. And then on September 30: "Blacks' have accepted *Silver* – if I can find an adequate illustrator. Laugh at that if you can ... There's bridges to cross yet ... but Black's letter is sufficient reward without any more! WHAT A DAY."

By early October he could no longer ignore family pressure to contact the C.C.S. It now seemed that a university degree was required for acceptance, but it was possible they might give him an appointment to the police force somewhere in Africa. "What a prospect!" And that is the last we hear of the Colonial Civil Service. In a letter to Ann Elmore that same month, he said: "I often long to be back on the Pacific Coast ... Seattle has two very pleasant memories: Hartman's bookshop & Marian Fisken's house. Vancouver Island has thousands upon thousands." He also mentioned reading *Vile Bodies*, by Evelyn Waugh – "brilliantly clever," and *The Well of Loneliness* – "very, very beautiful." Black's found an illustrator for *Silver*.

Then Uncle Harold announced he would no longer get his four pounds a week unless he got a job. Eventually it was agreed that the allowance would continue but be decreased by any amount that Roddy earned. In late October he was "off to Ealing to marry my Aunt Katie ... With dignity she walked up the aisle on my arm and I gave her away to my new uncle." Katie was fifty-one and this was her first marriage.

In November his mother came up to London, decided he wasn't too well and took him home for a week in the country. He returned to London to a new and better room and continued trying to write the philosophical book without success, probably because his worldly experience was still a little limited for such weighty matters. He had described it to Ann as: "... called *Impertinences*, which attempts to set forward the views of Youth. Everyone is talking about Youth in England now." But he was also writing short stories and selling some of them. Then in the Christmas holidays when "a gale of wind and lots of rain" kept him from shooting at Wrackleford for the third day in a row he "settled to work. Work consisted largely of reading *Tarka the Otter* by Henry Williamson [still much-admired by those who come across it] and trying to think of a way to write the book that I want to write about the Nimpkish River and all the animals and Indians." At the same time he was working on three other stories, all of which eventually were published. He did think of a way to write the book, which became *Pool and Rapid*, a combination of a legend of the Nimpkish River and its origins, and a story of a struggle over a potential dam on the river.

Christine Eliot became a most serious love of Roddy's life during 1931. Our father often told us of his family's strenuous objections to their association. He was finally forbidden to see her, but, assuming London to be big enough to go about unnoticed, he continued to, and was seen by an aunt who immediately reported to all. Christine was older, had a child, had been (and was later) a "kept" woman and lived in the film and stage world. We can only imagine what the aunts and uncles said, but it was no doubt much like the dialogue of Edwardian novels in similar circumstances.

What we do know is that *Silver* was published in 1931 and that *Pool and Rapid* was well under way. The London *Times* review of *Silver* said: "A remarkably successful example of a class of work which, for all its popularity, is very rarely altogether satisfactory. There is no 'nature faking.' He evidently knows his subject from end to end, both from the standpoint of a naturalist and from that of an angler." Sixty-five years later the book is still in print. Roddy lived in his Chelsea room, did some more work as a film extra and continued to write, and sometimes sell, articles. But by the summer he was back at Wrackleford recuperating from an unspecified illness. (The illness, if it did not soften his grandfather's heart, at least allowed him to be tolerated.) He spent several weeks there working on his manuscript in the garden. Christine was away in France.

In the fall he returned to London and Christine. Aside from continuing family disapproval, it was also obvious that Roddy could not support Christine in the style to which she was accustomed, so marriage was out. Nor would Christine have lasted for a moment in the forests of Vancouver Island where Roddy had decided he belonged.

On November 6, he began a new notebook labelled "Canal Diary." He was "aboard *M.S. Pacific Shipper*, bound for Canada via Panama Canal." Enough of the huge, interfering families. At least he could lead his own life at the Nimpkish. He wrote, "Last night certainly was a night but there was no end [of sorrows] to be drowned. I think I've never known anything like the hell of leaving Christine – certainly I've never felt that on leaving anyone else ... to walk away from a train crying like a baby and then have to walk fast along half a dozen streets with fists clenched tight and eyes staring straight ahead, half crying all the time is something strange for me."

But Roddy was soon watching with interest as the ship moved out into the Mersey, and by the next day they were "coming into the fishing fleets on the edge of the Atlantic." His friend Peter Bower from Dorset was travelling with him. Roddy planned to work on revising *Pool and Rapid*, but the weather was rough and the ship rolled and pitched too much for writing. One wave smashed a hole in the bridge. He missed Christine. "I don't want to let myself lose her or let her lose me in the next year or two ... I'm afraid of the changes that separation may bring about." After five days of rough weather, they neared the Azores and calm prevailed. Roddy worked on a short story about a girl logger and the other passengers all read his copy of *Silver*. He polished a second story and got on to the book revision. The work was rough and so was the sea, but flying fish appeared and cheered him a little.

The weather warmed as they neared the canal, and deck tennis and swimming became the order of the day. The book progressed, but slowly.

The canal fascinated him – the locks, the other boats, the birds and fish and the tropical sunsets. As they entered the Pacific, they were well ahead of schedule so the captain let the boat drift and Roddy took the chance to try a little fishing. No luck. After loading bananas, they headed up the coast toward Los Angeles, with each day surpassing the previous one in warmth and beauty, and Rod's spirits soared.

On December 9, after a month at sea, they arrived in Los Angeles – in the rain. But there was mail – a newsy letter from his mother; one from Mrs. Lansdowne at the Nimpkish, telling of the depression in B.C.; and "the most wonderful, wonderful letter from Christine." Five days later, having welcomed the gray skies and gray seas of the northern climate and done some good work on the book, Roddy wrote, "British Columbia again after two long years away." A letter in Victoria from Mrs. Lansdowne said that she was at the farm and that he and Peter were welcome to come up. Two letters from Christine, and he wrote, "I hate to think of her lonely and sad in London while I'm happy out here with a thousand wonderful things ahead."

The final entry in the canal diary is a long one written at the Nimpkish two weeks later. It tells of arriving at the Vancouver immigration office: "Real circus here and things looked almighty bad for a moment or two, then the atmosphere cleared in a flash and we were through as immigrants – 'they're a fine clean-looking pair of boys; may's well let 'em in'." After a couple of days in Vancouver getting gear together and partying with old friends, Roddy and Pete boarded the coastal steamer for Alert Bay on Cormorant Island in Johnstone Strait, near the mouth of the Nimpkish. They were dropped off at 4 a.m. on a cold, gray morning to a sleeping town, but eventually got breakfast. "Then a ride across to the River in Meunes's boat. *Kathleen* – remodelled out of all recognition – was in the bend, and Ed was aboard. That was that; we were home again."

Plans evolved quickly – a dude ranch for Roddy and Ed Lansdowne – they planned to bring tourists up for hunting and fishing. For $150 Roddy bought a sixty-foot yacht, *Chakawana*, that had caught fire and sunk. Pete, who was clearly not for the woods, but mad about boats, was to partner with Buster in attempting to raise her. In the midst of it all, Roddy worked hard on *Pool and Rapid*. The diary for 1932 was kept in occasional long entries, instead of daily ones, at Christine's urging. She felt that daily entries were "too much a catalogue of events, too little a concrete expression of my thoughts."

The revision of *Pool and Rapid* was sent off to the typist in Vancouver on January 19. Roddy thought the first ten chapters the best, especially six and seven which he wrote aboard the *Pacific Shipper*, but felt the remaining chapters did not have enough about the river. Pete and Buster went to Vancouver (Mrs. Lansdowne was already there for the winter) so Roddy and Ed were alone. Attempts to get on with the writing were interspersed with tending a trap line along the beach and sometimes-harrowing, wind-whipped trips across the strait to Alert Bay for mail and groceries, and even a dance. Once the local policeman warned them not to go home that day, little knowing they had come across the previous afternoon in even worse weather – another story we loved to hear whenever it came up.

The rest of the Lansdowne family returned in late January and even less writing and reading got done. Roddy and Ed came very close to drowning when they upset their canoe at Siwash Rock in the river, to say nothing of nearly freezing to death when they did get themselves out. Days passed in wood-cutting, hunting the cougars that were raiding the chicken house (they got one) and checking the trap line, but very little writing. Roddy scolded himself for this and felt that if he were back in London amid the world of writers and publishers and newspapers and books, he could get on with it. On the other hand he loved the freedom and the outdoors and wrote mini-essays in the diary on the glories of a winter sunset, the pleasure of tracking a cougar in snowy woods, the look of ragged firs against the skyline and the life of eagles. He recognized that his and Christine's letters were getting shorter and less intense and admitted to himself that he would not likely keep his promise to return in a year.

News came in mid-March of 1932 that Black's would publish *Pool and Rapid* in the fall, but a book of short stories about Canada for Dent's was rejected. He attempted a film script for Christine, but it did not go well. The dude ranch idea progressed. Practical jobs like cutting the canoe poles were interspersed with letters to family and friends urging them to drum up business. Buster built skiffs and they got guide's licenses.

But they needed more money. Roddy craved a quiet place to live alone, or perhaps with his mother or a woman who would understand and encourage his work. He knew what he needed in order to be a successful writer, but little knew how close he was to realizing it. Trout fishing in April lifted his spirits, and then a nice letter from Ann Elmore. "I'm fond of her with her love of books and her red hair. Soon I'll go down to Seattle and see her; she said she'd come up to Vancouver or Victoria and meet me there if I couldn't get down to Seattle, but that scarcely seems a very proper suggestion from a young lady. God, what fools we are! Why shouldn't it be perfectly proper?"

Work began on a shack to house the dudes in the fall and some thought went into books about the Panama Canal trip and on nature for children. This was interrupted by a week-long trip with the Alert Bay game warden, Mottishaw, to Knight Inlet to try to catch some fur thieves. Suddenly, on May 26, a cable from Christine to say that Dinky, her little boy, was dying. Two more cables and then one on June 1 to say he had died. There was nothing to do but write Christine a consoling letter and console himself a little by writing about Dinky and the unfairness of it all.

But by the end of June: "It's been a congested upside down week of interruptions [like most of them] ... but it's been worth it; I've got a new book; the book I've always longed for, the book I promised Blacks', the book I'm actually looking for. I'll tell you about it. Cecil Smith's the source of inspiration; 'Cougar' Smith, and the book's to be the life story of a Panther." Smith was a government cougar hunter and had been called up from Comox, farther south on Vancouver Island, to pursue a cougar that was bothering the logging camps. Roddy and the Lansdownes hunted with him and the book idea evolved rapidly over a week of conversation with Smith. By the time he left, it was agreed that Roddy would hunt with him the next winter to learn more about cougars.

The panther book was to be the driving force of much of the next year, but, before Roddy could get truly started, there were several frustrating months to be put in attempting to carry out the guiding scheme. The shack was finished, a few people came and caught a few fish, but all the usual givens of rain, fish not in, greedy guests, etc., made the experience far from exciting – or lucrative. The best part of the summer had been a two-week trip to Vancouver and civilization. On August 15, he wrote: "Tomorrow I have to go back up to Nimpkish. My ticket's bought and God knows how I hate the thought of it. I'm getting used to being alive, to having people about me, to avoiding cars when I cross the road, to reading today's paper today, to being able to go in and see a film when I feel like it or browse around a bookshop. And now I have to go back and bury myself for another three or four months, row a bunch of idiots around from dawn till dark, catch a few fish that don't matter much, kill a few animals that should be allowed to go on living. Yet it shouldn't really be so terribly bad; there'll be sunsets and sunrises; the stillness of big tides at the River and the dusky red light on the sandbars at dead-low tide in the evening; big fish finning or rolling out of the water; maybe a good companion or two; maybe a pleasant trip in the woods." There was also another cougar hunt that became Chapter 25 in *Panther*. And Roddy resolved to write a book about Pacific salmon: "I'm going to show up all the ignorance of the officials, all the graft and abuses and stupid little blindness that's destroying – has destroyed – one of the greatest natural resources any country ever had. It'll be a dam' fine book, but I wonder if I can make it so that it'll sell?"

Pool and Rapid was published on September 22, and Roddy received his copies in early October. He admired the book, but objected to the dust jacket: "All these aids to sales are very wrong ... the text of the book should sell [it]. Much the same applies to the blurb ... All the details of the author himself and his mode of living are quite ridiculous ... I'm author, pure and simple and anything else I do in this life is merely done in pursuit of that profession." A review in the London *Times* said: "Mr. Haig-Brown is at his best as a descriptive writer; the culminating passage telling of the great flood which thwarts the damming project, is particularly thrilling, but throughout the work the author contrives a happy blend of realistic observation and poetic fancy which cannot fail to have wide appeal among the varied tastes of lovers of nature."

Other mail included letters from his mother and his Uncle Decie congratulating him on *Pool and Rapid*, from Ann Elmore about reading Virginia Woolf and D.H. Lawrence and theorizing about the two of them going off to Mexico, an invitation from Marian Fisken to spend Christmas with them in Seattle, and one from Christine in Biarritz, where she had acquired a string of potential lovers. Roddy's only complaint about this last was that the men were not good enough for her.

When there were no dudes the shack became a quiet sanctuary for reading and letter-writing, but it was a relief to finally be away at the beginning of November. Although he worried: "I'm afraid of the Nimpkish now. She's only a little, unimportant streamlet in a very dead part of the world, but she's got a tremendous grip on me now."

He got off the boat in Campbell River, then the end of the road on Vancouver Island, where Cecil Smith's son met him. "We drove to Herbert Pidcock's house and there found Cecil and Mrs. Smith ..., Herbert and his wife; he's a guide at Campbell River and a panther hunter when the bounty's on. And Reg Pidcock, a bold, bad bachelor uncle, very popular with his nephews and nieces." From there, they drove to Cecil's pleasant house at Comox, thirty miles south. The next month passed in sometimes very hard work hunting cougars in the snow and cold, but learning every day, contrasted with enjoying the green and openness of the Comox Valley and the people there.

Ann's letters became almost weekly and she was "on tiptoe" with excitement at his coming to Seattle at Christmas. They had only met briefly in 1929 before Roddy went back to England, but the attraction that was there then and kept up in occasional correspondence over the three-year interval had bloomed rapidly in the last few months.

.2.

Ann (1908 – 1932)

My mother, Ann Elmore, was born on May 3, 1908, in Seattle, Washington. She was the first child of Bruce Elmore and Annetta Maud Wright. They had met when Bruce was an intern at Roosevelt Hospital in New York City where Annetta was nursing, and moved to Seattle shortly after their marriage in 1906. Seattle at that time had a small tight-knit group of social leaders, and the charming young doctor and his wife were no doubt welcomed into the circle. There would have been both university and naval connections of Bruce's who introduced them to the "right" people.

Many years later, when a granddaughter was doing a family tree for school, Ann wrote a brief history of her family for her, perhaps partly to counteract the very well-documented history of the Haig-Brown side of the family. From this we know that her father Bruce came from a family of five children. His father, also Bruce, was in the 173rd New York Volunteer Regiment and is said to have been the youngest officer on General Sherman's staff in the Civil War. He died just before his son was born. Bruce's mother died of tuberculosis when he was thirteen. His sister Mary, who was twenty years older and a teacher and public school principal in Brooklyn, helped Bruce earn his way to, first, an arts degree at Columbia in New York, and then a medical degree, also at Columbia, where he came third in the class of 1904. Another sister, Jen, was married to a Presbyterian missionary to China. They were at Canton Christian

College, and their two children survived the Boxer Rebellion because they were hidden by their nurse. The others were a brother, William, and a sister, Leil.

Bruce had served briefly in the navy during the Spanish-American War and in 1905 rejoined, again briefly, and was stationed at the U.S. Naval Hospital in Washington, D.C. He was later on active service in Seattle during the First World War.

Annetta, or Annette as she preferred to be known, was the daughter of Emerson Wright of St. Catharines, Ontario, who was an engineer and worked on building parts of the Welland Canal. He later became a pilot on the Great Lakes. She had a sister, Mary Elizabeth, and a brother, Charles, who died at twenty-one when he fell from a train. Annette trained as a nurse, then went to New York where she took a three-month course at Sloan Maternity Hospital in 1902. When she and Bruce met, she was head operating room nurse at Roosevelt Hospital.

The year after Ann was born, her sister Mary followed. Her brother Bruce was born in 1912, the same year that Ann started at St. Nicholas' School. In 1916, her youngest sibling, Daniel, was born. The family lived in a large white clapboard house on Federal Avenue, on a hillside not far from the center of Seattle, which backed on the green space of a graveyard adjoining Volunteer Park. My mother's brother Danny told me some of the details of their lives in those days. Annette was very socially oriented (she even subscribed to a clipping service to be sure of seeing every mention of the family in the Seattle press, he said), but Bruce was mainly interested in medicine and golf. They had a wonderful woman named Jenny who was both nursemaid and cook, and who had originally been a patient of Dr. Elmore's. Custom was that Jenny's excellent waffles were always waiting on the sideboard on Sunday morning after Annette and the children had been to Mass (Annette was a devoted Catholic, as were all her children), and Bruce had played golf, usually with medical colleagues, who often joined him for breakfast.

Jenny was very important to all the children. My uncle said perhaps it was because she "was the warmth that Annette never had or wouldn't show." I remember my mother coming across a photograph of Jenny and "her Danny" in some things of their mother's when the house in Seattle was being sold, and clasping it to her with obvious affection. At one point, Danny said, Jenny went back to her relatives, but missed the Elmores so that she came back to the household. Also helping with the household was a succession of Filipino house "boys" (quite common in Seattle in those days). Annette usually had a large vegetable garden in the backyard, and these men worked along with her in the garden, as well as doing the heavy chores. Some of them also went to school while they were with the Elmores.

My mother used to describe two trips the family took – one, when she was very young, by train to visit family in the eastern U.S. and Canada, and the other, in 1919, to spend the summer in Hollywood, then a quiet California town, with some of her mother's family. The next year they spent the summer in Victoria, B.C., where Ann's two brothers eventually went to school at Brentwood College, so that they could share some of their mother's Canadian background. Ann herself entered Forest Ridge Convent, the Seattle school of the Sisters of the Sacred Heart, in 1920. Her mother had attended a Catholic high school in Ontario. She finished school there in 1924 at the age of sixteen, two years ahead of her age group. An important part of her life at that time was Campfire Girls, an organization much like Girl Guides or Scouts. The leader was Ruth Brown with whom Ann kept in touch for many years. One of their activities was a Magic Ring in which the girls recited favorite poems around the campfire. A book of these poems was on our shelves when we were children.

In the fall of 1924, Ann went to the University of Washington to take a general arts course. Both her mother and father were well-educated and accustomed to women in the family going on to higher education in some form, so this would have been a natural course of events. In addition there was Ann's "braininess." A printed card dated January 16, 1925, from the psychology department of the university reports Ann's score on an intelligence test as equalling or exceeding the score made by 100% of the students, presumably indicating that she had achieved the highest possible score. Her courses included English, French, Latin, Greek, journalism, history and philosophy. Danny described the family dinner table in those days thus: "Daddy, with Ann at his right and Mary at his left, exchanging Greek quotes with Ann and Latin with Mary; Bucky and me on either side of our mother where Bucky held his own, and I told tall tales to get my share of the attention."

After three years at Washington, Ann transferred to the University of California at Berkeley. At California she studied Greek, paleontology, physics, English and play producing in the fall and Greek, zoology, English and French in the spring semester. Ann was by this time a member of Delta Zeta sorority and lived in the sorority house. Her mother wrote frequent long letters as did several Seattle friends, which Ann kept. When I was sorting these letters and others that followed her return to Seattle, a shower of engraved cards inviting attendance at dinners, teas, "at homes" and weddings slid out from between the pages. It was an Elmore custom to be at home to friends for tea on Sunday afternoon and some of the letters to California report Ann's friends dropping in on the family. What with Jenny's waffle breakfasts on Sunday morning and the afternoon tea, Sunday was certainly a social sort of day.

A typically breathless letter from Annette to her daughter was written from the Empress Hotel in Victoria on "September 6, 1927, 21st Anniversary of the Engagement of Your Parents. Ann darling, have you been neglected by Parents? Last week was busy – Tuesday night dinner at Fergusons – Wednesday the Adams had dinner for the Crosbys – lovely dinner – Thursday night we dined again with the Durands – Mr. and Mrs. Coulter of Atlanta, Georgia – formerly of Seattle. Well, Thursday night we realized it was Labor Day – the Durands were going to Victoria Sunday a.m. – We wished to come up to arrange about Buckie's school so – Bruce and Lillian telephoned for reservations – and here we are! Saturday night I was giving a dinner for the Chessmans – Friday Beatrice Perry gave a marvellous luncheon at the Sunset Club for Mrs. C. and Mrs. Staples of Havana. 47 people at luncheon – it was lovely. I sat between Clara Stimson and Mrs. Hargrove ... Friday night the Farnsworths gave a buffet dinner for 50 – bridge, poker and mah jong were after dinner entertainment. And then came Sunday. We took the car – Jane Chessman stayed with Mary. I went to 7 a.m. Mass – then dashed – We had a huge drawing room cabin effect – we played bridge. Then we got stowed into quarters at the Empress ..." and the letter dashes on in similar fashion describing two days in Victoria.

Aside from her mother's letters, Ann's papers include frequent correspondence with two men, Sidney Patzer, editor of *Columns*, a University of Washington magazine, and Clyde Rapp, who was clearly smitten with her, but not nearly as clever and witty as Sidney obviously was. Sidney and she exchanged gossip about university publications – Ann had worked on the Washington daily newspaper, an experience she often mentioned with pleasure. (Sidney was fired for pushing too close to the line in his editorial opinions – on what subject isn't clear.) Both men mention seeing her sister Mary around the campus. Ann used to say that she had missed out on university social life to some extent because of being two years younger than most people in her class, but she certainly seems to have been involved in more than just her classes. But her brains would probably have kept some at a distance in those days, too.

Ann's mother's letters from early 1928 report on a visit to Vancouver, mostly to shop; the sensational elopement of friends; the equally sensational murder of a friend's cook by her Greek lover right on Federal Avenue (the lover immediately shot himself). Her parents were elected to the Olympic Riding and Driving Club and would join as soon as they had the necessary funds – this was for the sake of her father's health – his blood pressure was a worry. All of this is punctuated by many dinner parties, often with friends from Bruce's navy years or the parents of people who became lifelong friends of my mother and father – many of the family names are familiar from our visits to Seattle and return visits of these friends to Campbell River.

Frequent reference is made in Ann's correspondence with her mother to Father White. There are also occasional letters from him in Ann's papers. Danny told me that he was a "fabulous" Jesuit priest who used to give sermons at St. Joseph's Cathedral in Seattle, just across the park from the Elmore house, and was a friend of the family. By the time Ann went to Berkeley, he was also in California and she saw him there as well. When Ann was in Seattle for the summer of 1928, he wrote her from St. Ignatius College in San Francisco. The letter begins with a long apology for being slow to answer and continues, "... it *is* difficult to do this father confessor thing by means of pen and paper! Vis-à-vis I know I would achieve more satisfactory results. Still, if I may be permitted to cut through the general inquiry to the specific instance that prompted it, I should say that, waking or sleeping you were wholly within the law ... it's the Teaching Church which tells us that to incur grave guilt we must be *fully* conscious of what we are doing and give *full* consent to the doing of it ... When next we meet, I shall elaborate on this principle and give appropriate examples ... My love to *all* the Clan Elmore and my deepest sympathy to Jenny – so sorry she got a misery in her shins and laigs!" This letter is certainly indicative of Ann's constant, thoughtful, questioning approach to her deeply felt Catholicism, which stayed with her most strongly all her life. There is no indication what the "specific instance" was that prompted the inquiry.

Ann had returned to Seattle for the summer of 1928 after graduating *summa cum laude* and took two English courses at Washington that summer. In the fall she returned to Berkeley for a final semester. A long letter from her mother described the week at home. "Pam had tea with Mary. I was going to write letters – Daddie came home early. Jay and Lillian arrived – they left soon and I gave Bruce some supper and we went to a Talkie Movie – Buck was at the Country Club ... Wednesday I went to a small luncheon Mrs. F.R. Greene gave at Sunset Club ... Bruce went to a medical dinner at the Olympic. Mary and I dressed for wedding. Buck drove us down to hotel. We picked up Daddie – K. Salmon looked lovely – the man is a dear – grandson of the late Pres. Dwight of Yale – He himself is an instructor at Columbia. Mrs. Blodel – Charlotte

— we talked to — Mary had a fine time flitting — the food was awful — the music *one* piano — however everyone was there. When we came home there was a message that Dr. Paul Ringen was at the Olympic (internes together at Roosevelt) — we made dates for next day ... Friday was Mrs. Hughes perfectly stunning tea for Janie — quite too lovely — Janie wore a gorgeous corsage presented by Bobbie Greer ... At the Salmon wedding Neva Douglas asked Mary for dinner before the Somerwell dance — of course she accepted — Dick Lesh took her — corsage — spiffy car — grand time — perfect party — Buckie also invited — stagged ... Saturday Bruce and I drove to Marysville to see Bruce's broken-backed man — the one who carelessly fell out of the aeroplane — he is walking with crutches — Bruce and I dined at the hotel in Everett ..." And on the letter dashes, as usual.

In one of his rare letters, at about the same time, Ann's father wrote, "Two weeks from tomorrow we ship dear, beautiful Mary to you and start on our own argosy — what in hell is an argosy anyhow? However, it's a fine sounding name for a trip East. Saw Dan yesterday. How he loves the hard-boiled life of a military school. Naturally he has completely outgrown childish things in one week. My love to Father White and my other friends ... I love you Ann, Daddy." Mary joined Ann to go to the Sacred Heart College in San Francisco. Danny was at Marymount Military Academy in Tacoma, Washington, and Bucky (Bruce) was at Brentwood College, near Victoria. (Danny later went there also.) Their parents spent several weeks that fall travelling by train through Canada to Montreal, on to Boston and New York for a meeting of the American College of Surgeons and eventually home via New Orleans and San Francisco. At Berkeley that semester Ann took one course in Greek and four in English and then wrote her comprehensive examination to qualify for graduate work. She did extremely well (91%) and returned to Seattle at Christmas.

On December 27, Ann's parents gave a party for her. A clipping among Ann's papers describes the occasion.

> *Invitations went out this week for a dancing party which Dr. and Mrs. Bruce Elmore are giving at the Sunset Club on Thursday evening, December 27 to formally introduce their daughter, Miss Ann Elmore, to society.*
>
> *Miss Elmore, one of the most charming and interesting of the younger group of girls, graduated from the University of California last June and returned this autumn for post-graduate work. She will come up for the Christmas holidays accompanied by her sister, Miss*

Mary, who is a student at the College of the Sacred Heart at Menlo Park.

The invitations for the dance are limited to the younger set, but Miss Elmore will receive with her parents on Christmas Day at their annual at home to their friends. (Ann was now "out among the people" or grown up, so would be eligible to "receive" guests.)

A bundle of tiny cards tied with silver ribbon is also among the papers and is marked "Coming out flowers and presents. Christmas 1928." It is perhaps indicative of my mother's values that I do not remember her talking of this party. In contrast, she talked often of her university studies and the books she read then. An application to Radcliffe the following spring for graduate studies was unsuccessful, probably fortunately for the ultimate course of events. Ann's 1929 correspondence still contained letters from Sid and Clyde – Sid was working and travelling in Europe and North Africa, and Clyde was working in New York – but there do not seem to be any serious suitors, although she used to mention being rather fond of one or two other men before she was married. From early 1930 to mid-1932 there are letters from U.S. Navy Ensign Donald Stillman, but the correspondence ends sadly with clippings that tell of Stillman's disappearance overboard from his ship in the South China Sea. In May of 1929, Ann was elected to the Junior League of Seattle, a women's service organization with a strong social cachet. By the summer Ann was learning to type braille. Ann and Mary were also members of the Junior Club, and took riding lessons at the Olympic Riding Club. Danny has a silver cup that he and Mary won in a treasure hunt there in May of 1931.

Ann began working in Harry Hartman's bookstore in the fall of 1929. Hartman's was *the* bookstore in Seattle at that time and included a lending library, of which Ann had charge, as well. The lending library was very popular because it had a better selection of current books than the public library. Ann also wrote reviews for the store's monthly newsletter, *The Lantern*. It was at Hartman's that Marian Fisken introduced Ann and Roddy that same fall. Roddy spent a lot of time in the store during the month he was in Seattle on his way back to England, and mentions occasionally over the next two years that he has received a letter from Ann.

In mid-May of 1930, a note from a friend in Portland expresses her sympathy at both Ann's father and her sister Mary being in hospital. Mary had had an operation for goiter problems from which she recovered, but Ann's father, who had had a problem with high blood pressure for some time, died of a cerebral hemorrhage a few days later. It was thought that the hemorrhage might have been related to an injury caused by a fall on board ship during navy service in the Spanish-American War. According to my Uncle Danny, his father became a Catholic on his deathbed. A few letters written to Ann then survive, and they leave little doubt that, when read beyond the consoling cliches usual in such letters, he was a very much-loved man. Danny told me of being taken to lunch by the editor of the Honolulu paper years later when he was there with the navy because the man remembered his father with such respect. As a young reporter in Seattle, the editor had done a series on botched abortions and Dr. Elmore had been one of the few doctors willing to speak out on the subject.

After her father's death, Ann continued to work in the bookstore, and her mother, of necessity, became a successful insurance and, later, real estate saleswoman. Annette worked for North American Life and, according to Danny, her sales technique included approaching Bruce's friends and pointing out that she was there partly because Bruce had died without insurance, and they should not let the same thing happen to their wives. In the fall of 1932, Annette won a trip to eastern Canada as one of the company's top salespeople.

During the Nimpkish year that followed Roddy's return from England in late 1931 (he came via Vancouver and the two did not see each other), Ann wrote more and more frequently and the letters were most important to him. Mother told me that Marian Fisken had urged her to write regularly because she thought from Roddy's letters to her that he was quite lonely. Marian certainly encouraged the right person to ease that loneliness. No doubt the attraction that had caused Roddy to wonder if he should kiss her as he left for England in 1929 had been at least somewhat mutual. And the letters of the last few weeks between Seattle and Comox, where Roddy was following the cougars, must have revealed a mind that caught Ann's interest most strongly to produce her "on tiptoe" excitement at his imminent arrival in Seattle for Christmas of 1932.

·3·

Love and Letters (1933)

If ever there was a romance made from books, it is most obvious, even without their letters to tell us, that this was it. The lovers were introduced in a bookstore, the early letters are mainly about books – when you are getting to know someone by mail, books are a safe and revealing subject and, in this case, a very basic common interest. Books remained a constant in the correspondence even as they got to know each other better. And books, writing and reading them, were the constant theme of their lives. Over their years together my parents collected at least four thousand books.

After a three-year absence Roddy arrived in Seattle from Comox to stay with Keith and Marian Fisken for the 1932 Christmas holidays as planned. His diary entry for the night he arrived notes that he went "to *Prunella*, by the Junior League: a poor, poor show, but Ann was sitting in front. [No doubt Marian had made the arrangements, knowing that Ann, as a Junior League member, would be going to the performance.] There was no chance to talk – just hullo and one or two inanities. What a damn silly world it is. We've been waiting for ages and ages, then it has to be that ... We couldn't have looked at one another, then faded away together to talk and talk and talk and do all the things we wanted to do without offending dozens of people. Still, it's no good raving about that: that's only the very beginning, and I loved to see her again. She's a sweet person and I'm a dumb fool." My mother's version is shorter: she told me more than once that she was thrilled to see him at the play and dying to talk to him, but disappointed when he hardly said a word. Typical of quiet, diffident Roddy, the reticent Englishman, but also part of his appeal to Ann – most of the time.

Ann and Roddy met daily in a little sandwich shop on Fifth Avenue for Ann's half-hour lunch break from Hartman's, still feeling that it was all impossible, but lovely. "One night," Roddy wrote, "Marian had Ann to dinner. I was tongue-tied, almost miserable, then they made me talk panthers. That too was horrible." There were dinners at Ann's mother's house, walks, movies, parties and the flu. Roddy visited Ann as she was recovering, leaving her Henry Williamson's *Tarka the Otter* to read, and a few days later she returned the visit. "Ann came to see me and she was very sweet. She sat in a chair and she was going to be oh, so sensible. Then she walked across the room and kissed me, very firmly, very adorable, on the lips. After that she blushed and went away and I was left to think it over."

On another day "... we went back to Ann's house and I learned a little of the Elmore family. Mrs. E. is very nice and intelligent. Mary, Ann's sister, is shy, brilliant, rather startling to look at, but attractive. Buckie, the elder brother is a fascinating person. Slow and tough by nature, made unnaturally intelligent by his sisters; interested in ships and shipping; a good fellow, very upright and courageous; he's travelled a lot as a fireman and deckhand on ships, for which I admire him. And lastly there's Danny. He's nice; a youngster of about sixteen, at school near Victoria. Manners perfect – somehow a little too well-trained. Calls me 'sir' which is embarrassing, but it won't last. Altogether a very nice family and a tribute to intelligent upbringing."

Toward the end of January, Roddy returned to Comox and the cougars with his life unfolding in new directions. He and Ann had agreed privately to marry when he could be sure of a more certain income. Finishing the cougar book would, they hoped, do that. Harry Hartman, the bookseller Ann worked for, wrote a friend at Scribner's, who provided the names of New York literary agents. Roddy selected Harold Ober, and the firm has continued as agent for the Haig-Brown rights ever since. Roddy had also agreed to go back to the Nimpkish in the fall to work the guiding business with Ed Lansdowne.

The 1933 diary is full of pages of praise for Ann and delight at their love, as are their letters, now almost daily. In mid-February, Ann wrote: "You're quite right about our knowing each other even better through letters. I always found looking at you very distracting to my thoughts. And now I've been sad to find, too, that I can't vizualize your darling face. I have a very distinct picture of your grey flannel suit that I like, and your very English shirts and your brown gloves. And I love them and I love you." She was reading Sigrid Undset's *Kirsten Lavransdatter* with great delight. She later sent Roddy her copy and got another so they could both read it at the same time and compare their future together with that of the people in the novel.

But cougar hunting was the order of the day for Roddy now. Travelling in the deep Pacific Coast snow and brush was hard work and he had trouble with his knees – he treated them with coal oil poultices, which blistered his skin. He spent some time studying the behavior of two cubs he and Cecil Smith picked up after killing the mother and learned more for the panther book. (The cubs eventually went to a zoo.) It soon becomes apparent from the letters that Roddy and Ann plan to marry in 1934, even without much money. Roddy sent his manuscripts to Ann for typing and comment and began to plan the book. Letters from his mother approved of the marriage, but warned of the difficulties of living without a proper income, clearly reflecting her own early married years. She planned to come to the wedding, but decided finally that, ever the dutiful daughter, she had to stay with her father, now ninety, and a baby nephew whose parents were with the army in Egypt. The fact that there was a house full of servants and other family members who could have filled in so that she could go to her beloved Roddy's wedding seems not to have been considered.

In March Roddy went to Campbell River to stay with Reg Pidcock and fish for steelhead in the Campbell for the first time. This visit and the fishing are described in "House Hunting" in *A River Never Sleeps*. An agreement was reached for Roddy to live with Reg in the summer at Reg's invitation and write his cougar book. But first, back to Seattle. His aunt, Elspeth (Uncle Decie's wife and Marian Fisken's sister), arrived in Victoria from England in early April, so he met her ship and they went on to Seattle together. Love and the social round made work difficult, but eventually the Fisken household moved to their country house on Bainbridge Island in Puget Sound and the book got under way in a quieter setting. Roddy had to return to Seattle toward the end of June to see a doctor after a tonsil operation and, "a tiny bit to my surprise I found that I was staying the weekend at the Elmore's – which thing seemed very good to me." Ann's mother clearly also approved of their relationship. There Roddy's habit of keeping a regular diary ended, partly because he recognized that the letters to Ann were taking its place.

In a thank you note to Mrs. Elmore for that weekend visit, written on the Victoria ferry on the way back to Campbell River, Roddy urges her to come with Ann's sister, Mary, to visit him there so "you'll be able to gauge your daughter's needs ... but chiefly because I want to see you." She didn't get there, but his genuine affection for her is already clear.

Except during two weekend visits in Vancouver, for the rest of the time until their wedding in January of 1934, communication between Roddy and Ann was by mail. Roddy's letters were usually two long foolscap pages in his small, fine script, often written over a couple of days. Much of each letter concerned their love, as would be expected, which makes for rather repetitive reading to anyone else, but the letters were undoubtedly treasured then and for the rest of their lives, as all good love letters should be. The rest was a chronicle of the small details of daily life and the progress of the panther book. Ann's letters were usually written on heavy folded notepaper with deckle edges in her large, rounded handwriting. But some days they were from Harry Hartman's shop on little sheets from a notepad so that no one would notice her writing a letter. The letters were so frequent that they regularly crossed in the mail.

By mid-June Roddy was staying for two weeks in Room 309 of the Sylvia Court apartment hotel on English Bay in Vancouver. From there he wrote on June 14: "Sweetest and best, know you're lovely every way, mind and soul, heart and soul's soul, face and body, movements and thoughts and dreams. I adore you, darling heart, and six months will slip away somehow; even if it had to be six months of solid, unbroken agony, it'd be gone in the end. And we understand. We can break our own agony a little, steal away from it in doing things, awaken it and calm it at the same time by writing to one another. I love you, sweet, for always, but don't let's go away from each other when we're married.

I'm going up town now, to post this and do one or two odd jobs – amongst them get that picture of you framed, in a little leather frame if it doesn't cost too dam' much!"

Ann wrote, "This letter will do you no good, darling heart. I'm being selfish but after the first awful stab of waking up in the morning when all the conscious defenses are down and I only know that you've gone, I'm afraid to feel at all because it would surely hurt. And there are a thousand things to do, so I only do them with the feeling that, as you say, the world is vaguely empty. But I do belong to you, dearest, every second of every day, don't I?"

And on the 16th Roddy wrote: "I've not done a very good morning's work. I turned to last year's diary to look up something about that Panther at Nimpkish last August, then began looking through it, searching for little scraps about you. But I've written three pages of [Chapter] XXIV and I think I have the rest fairly clearly in my mind."

The parts of the book go back and forth for typing and comment and proofreading. Ann wrote late one night: "I've read to the end of XXIV, darling, and I could easily go on to the end only I don't think I'd take in much of it. I'm inclined to believe that it really is rather a presentable book, though it has it's bad spots. I wish you were here, so that you could read it straight through without stopping and tell me what you think."

Ann, and her mother as chaperon, came up to Vancouver and stayed at the Georgia Hotel for a couple of days. It would have been improper to stay in the same hotel as Roddy. The day before she came, Ann wrote: "I was so thrilled to get to the end of *Ki-yu* that I read it last night instead of writing you. I think it's a grand book, Roddy, and finishes exactly right. I can tell you more and better when I see you ... started to read a 1300-page novel called *Anthony Adverse* that I like very much."

Just before she arrived Roddy wrote: "In four hours time I'll be with you, dearest. I can't work; haven't done anything worth calling work for ages. Can't even sit down and write much to you. But I wonder, will we have chances to be alone and talk today and tomorrow? I've got such a lot of things I must tell you and I don't want to write them to you. Oh, I wish you were here for good. I'm in a mess now, Beloved; can't think, can't wait, can't work. I want to see you and be with you and talk to you. Sweetest heart, you're precious – so precious."

In the following week Roddy began the revision of the panther book, which eventually spread out over most of the next six weeks. But he also kept up with his correspondence and sent out some of his short stories (typed by Ann) to the new agent in New York. He wrote also to *Sporting and Dramatic* in England with story ideas, and *Oxford and Cambridge* magazine wrote him asking for submissions. And he worried about money and whether they would have enough to live on. He also wrote about the books and magazines he was reading – *Texts and Pretexts*, *War and Peace* (in a bad translation), *The New Yorker* (which became a lifelong habit) and the movies he saw – *Reunion in Vienna*, for one.

At the end of June Roddy left the Sylvia Court to spend two months at Reg Pidcock's house on his small farm at the edge of Campbell River. "This going farther away from you is quite beastly and yet somehow I don't have to mind much really because I can say to myself: 'Farther away, yes, but really nearer in the end. Every day is nearer, every place I go to and every place I leave is all on the way.'"

From Campbell River on July 1, he wrote: "My immediate jobs are clear enough and sufficiently difficult – to finish *Ki-yu* by the end of the month and live until the 18th or 20th on $10! Isn't that an awful confession to make to a woman you're going to marry in six months time? Darling, I can support you beautifully: 'I have ten dollars and I can spend it *all* if I want, in three weeks!' Tell me I'm hopeless, will you please, Beloved?" and: "I often think when I'm writing to you or reading one of your letters of the eternal stupid complaint of people who collect letters and make them into books. Remember it? 'In the hurry and rush of this modern age, when telephones and automobiles cut distances to nothing and people live in a mad whirl of gaiety from day's end to day's end, there is no time for the graceful art of writing letters.' But we find time – and need – don't we? And I'm rather glad we do, though I shan't be able to stand much more of it by the time October comes along and I can see you again."

To which Ann replied: "I need every word that you have a second to write. I wish I could write you more. But I don't seem to have very much time, and then when I do, there's so overwhelmingly much to say that I sit thinking instead of writing. I don't know why your confession about the ten dollars you have to live on makes me laugh. You won't go hungry though, will you?"

The next letter from Roddy contained a long description of the house and the surrounding orchard and garden, because Reg had agreed to rent it to them after they were married. The house was badly in need of furniture, he said, "but I think we'll make out alright. We can take down all the pictures and scatter some books about and have a few cushions and – oh, you know how a house grows like the people that are living in it." But he does continue to worry in quite a bit of detail over the coming months about domestic arrangements including fresh paint, building cupboards and bookshelves, and how big their bed should be. And he was already planning to grow sweet peas, which he did do in considerable profusion. Roddy's concern over the domestic side was probably brought on by a comparison of the amenities of the little house with those of his grandfather's establishment and Ann's family's simpler, but still very comfortable, Seattle household. He also cared about having pleasant surroundings for himself – he liked a nicely set table, flowers in the rooms and other touches of elegance.

Once, when asked if they had decided on Campbell River because of the river and Discovery Passage and the fish, Roddy replied, "No, because I had all those things pretty much in the Nimpkish too, ... but when I was going to get married, I realized that there was no road up there and there was no hospital within easy reach – there just wasn't anything, so the main attraction to Campbell River was that it was the end of the road, it had a hospital and had a school." Campbell River at the time was a small village with a few stores and a government wharf where the steamboats that carried the people and mail up and down the B.C. coast stopped. As with so many small coastal communities then, the economy was based on logging, fishing and tourism. It was, and still is, a supply center for the people who live on the islands between it and the mainland.

Amidst the domestic planning, the work of revising the panther book continued: "I've just finished Chapter III. Had an awful fight most of the day to get a decent description of David and King – remember it? I made it a good deal longer, but I'm not sure how you'll like it. Maybe it's too long now and some of the additions are awful. I wish you were here – and not for that one reason only!"

And more planning for their life in Campbell River: "Then I'm going to try and bring one of my skiffs down from the Nimpkish, so that we can have a good boat to keep up at the [Sandy] Pool and to take us up and down the river. Next year I can get a perfect 14-foot row-boat *that really will sail* from Painter for $30 or $40." Ann bought a typewriter at a good price for which Roddy congratulated her. She had obviously already become an important part of the work as a reader, but she was a particularly fast and accurate typist as well, which made a major contribution over many years.

During her holidays in July, Ann took over the family marketing and cooking in order to learn more of that aspect of married life. "I think an intensive two-week course will improve me considerably." Her letters in this period often mention the dinner menus. Ann reported with pleasure the comments of friends as news of their engagement gradually spread – the formal announcement would not be made until a few weeks before the wedding.

Roddy, the nominal Anglican, investigated the Campbell River church situation for Ann, the Catholic. "I found that there's mass at 10 a.m. on Sundays and 6 a.m. every day and Benediction at 7 p.m. on Sundays in the chapel at the hospital. So things are not so bad, are they?" (This was the chapel of Lourdes Hospital which was run by the Sisters of St. Anne and which was the only Catholic church in Campbell River for many years.)

The revision of the book continued: "I pitched hay again today and finished Chapter VIII tonight – remember the bad patches in it, about the ordinances of nature and so on? I've squashed them out, more or less, but I'm not sure if I've done it really well." To which Ann responded on July 20: "I didn't do anything but sit and go to bed early and read *Ki-yu*. I think the last draft is a great improvement and every word that's crossed out and replaced seems to have been for the better. I hope the typing's going to go as fast as I think it is because I haven't started." (It did.) Roddy replied: "It's a relief to know that you think the new draft of *Ki-yu* is an improvement. I should stop and work now, but I want to write to you for just a little more, please."

On July 22, Ann wrote about a literary lunch arranged by Miss Andrus, head of the Hartman rival, the book department of Frederick and Nelson, Seattle's major department store. "It was perfectly grand book-talk and publishing gossip that was tremendously exhilarating because I could let out to the full extent of my book knowledge and just fit in to the conversation. But Miss Andrus kept insisting all through lunch that I was to be her successor, so afterwards I told her why I couldn't and she delighted my soul by observing that she hadn't met you but that the author of *Silver* should be just about the right sort of person."

A week later Roddy discussed the matter of writing to each other: "... *I* like it and *I'm* doing it, so it can't be worth doing and it must be bad to like it. But I love writing to you and I'm going to keep on for a little longer anyway. Do you mind the bad writing from holding the paper on my knee with my feet on the mantelpiece? It's so good to get away from that dam' table for a little."

Ann on the same subject said, "Darling, you know I'd like more than anything to be calm and quiet with you, yet my letters when I read them over always sound rushed & breathless & disjointed. The thing is that when I start it seems absolutely essential to tell you every one of the thousand things that have made an impression on me during the day; but when I begin to write them, it seems that nothing is important except that I love you and want to be with you and am not. But I will be, won't I, beloved, soon? And for always."

Roddy sends Ann a thought of the future: "... I look forward to December in a picture —yourself and myself in some dam' little restaurant, with Lucky Strikes and coffee! Ann and coffee and Luckies! I don't know why; I still have some Luckies and I could go out and make some coffee, yet I don't want either. But if I were in Seattle now I should want to go out with you and have both ... On Sunday I shall go to Mass, I think, though I'm afraid without you in such a small place. They'll unmask me as a heretic. But the nuns would be kind because I would tell them I love a convent girl."

Part of Ann's share of the arrangements for their new life was to buy a new car and at the end of July she reported: "I've finished typing the first six chapters and I've got our Ford. It's a light grey-brown sort of a coupe with room in back for two steamer trunks —no rumble seat. It's a new one because I figured I might as well put the money in that, and then it'll be worth that much more when we come to sell it. I couldn't get much for the LaSalle — just how much depends on what the Ford people sell it for, but I'm delighted with the whole situation and I hope you are."

There is a gap in Roddy's letters that lasts from early August until one mailed from Alert Bay in late September. But it is clear from Ann's letters that Roddy mailed a letter whenever he could get to a post office, that Keith and Marian Fisken came to Campbell River in August to visit Roddy and fish for salmon, the revision of *Ki-yu* was completed and Roddy moved on up to the Nimpkish to keep his commitment to Ed Lansdowne to work the guiding business for the fall. The fish were running well and the guests were due to come just as the earliest fall rains in ten years came, making the fishing hopeless, so they had to call the guests and tell them not to come.

In a letter to Mrs. Elmore at the same time, Roddy wrote of his admiration for her whole family and sketched his schedule until he would arrive in Seattle in December. He also told her he really was finished the panther book at last — "... unless Ann says once more: 'That won't do at all' ... Then I shall do it half a dozen more times." Ann's enthusiasm for and encouragement of Roddy's work and his respect for her knowledgeable, educated opinion were already a key complementary part of their relationship.

Roddy wrote Ann of his frustration over the rain and she replied, "Precious, I'm sick about the rain. It hasn't stopped much down here, so I'm afraid it must have got worse than it was when you wanted to shoot holes in the roof. Aren't you bad though! I shan't let you get so furious about things that can't be helped and couldn't have been — like rain. And yet I love you because you do. And it is damned annoying." But the next day, feeling discouraged about things in general, she wrote: "I wish I could remember what I told you about not getting wrought up over things that can't be helped. All I can remember is your very good idea about the rifle-shots through the roof. Fortunately, I have no rifle."

The English magazine *Sporting and Dramatic* had accepted two more stories which paid enough for the ring Roddy wanted to buy. "A little thin one, sapphires all the way round and about five small diamonds set at regular intervals among the sapphires? Tell me if you think that's alright." Ann wrote back: "Do give me that ring when I am in Vancouver. I want it. But if you don't mind, I really don't like anything blue very well at all, and I'd rather, unoriginally, have any kind of a one wee diamond on a thin-as-can-be, plain ring," to which Roddy replied: "... I like your choice better than mine ... the only thing is that the single diamond on its narrow band seems top heavy ... But I think the jewellers have some means of off-setting that."

And in another exchange Roddy began: "And there's one important thing that I'm going to try and study a bit more thoroughly than we have so far – the art of not having children. Do you think it would be a good idea to invest in a copy of this Marie Stopes book? It sounds as if it might be very complete and very sound. Shall I? ... Do you suppose they allow this book in Canada? If not, do they in the States? I can get a copy from England anyway, I guess, and the Customs people probably wouldn't bother to look and see what it was." Ann replied: "I guess it would be a good idea to get that Stopes book. I don't know whether they allow it in the States or not, but I doubt it. If they do, it probably hasn't much practical in it. I think we better ask your doctor friend in Vancouver." They were obviously agreed on the necessity of birth control in spite of Ann's Catholic faith – in fact, they considered not having children, given the state of the world at the time. The English doctor Marie Stopes' pioneering work on sexuality and birth control was not available in either country and Roddy did consult his doctor.

Without the dudes Ed and Roddy were free to go over to Kingcome Inlet on the B.C. mainland for an excursion into the mountains as research for further stories, or as Roddy put it in a letter to Mrs. Elmore, "collect stories from various intelligent liars." They stayed with Lansdowne cousins there who were a "wild and woolly" lot and Roddy thoroughly enjoyed himself. After an unsuccessful attempt to kill a wild cow for beef, Ed, Roddy and Ed's uncle, Hilly, set out up Kirby's Gully. They spent a couple of days up there and Roddy came back full of enthusiasm for the place. It would seem likely from his description that Kirby's Gully became the setting for parts of Roddy's novel *On the Highest Hill* many years later.

Roddy's next letter was from Reg Pidcock's Campbell River farm again, where he had gone to prepare the house as best he could for Ann's arrival – Reg was still living there and wanted Roddy to hunt deer and fish for the larder and leave the painting to him to do after Roddy went back to Vancouver. Wedding arrangements were moving along: "I've got to be practical for a minute or two ... Do whatever you like about announcements and so on – whatever your Mother likes. My name is RODERICK LANGMERE HAIG HAIG-BROWN. I've written it out in full because it's really more respectable for a girl to know her husband's name before she marries him."

Ann wrote: "This business of being officially engaged seems as though it would be rather pleasant, because it's something definite. But not as definite as seeing you would be. And it will make this Christmas holidays harder than the last one was, because we can't go our secret ways so much and I shall have to ask you to do things you may not like very well. How foul all this sounds. I'll stop, beloved."

Roddy, alarmed, replied: "What will you have to ask me to do that I shan't like very well? Go out and be inspected? I'll hate that but I'll stand it somehow. Go to dull parties and not be rude to people? If I'm not to be rude I shall have to be duller than the dullest – probably sulky ... Shall we come straight up [to Campbell River] or go somewhere first? ... I think I couldn't possibly stand a stag dinner the night before the day though; they won't make me do that, will they?" The formal announcement of the engagement brought a flurry of excitement and much praise of Roddy, and Ann said it "seemed to change the face of things vastly for the better."

On November 2, Roddy wrote from the CPR ferry from Nanaimo to Vancouver that he had left a carbon of the *Ki-yu* typescript with Cecil Smith when he stopped in Comox on the way down, and was making plans to travel with him again. But most important, Ann and her mother were coming to spend the weekend in Vancouver: "Isn't it good to be able to say 'day after tomorrow'? Feels wonderful to me." He had had a story accepted by *Canadian Forest and Outdoors*, but an acquaintance who also wrote for them said they were bad about paying. "... if they don't pay me I'll take much pleasure in using some bad language on paper. Some magazine editors are the scum of the earth and need to be told so."

In Vancouver, Roddy settled into Room 410 in the Sylvia Court. His stay there began with a glorious weekend with Ann. The engagement ring with the single diamond was duly presented. Ann and her mother stayed at the York Hotel, but my mother told me she and Roddy actually got engaged at the Sylvia. A veiled reference in a later letter implies that they perhaps did more than get formally engaged there. From then on Roddy's letters become more and more rhapsodic on the wonders of Ann – he is clearly more than ready to love a woman who is his intellectual equal and whom he sees as being both stimulating and supportive. It is as if he has found a haven at last after wandering, both literally and figuratively, for a number of years. The letters from these last six weeks cover ninety-five long foolscap pages in Roddy's fine, small handwriting and a few could be missing.

"I thought of 1926, 1927, 1928. All years in which I passed through Seattle and did not know you. I thought of 1929 and how it seemed only a little sad when I had to sail for England. Of 1930 and 1931 when a hundred things might have happened differently to keep me from coming back to this country. Of 1932, when a hundred things might have happened to send me away again without having seen you. And none of these things happened so the world is more glorious to me than I had thought it ever could be."

One evening he visited with friends and reported, "quite nice, except for one thing. They all sit there and hang upon the words of Professor Hill-Tout – I've told you that before haven't I? Well, he had read *Silver* before I saw him last time; but since then he's read *Pool and Rapid* too, and when I came into the room he proceeded to deliver a eulogy of both books. It was an extravagant eulogy and I was very, very embarrassed – knocked clean into mumbling incoherence, and if there's one state I hate more than any other, it's exactly that." Ann replied: "How do you go on writing me lovelier and lovelier letters after you've written me perfect ones since you first began? I wish I'd heard Professor Hill-Tout's eulogy, but I'm glad I wasn't there, because if you were embarrassed I'd have been."

Roddy was worried about the possibility of long term effects from his undefined illness in England in the summer of 1931, and began a regimen of exercise on the advice of his doctor who said he was feeling lazy because city life was too sedentary for an active man. The exercise therapist "looked at me for about two seconds and said, 'What do you do? Invent or write books or write music or paint pictures?'" and told him to come four times a week for "lazy, slack-muscled exercises" to relax him. He bought a three-quarter bed at Spencer's department store, and a .22 rifle with a gold sight for Ann [she may have been a little dismayed at that – there is no mention of it in her letters, but the rifle is still in the family], ordered a plain gold wedding band and asked his mother to send his "tailcoat and a couple of white waistcoats."

He waited also, with growing trepidation, for news from his London agent of Black's acceptance of *Panther*. At the same time Ober was attempting to find a U.S. publisher. Eventually Blacks turned the book down because of too much violence and disagreement over the need for illustrations – they wanted them, Roddy didn't, partly because his royalties would be less, but mainly because he didn't feel that a well-written book needed them and he had confidence in *Ki-yu*. (British publishing rights were finally sold to Jonathan Cape on March 23, 1934, and the book was published that fall without illustrations. U.S. and Canadian rights went to Houghton Mifflin on March 14 and they also published in the fall, with illustrations by Kurt Weise.)

But well over half the pages of the letters are filled with words of love in all their permutations and combinations. Roddy said, "I'm going to marry you because I love you, and I want you because I love you, and

I need you because I love you. But when you're married to me you'll be filling a thousand *concrete* needs of mine, giving me a host of things that I have to have. You'll have to think seriously and make quite sure that I'm not marrying you in the good old backwoods spirit – 'She's a good cook and a tolerable tidy woman. She can milk the cows and cut wood and carry a couple of pails full of water.'" Shortly afterwards Ann wrote that she had slept till noon that Sunday and was now trying to make things "tolerable tidy."

Roddy added eye exercises, swimming and a chiropodist to his regimen. This was going to be a very healthy bridegroom! And well-dressed. After considerable debate because of the cost, Roddy decided he must have a new gray flannel suit made in order to look decent at the wedding parties – he had been brought up to dress well and a good gray flannel suit was the basis of his city wardrobe all his life. Ann told him: "I shall gasp with wonder at your new suit as often as you like. It won't be hard, because you know I have a strong tendency to gasp with wonder and delight every time I see you – every time I think of you even." Ann never did stop gasping in wonder at Roddy – and not just when he was dressed in a new gray flannel suit.

Roddy filled his free hours with movies and books. On one occasion he "... found a movie theatre I've been looking for – one showing Edward Robinson in *Little Giant* and *Rome Express* – two pretty decent movies for 15 cents ... My eyes didn't hurt when I got home, until I had read about 50 pages of Proust ... I like your Proust, but one must be quiescent for him, in a mood to read slowly, to savour and enjoy what is often pure (I think this is the right word) virtuosity."

There was, of course, much more discussion of Proust in the next few letters, and other writers too. Mrs. Blackmore (who provided his meals at her boarding house – probably cheaper than the hotel dining room) confessed that her favorite author – she couldn't remember his name – had written a lot of stories about one Fu Manchu, and that a friend of hers had seventeen volumes of his works "... 'all beautifully bound in black and gold.' Game, set and match to Sax Rohmer. Why does one bother to write?"

Roddy continued to shop for the house – found paint on sale – and other equipment. "I've worked out a rather good idea about the sleeping bags and told Jones [Tent and Awning] about it today. I'm going to have two light bags made, each with a zip fastener all down one side and across the bottom. Then one bag can be laid out flat, the other laid on top of it and ... make a perfect double bag. Or, if we want, we have two single bags. Doesn't that sound good darling?" Congratulatory letters on their engagement came from friends and relations and had to be answered, and there were regular letters to his mother and Uncle Decie, as well as correspondence with his agents.

"The letter you forwarded was from the governess who taught me to read and write – she had seen the notice mother put in the *Times*. I'll send you her letter soon because it's a good letter, probably good because she hasn't seen me since, I think, about 1914 or even earlier!" The "governess's" name was Angela Beanlands and she was actually Roddy's form mistress at his first school in Shoreham. She sent Christmas cards and little presents for us for many years. The sound of her name always fascinated me.

Roddy wrote also to Mrs. Elmore. In reply to hers about whom to send wedding invitations to, he said, "Marian and Keith and Mr. and Mrs. McEwan. But I've a suspicion that won't do." In the end he left it up to Ann to advise in conjunction with Marian and said he would accept their decision. (But a list in Roddy's handwriting of some forty names and addresses of family and friends in England and a few in B.C. is among the letters, so he obviously put his mind to it eventually.) Later in the same letter Roddy says, "Mother ... is still convinced she'll get out in May. I'm not, but I'm hoping for the best ... Poor Mother. She spends a lifetime trying to keep a son from making mistakes and defending him when he does, and then she's denied the chance of watching him do the one really sensible thing he's ever managed to do."

Roddy's new agent in New York, Harold Ober, sent back two animal stories because they were too cruel – the natural world wasn't tame enough for readers of the day. Roddy was also dealing with Black's objections to *Ki-yu* on the same grounds. "What am I to do. Write wishy-washy, tolerable stuff, of the type that's been written for years and years ... I don't think of it as cruel, you see; animals can't be 'cruel' or 'kind'. The things they do are natural things ..."

He fussed regularly about all the pre-wedding parties, and Ann had begun to worry about inflicting them on him. "And you can stop, altogether, worrying about me and the parties ... I write you that I'm terrified of the parties and so on and so on, because it's quite easy to write all that, because I probably shall be a bit embarrassed now and then, and because I wouldn't go to a whole bunch of parties of any kind from choice. But, Lord alive, I don't really care; I shall probably enjoy them far more than I expect to – parties affect me much as boxing used to; I'm panic-stricken before I get into the ring, but quite happy once I'm there. And we can't cram an awful pile of them into five weeks." Roddy didn't change his attitude toward parties much over his lifetime, but his own assessment was right in that he enjoyed them once he got there and invariably charmed his fellow guests, especially the women.

At last December 13th arrived. The doctor had declared him fit and healthy, he had gained some weight and put on "some good smooth muscle" and the optician declared that his eyes had improved in record time. And a letter from his mother, "enclosing a windfall, a cheque for £25 from the niece of one of my godfathers, with instructions to buy myself a 'book or something to remember him by.' So ... I bought that little Shakespeare that I coveted." Roddy had described it in an earlier letter as "little light volumes with good paper and clear, clear print, easy to hold up and easy to read. But, of course, the infernal things had to be bound in real leather, which appealed to the second-hand bookstore man a lot and to me not at all, with the result that he wanted $7." His mother was now planning to buy a steamer ticket for May 12, to his delight.

And so the letters ended and Roddy took the boat to Seattle to stay with Keith and Marian until January 20, 1934. Two people who had started the journey through the first twenty-five years of their lives a continent and an ocean apart, yet were still introduced in correct fashion through family and friends, were about to test their own certainty that they would magnificently enhance each other's lives.

·4· Ann and Roddy (1934 — 1936)

Once Roddy arrived in Seattle, shortly before Christmas 1933, the social round got going in earnest. Ann was committed to her job at Hartman's until the Christmas rush was over and, as in the previous year, would have had little time for lunch, but just being together, now formally engaged, and probably spending all their evenings in each other's company must have been sheer joy.

There is a tiny 1934 pocket diary of Roddy's that begins with a list of wedding present checks, mostly from English relatives for £5 or £10 and including one from "Grandfather" [Pope] for £50. These must have eased the financial worries considerably – Roddy wanted to have a nest egg of $500, but the new gray flannel suit had cost $75 and made that goal seem distant a few weeks earlier. My mother told me that one thing Roddy bought with this money was a pair of silver candlesticks at Birks in Vancouver. They would have seemed to him a necessity for a nicely arranged dinner table, which he very much appreciated. We certainly used them on countless occasions over the years.

The tiny diary begins listing, on January 4, a series of lunches, teas and dinners, many with people who remained lifelong friends of the family and visited Campbell River regularly, especially Edward Dunn, who was best man at the wedding. Mixed with the social engagements are a couple of dentist appointments and, on January 8, the words "Marriage license" appear. On Saturday, January 20, 1934, the wedding day,

Roddy wrote simply, "Ann." They were married in the vestry of the church because mixed marriages were not allowed in the church proper in those days.

For the following two and a half weeks the little book lists the places Ann and Roddy travelled to on their wedding trip. The trip took them south into California at Yreka, to Carson City via Truckee and Reno and on to Crestview where they stayed for two days high in the mountains. Ann described it in a letter to her mother as "an absolutely perfect place seven thousand feet up though there's only a little snow and there's been bright sun all day and a marvellous moon to-night." From there they went to Barstow and on to Big Bear Lake via San Bernadino. They travelled south to the Mexican border via Palm Springs where they spent the day with Seattle friends, but didn't stay because it was too expensive. After looking over the border at Mexico, they started back north via Escondido, where, as Roddy described it to Mrs. Elmore, they "found a little old hotel in an orange grove with eucalyptus trees behind it, and geraniums and roses and lots of nice things." They then stopped with a friend in Pasadena and visited the Huntington Galleries. Then it was homeward via Santa Maria and Berkeley, where Ann no doubt showed Roddy some of the important places from her university days. They continued north via Santa Rosa and Crescent City and through the redwoods to Salem via Grant's Pass. They arrived back in Seattle at 5:45 p.m. on February 8. There followed another ten days of lunches and dinners and, no doubt, packing up the Ford. Because Ann had bought this car with her earnings, the family cars were kept in her name for a number of years in continued acknowledgement of that initial purchase.

Ann and Roddy left Seattle on February 19th to spend a few days in Vancouver at the Sylvia Court. Ann wrote her mother from there that she had at last seen her gun. The gun, the sleeping bags and other outdoor equipment that my father bought indicate a vision of taking his city girl out into the woods to enjoy the good parts of the life he had lived up at the Nimpkish. This happened only rarely and my mother, although she enjoyed the natural world, did not become an avid camper or outdoorswoman, partly because of children, but also, I think, because both she and my father preferred the comforts of their own house. Ann and Roddy went to Campbell River on February 24th.

My mother told me, years later, that she cried when she arrived at the rented farmhouse. Reg Pidcock was still in residence, which would have been a bit dismaying – newly married couples don't generally want to share their living space. Either Roddy did not know Reg would still be there or he did not think to tell Ann – probably the former. However, Reg seems to have stayed only long enough to welcome them; he customarily went to visit relatives in California after Christmas. The basement was full of wood, which was essential for both heating and cooking, though whether the walls were painted or not wasn't mentioned. On March 9, a note says: "Furniture arrived." This would have been furniture Roddy had bought in Vancouver. On the same day Roddy wrote: "News of [Jonathan] Cape's acceptance of *Ki-yu*," which must have made that a momentous day after all the waiting and worrying of the previous year while Black's balked over the manuscript because they thought the story cruel.

In a March letter to her mother Ann told of settling in, buying gingham material for curtains, having the local priest to tea, eating dinner on a mahogany gate-leg table brought from Seattle. She also let her mother know that: "We really have four guns over our living room fireplace." And "I really made that butter Roddy told you about." Ann told of starting on a garden and wished they had her sister Mary's expert help, and of the ordeal of being hostess for a hospital fund monthly bridge party.

A few pages of Roddy's tiny diary contain lists of both long and short wave radio broadcast schedules. Many of the listings are for classical music programs and include Kirsten Flagstad, Lily Pons, Laurence Tibbett and John Charles Thomas. There are also times listed for "Lux Radio Theatre," "March of Time," "Firestone Hour" and "Richfield" every night at 10. Mother told me they used to sit in front of the fire, smoke and listen to Jack Benny, Burns and Allen, and Ed Wynn, among others. In one of numerous writer's notebooks kept over the years, Roddy wrote of a perhaps typical winter evening: "Peer Gynt Suite No. 2. Little blue disk on the radio, with glass in front of it. Ann's turquoise blue dressing gown reflected against the dark blue disc, seeming luminous. Her white hands on the typewriter keys, moving busily. Every now and then one hand reached out to throw the carriage back, revealing a little of her arm. Blue smoke from pipe going up across the reflection. A yellow room and yellow light. Dark brown of gunstocks. Warmth. George Santayana's *Last Puritan* just started, lying on the bed for a moment as the cradle song reaches its perfection."

In early May Roddy wrote Mrs. Elmore to say that she could not have Mary, who had come to visit, back yet as "she's really done wonders for us. The flower garden looks like something. Another set of curtains is almost finished. Yesterday she helped me bring a skiff up the river and landed a trout." Roddy's own first efforts at growing vegetables pleased him, too. In the end, Mrs. Elmore came and picked Mary up, thus also paying her first visit to Campbell River.

A few days later, pain in Ann's side caused some worry. It was eventually diagnosed by a Victoria doctor as a slightly displaced uterus and an adherent appendix. This also explained why she was not yet pregnant as she had hoped to be. An operation was planned, but had to be coordinated with the next big event in the new family's life. The last note in the little diary was on May 12: "Mother sails from England." In a letter to Mrs. Elmore from Vancouver the previous November, Roddy had said: "It will be fun, won't it? She'll be very amazed at everything and probably quite frightened. Maybe Ann and I had better acclimatise her at Campbell River before we rush her down to Seattle!" But Mrs. Haig-Brown had only a few days in Campbell River before they all went to Seattle to Ann's brother Bucky's formal wedding to Charlotte (Gar) Eddy – they had actually eloped the fall before. Roddy's mother stayed in Seattle with Ann's mother, while the newlyweds and the almost newlyweds returned to Campbell River. But then came cables from England saying that Mrs. Haig-Brown's father really was dying and she had to return there, sadly for everyone.

Photographs taken in the summers of 1934 and '35 show Seattle friends up for the salmon fishing, sometimes guided by Roddy and sometimes by professional guides such as the Pidcocks. Some friends stayed with Ann and Roddy and some at the camp on the Spit at the mouth of the river run by Ned and June Painter. (This camp was the beginning of the famous Painter's Lodge, built across the river mouth from the Spit.) In August of 1934 Ann caught a 33½ pound tyee salmon, to Roddy's great delight. The Painters themselves soon became lifelong friends, as did Tom and Mavis Hudson (Tom had also gone to Charterhouse, although the two men had not known each other there. Ann had given a tea welcoming Mavis to Campbell River after their June marriage in Victoria), Joe and Marjorie Meredith (Joe was a guide, too) and Bathurst and Dorothy Hall (he was the doctor).

During those first two years of marriage Ann and Roddy acquired a cocker spaniel for Ann, two Labradors named Souse ("Black Fisherman" in *Woods and River Tales*) and Nellie in hopes of breeding and selling puppies and, one summer, a cougar kitten, which did not live, but was the subject of a story sold to a British magazine. The spaniel was perhaps another example of Roddy's assuming that Ann would be a sort of British countrywoman – my mother was never very fond of dogs, or cats, and the very idea of her being a doggy person seems quite funny in retrospect. They gardened with some success (in "The Garden" in *Measure of the Year*). Finances were always tight, according to my mother, but Roddy's mother, no doubt remembering the financial difficulties of her own early married life and having inherited money when her father died, did send £200 a year until Second World War currency restrictions prevented it. Some of the money may have been the remains of Roddy's education fund.

They lived on the Spit at the mouth of the Campbell in a tent for a week or two the first summer while Roddy guided tyee fishermen, but Ann confessed to her mother that she did not much enjoy it, and Roddy had never been very keen on guiding. The cow ate the vegetable garden while they were gone. Mary came again in the fall, and Ann joined Roddy and Cecil Smith in a couple of cougar hunts, "but missed the time they got one." The first year of the marriage concluded with Mrs. Elmore, Mary and Danny coming to Campbell River for Christmas.

Ki-yu: A Story of Panthers was published in November of 1934 in both England and the U.S. The *New York Times* reviewer, B.L. Buell, wrote: "A superbly written biography of a panther, Ki-yu ... It is also a story of the wild life of the northern forest told with the veracity of a man who has known this life for a long time, and who can translate the majesty as well as the cruelty of the eternal struggle for existence among animals into vivid, swinging prose." But Buell also thought the book too long.

Plans for the new year included a visit from Roddy's sisters, for whom Reg made two bedrooms in the attic of the house during the spring. Gardening began again, with help from Mary. Mrs. Elmore entertained Lord and Lady Baden-Powell, who were on a tour of the U.S. as leaders of the Scout movement, while they were in Seattle. Roddy only felt a little guilty about not rushing down to see his godfather.

In May, Roddy's sisters and his mother arrived to take up the interrupted visit of the previous year. Now that Mrs. Haig-Brown was not tied by her father, they were on a round-the-world trip. But the operation Ann needed could no longer be put off, so in mid-June they all went to Victoria. Roddy and his mother stayed there with friends until Ann could travel, and his sisters went on to Seattle. The doctor who performed the surgery was an old friend of Ann's father's. In a note to Roddy he said: "There is still a case of champagne in our basement which Dr. Elmore was reserving for [Ann's] wedding. When prohibition came in I ordered a stock of various wines and Dr. Elmore got me to get him some. When he came over to see young Buck at school here, he usually carried off a bottle or two for his friends at the hotel, but asked me to keep intact the case of champagne. I shall be glad to hand this over." The reason that the champagne had not been used for the wedding, even though Prohibition was ended, was probably because, with Ann's father dead, no one remembered that it was in Victoria.

Once Ann recovered enough to travel, she and Roddy and his mother went to Seattle. From there Roddy's mother and the girls travelled on to the Orient. Ann and Roddy were back in Campbell River by mid-July. That fall they spent several weeks in Seattle and the Elmores came to Campbell River for Christmas again. Ann's operation had proved successful and she was expecting a baby in April.

Roddy kept a diary titled *ANYBODY'S DAUGHTER* for the baby, Valerie Joan. He started it after I was born on April 21, but backtracked and chronicled the events of the weeks before the birth as well. He begins: "Why it should be written, I don't know; except perhaps that it will one day amuse her (or disgust her) and that it will keep for me a record of how small things grow and develop." In the end he concluded that babies didn't develop very much like cougar kittens, the small animals he knew best at that time. Along with details of my mother's health and my progress, the diary tells quite a lot of family life.

The baby diary tells us that Ann and Roddy made the then day-long drive to Victoria in January and Ann went to Seattle to be checked by her doctor. It had been decided to have the baby there so that specialists (who would have been family friends) could assist, and Ann would have the help of her mother and sister with the new baby. This also meant that the baby would have dual citizenship. Roddy stayed in Victoria with a friend "for reasons of economy." When they returned to Campbell River, the weather turned cold and snowy, but "I managed to get up the river with Ann now and then for the last oddments of duck-shooting season and to try for steelhead." In February Roddy hurt his back and spent two weeks lying prone. "We found a boy who brought up wood and split it, but at ten or eleven o'clock each night Ann would have to plough her way through the snow to the smokehouse and bank up the fire." The smokehouse, which was probably in the base of the water tower, would have contained either venison or salmon, and was important because, with no electricity, the only other method of preservation was canning. In spite of the back he says, "I worked well this year from Christmas to the middle of March." He would have been beginning work on *The Western Angler* as well as writing articles and stories.

In early March "... I began to work hard on the garden, filling sweet pea trenches, making the big new square bed in front of the house and, finally, planting sweet pea seeds. It was only just possible to get them safely in in time to leave for Seattle at the right moment ... Ann came out to indulge in her little spring trick of burning [dead grass] along the fences." They made the trip to Seattle via Vancouver where they stayed at the York Hotel. Souse was entered in a dog show there where he took his "fourth Best of Breed ribbon." Several close Seattle friends were also pregnant, including Gertrude Dunn Jackson and Ann's sister-in-law, Gar. I was born four days after my cousin Mary Ann (Garby), both of us in the Swedish Hospital. On May 9, they brought me home from the hospital to my maternal grandmother's house and settled me in a woven basket with folding legs that Roddy had bought. This basket has since held most of the family babies, including a couple of great-grandchildren.

On May 14, Ann wrote in the baby diary, "Father has gone sorrowfully on a very necessary two weeks' trip to the interior of B.C." But he wrote every other day with details of the trip described in "On the Water and In the Mail" in *The Western Angler*. He also spent a few days at Vernon with Tommy and Becky Brayshaw, both of whom he thoroughly enjoyed. Brayshaw later did the illustrations for the second edition of *The Western Angler*. Roddy returned to Seattle on June 3, and on June 7, I was christened Valerie Joan, after Roddy's two sisters, at St. Patrick's Church. The next day they took the ferry to Victoria and the following day drove slowly up the Island, stopping at Cecil Smith's to show off the baby, and arrived home in time for the 10 o'clock bottle. "It looks like a good place for her, this house at Campbell River, with its hayfield and the flowers in the garden and the river flowing by."

Woven through the details of my early days are the comings and goings of Campbell River friends and neighbors (my mother gave a tea for me a few days after their return), as well as Seattle people and Uncle Decie. Roddy spent a week in late June helping Reg with the haymaking. In mid-July Edward Dunn came to go to Buttle Lake with Roddy on a research trip for *The Western Angler*. His sister Dorothy and her husband, Emery Bayley, came shortly afterwards on their honeymoon. Paul Jackson, who was my godfather and married to Edward's sister Gertrude, came for ten days. In mid-August Ann and I made a quick trip to Seattle to see the doctor for a checkup, and Ann's sister Mary came back with us to stay for a month. The list of Seattle visitors grew and Roddy wrote: "Full days these, the 'season' for the place and the season for ourselves also. So many of our friends come up, some simply to see us, some primarily to catch fish. Even now it makes life exciting for V.J. and in time it will be really valuable to her, counteracting the only disadvantage of living in the country which is lack of people."

On September 3, the baby diary reads: "Today she stayed at home with Aunt Mary while Ann and I went to Courtenay to arrange about the new house." Roddy's grandfather had left a legacy of £1000, which made it possible for Ann and Roddy to buy Herbert Pidcock's house a hundred yards up the river from the house they were renting. In a letter to Mrs.

Elmore, Roddy describes the transaction thus: "$4600, the full price for a piece of property described as Lot 3 (20 acres) sub-division of part of Lot 66, Plan 2596, Sayward District, Comox Assessment District, B.C. The assessed values are Land: $2500, Improvements $3220, on which we have to pay a tax of $21.10 with an additional school tax of $37.15. The insurance rates are $20.00 per thousand for three years on both house and personal property." My grandmother was selling both insurance and real estate and would have been interested in the details. Roddy thought they might live there ten years or so. "She'll like it for as long as that I know," Roddy wrote in the baby diary, "and be happy with so much space to play in, with the garden and the lawn, the clump of maples and fir behind the garage, the barn and the alder bottom that runs into the pasture across the road. She'll swim in the river in summer time ..."

Buying a small farm of their own really plunged Ann and Roddy into country life. Roddy's Dorset country upbringing would have given him a feel for the life and he had pitched in at the Lansdownes', so knew what was involved in running a subsistence farm on Vancouver Island. He had also picked up some carpentry skills on the Nimpkish. But Ann, the city girl, took on her share just as solidly. Her mother had kept a vegetable garden in Seattle, so there was some feel for the earth in her background, too.

It took a couple of months to get the house ready and, in a late September letter from Roddy to Mrs. Elmore, he described an overnight camping trip he and Ann made to Buttle Lake. They left me with the nuns at the hospital and I came home singing in a high falsetto – Ann presumed in imitation of the voices of the nuns as they fussed over me. The letter told of Roddy's plans for the land – he was hoping to have a neighbor farm it for him. Ann's letters to her mother are more than ever full of house details and baby news. An October letter from Ann accepted with delight the offer of the twin beds that were in her Seattle bedroom. This meant that they would be able to afford a rug for the living room. The spinet desk that Ann's father had given her for her fourteenth birthday was to be shipped at the same time as the beds.

The Pidcock brothers had built their two houses in the early twenties and only the main floor rooms – kitchen, living room, bathroom and two bedrooms – were fully finished at the time. A small bedroom for me was created on the east side of the upstairs. Ann painted the room – "Three pale blue walls and pale blue ceiling. The fourth wall which has two windows looking out across the orchard and down the river, is yellow," wrote Roddy. (I still fondly remember waking up in the little blue and yellow room on sunny mornings.) "The carpenter put in a good closet in one corner and I laid new flooring." The carpenter also worked on kitchen cupboards, put some new windows in the living room, and built a bookcase for Roddy's study next to their bedroom on the main floor. Roddy "floored the upstairs and is planning to do over the Beaver-boarded guest room, so it will be rather a grand place by Christmas," said Ann to her mother.

On October 21 Roddy wrote in the diary: "Today is the last of the difficult times though, for we've resolved to move tomorrow even though nothing is ready or finished and the carpenter will not be able to come [again] for several days yet." And next day, "Joe [Meredith] came with the wagon this afternoon and we moved with remarkably little effort." Two days later, "Today and yesterday were busy days – the winter's wood supply. Johnny [Perkins] hauling cordwood from the alder bottom, Reg and myself cutting it with the circular saw and throwing it into the basement." Life in the new house was a reality.

·5· Above Tide (1936 – 1940)

It must have been enormously satisfying to Ann and Roddy to feel that they had their own roof over their heads. They had been married two and a half years ago with very little money and only the beginning of a writing career to support them. Now they had a farm with a cow and chickens, a baby to start their family, and the writing was beginning to add up, with three books in print.

In October 1936, on the first Sunday in the new house, Roddy wrote in the baby diary: "We let ourselves forget about moving and cutting wood and the new house and all such horrors today and so spent our first normal day under this roof. It was a nice day, cold and sunny, but we didn't go out much. There was the radio, symphony orchestras, comedians and all the other Sunday delights." And a couple of days later: "These are such glorious days. I cannot remember such a fall, ever. The wood is all cut and stowed in the basement. The house can look after itself for a while. The willow grouse season is in, the birds are in the crab-apple swamps and the swamps are dry underfoot. So the dogs and I go out and fight our way through hardhack and alder and poplar and crab-apple, finding birds here and there, missing quick shots and sometimes killing."

At the end of October Roddy wrote, "It is pleasant to feel that we are really in this house now, and settled for the winter. Good alder wood is piled right up to the basement ceiling. Potatoes and carrots are stored away. And the fruit is in hundreds of bottles, waiting quietly enough until Ann wants to use it. That readiness for winter is a good experience ... when one is conscious of it the house becomes a castle ready to stand siege."

In mid-November came two weeks of agony —even the baby's book is filled with it. The prize-winning Labrador retriever, Souse, and a visiting beagle ran off. The visiting dog came back in a couple of days but the search for Souse continued. On November 14, Roddy wrote, "I hunted for him again this afternoon until it was dark & I had to hurry out of the woods with the Cape Mudge foghorn as my guide." And later, "These five days have gone in vain & more & more hopeless searching. I shouldn't describe them in here I suppose, but the story of them accounts for my failure to pay much attention to V.J." Roddy walked as much as twenty miles a day whistling and calling, and a friend even consulted a psychic (who wasn't far wrong), before Souse was found after two weeks a few miles across the river in unfamiliar territory. He was "thin & with one ear torn, but well & strong and in good condition."

On December 1, "The river was in good shape yesterday so Reg and I went up to the pool and started the steelhead season. Caught a nice fish of nearly 15 pounds, a tiny part of which today made V.J.'s first taste of steelhead." And next day: "As though yesterday was not enough today she had venison for the first time. Reg killed the last buck of the season about ten days ago, a good big two-pointer who had hardly started to run."

Roddy reported to Mrs. Elmore in early December on the hospital dance "which minor calamity occurred last night ... there was no trouble, very little drinking, and good music, edible food, excellent coffee and a fair floor ... Ann has proved herself a capable president and those dear old ladies are not always easy to handle." Roddy loved to dance and did so smoothly and elegantly. He had once considered, in a moment of infatuation with an aspiring dancer-actress in England, becoming a professional dancer himself.

The pages of the baby's book are soon filled for several days with world events as Franklin Roosevelt is elected president of the U.S. and King Edward VIII abdicates the throne of England, the latter a great sorrow to Roddy and Ann who felt he needn't have. Roddy speculated on the possible effects of the abdication on his daughter's future. Canada was still very much part of the British Empire and a stable monarchy was seen as vital to the proper order of the state. On December 23, Ann's mother, sister Mary, and brother Danny arrived to spend the first Christmas in the new house.

The book is kept up for a few days into the new year, and on January 3: "A grim day for me ... Serious and almost insuperable trouble with the pump. Ann says that my silent – and sometimes not silent – rage, with its accompaniment of slamming doors upset [V.J.] quite a lot." The water system consisted for several years, until the house had electricity, of a small paddle wheel on a raft in the river. When the raft was winched out into the current the wheel powered a pump which filled a tank at the top of a tower near the house. The tank was high enough that gravity then fed the water into the house. It was partly because of the water system that the house got its name of Above Tide. In a note written during the time in Reg's house there is a passage titled "War Between Tide and River" that reads: "In its more magnificent moods, and in the river's gentler moods, the tide floods above the bridge. But you could only know that if you lived in our house." Observation of the river was a constant, but it was from the water system rafts that Roddy noticed the tide at Reg's and the lack of same in the new house.

The final entry concerns what I seem to see out the kitchen window. "The birds, hungry and coming close to the house for food we have put out, please her ... Juncos, chickadees, song sparrows and big spotted towhees. She watches for an hour or more at a time. She watches with a sort of wonder, though not much understanding. Quick movement, something for her eyes to follow; perhaps colours and perhaps occasionally a light beady eye whose light catches hers ... Swamp robins are such grand birds that I wish they'd come close too, but they won't. Shy and timid and quick, they stay in the mountain ash trees and the hawthorns."

The news of the household for the next decade or so comes largely from letters written to the two grandmothers. Roddy's sisters returned his to him after their mother died, and Ann's brother Danny carefully kept those to their mother. The letters to Roddy's mother describe all the regular events, while those to Ann's mother are more concerned with immediate details of gardening projects, or children's cute sayings and activities or visitors from Seattle.

The letters tell of me sprouting teeth, claim I am talking and report on continued and lasting snow. Ann made marmalade, Roddy went to Board of Trade meetings, kept writing and thanked Mrs. Elmore for a birthday subscription to the *Saturday Review of Literature*. [Campbell River was unincorporated in those days and the Board of Trade served as a kind of unofficial local council. Roddy was the secretary. Such public service would have seemed a given to Ann and Roddy – both their families considered community work a natural obligation.] Ann completed her second term as hospital auxiliary president with a successful dance and bazaar. With spring the garden of the new house is frequently described in all its glory, and Ann and Roddy worked to make it even more dramatic.

In May of 1937, a cable came from England saying: "PROPOSE SAILING CANADA AUGUST 21ST. CAN YOU DO WITH THREE. MOTHER." They cabled back: "THRILLED." A later letter said that the three were to be Roddy's mother, his sister Valerie and Judy Moss, their landlord's daughter. Roddy wrote back urging his mother to make her visit longer than the two months she planned. "But we can talk about that when you get here ... I will do my best to get the third upstairs bedroom finished before you arrive so that whenever Val and Judy are not off 'seeing the country' we can all be comfortably fixed here. Your friends in Seattle are going to be delighted to see you again and Val has plenty of friends down there too. Sorry Joan is not coming, but I expect she will have much more fun in England during the winter with hunting [on the horses she loved] and the dogs and all the people round about ... You needn't worry about fitting in here or the extra housework or anything as Ann is going to book little Dorothy Perkins to come in every day while you are here and she is very good. We've been having her quite a lot since V.J. arrived until recently when we've been trying to economize and pay off bills ... I shall do all I can to have as much as possible in bloom in the garden during September and October."

On the domestic side Roddy reported: "I've had to do some carpentering lately, a new book-case and a gate for the veranda and so on and Ann generally leaves V.J. to help me with jobs like that ... Ed Lansdowne, his wife Edna and their 5 months old baby have been staying with us the last few days, on their way north [to the Nimpkish]." The letter concludes: "Your very loving son, Rod."

In June Roddy wrote Mrs. Elmore, "A lot of my books came out from England just after the Stanilands were here [friends of Uncle Decie – part of the endless summer stream] and it took us nearly two days to sort them out and stow them away ... all the regular shelves are crammed and I've made a new bookcase."

In July Edward Dunn came again, I went to Seattle with Aunt Mary, and Ann, Roddy and Edward spent a week at Buttle Lake – more research for *The Western Angler*. Ann went down to Seattle with Edward, picked me up and came back with Bucky, Gar and their baby, Garby. Letters to her mother talk much of the two little cousins together.

The English family arrived and there is much back and forth about plans for entertaining them – the two girls, especially, who would be in Seattle for a while on their way to Judy's cousin in Mexico. Ann had already introduced them to Seattle friends who were in Campbell River.

My mother told me years later that she found the visit difficult because "the girls" were not very nice to her. They teased her, mostly about her American ways. (My mother never seemed very American to me. Her accent was Canadian, if anything – after all, her mother was Canadian – but to English girls inclined to tease, the difference would have been too subtle to bother noticing. Also Roddy's sisters were fairly open about the fact that they resented his staying in Canada, and would logically have blamed Ann for that.) Undoubtedly Val and Judy had no idea what it meant to have to cope with house guests, a small baby and all the work of canning and gathering the fall garden produce that was essential to the household economy – even with Dorothy Perkins to help. In addition to the usual cooking and baking there would have been milk to put through the separator so the cream could be sold or made into butter for the household, and the laundry was done in the bathtub. Ann reported to her mother during the visit that "dear Mrs. HB, having decided that it ain't fitten for the likes of Roddy to dig so much, is getting him a hired man all for himself."

After "the girls" left, Roddy's cousin Agatha arrived and she and Mrs. Haig-Brown were in Campbell River until after Christmas. They took care of me while Ann and Roddy spent a luxurious two days in Victoria when Roddy went as part of a delegation from the "Boards of Trade of Vancouver Island to present their resolutions – chiefly one on reforestation – to the Premier and Cabinet." They also saw the movie *Elephant Boy*, which Ann urged her mother to see in a later letter. A resolution on reforestation would have particularly appealed to Roddy, with his commitment to conservation that he had learned in England on his grandfather's estate and expanded during his Nimpkish years. His work as a logger would have given him credibility here, too.

Ann missed her mother at Christmas, but they all went to Seattle for New Year's and Mrs. Haig-Brown and Agatha sailed from Portland, Oregon, on January 12. While she was in Seattle, Ann went to see her obstetrician. She was happily pregnant again.

In late January Roddy wrote Mrs. Elmore about his work: "... back to my book again and stay with it pretty steadily until it's finished. I want to get it out of the way, because I don't think it will ever make money in proportion to the amount of work involved; but on the other hand I didn't want to hurry it too much because it has to be a pretty solid book to be of any value at all; it may do quite a lot to sell articles for me by establishing my reputation on Western fishing. Once it is safely out of the way I think I shall be able to turn out quite a lot of things that will stand a real chance of making money." In fact, things did work out very much as Roddy hoped.

Mary Charlotte was born on June 2, 1938, in Seattle. In a rarely kept, five-year diary which reports on both children the day's entry reads: "V.J.'s 'Baby Hisser', Mary Charlotte born 5 p.m. today. V.J. talked to her mother [from Campbell River] by phone less than an hour afterwards. Mother has been away so long now that I am not too sure the statement 'Mummy fetch baby, bring back soon. Baby drink bockle,' is still spoken with much faith."

Ann had left for Seattle a month before the birth and stayed until early July. The letters Roddy wrote her then tell of events on the little farm, tales of my activities and of the growing and maturing love between my parents. Work would have been progressing on *The Western Angler*, but very slowly if the details of gardening, pump troubles, haying, car troubles, making screens and drawers, various visitors, chickens, cows and one fishing day are any indication. Roddy reports, too, that pie cherries have been picked and sold to pay for the necessary materials for building projects. Ann's sister Mary was there to help and was kept busy canning and making jam as well as cooking (Roddy regularly sings her praises as a cook to Mrs. Elmore) and keeping up with a two-year-old. Mary also worked hard on the garden (she later had a landscaping business in Seattle and wrote on gardening for *Sunset* magazine) and she was frequently mentioned as planning and planting and arranging flowers.

One project of Roddy's was the addition of a sandbox to the play yard – an area as big as any city backyard, but tellingly referred to as "V.J's pen." No doubt it was intended to keep me from drowning in the river, especially with a new baby to distract my parents' attention, but all I remember of the pen part is standing at the gate screaming what would have been referred to as "bloody murder." The swing, the sandbox and the metal wading pool were delightful, but I expect the gate was rarely closed. Perhaps after that "Baby Hisser" could join me the pen worked.

Ann and Mary Charlotte returned to Campbell River in early July. Roddy wrote of his pleasure in his new little dark-haired daughter to his mother-in-law and said, "I can't tell you how pleased I am with the way Ann looks and seems. She has never been nearly so beautiful before." Mary stayed on a few days to help Ann settle in, but on July 20 the occasional diary reported that Ann took "Mary Charlotte and V.J. both to Victoria to be out of the way of the forest fire that has already got Forbes Landing [a few miles west on Lower Campbell Lake] and looks like getting most of the Island north of Nanaimo." And next day: "Ann back today. Decided to 'phone Mary [her sister] to take the children on down to Seattle tomorrow. Things are not exactly dangerous, but we are Forbes' next door neighbour and it feels better with them well out of the way." Ann wrote her mother worried letters about the effect all the disturbance might have on the children, especially the baby. "And I simply cannot say how long all this will go on ... it seems almost inevitable that it will surround us eventually, although Roddy feels quite confident that we will save the house. My job is to get everything moveable in order and to keep it so that we can get it out – probably down to the Spit – when necessary. There is absolutely no personal danger and we will leave by car probably; failing that, by boat down the river ..." But a week later the diary reads: "Ann brought the children back. They seem to have had a good time in Seattle. Plenty of fire about still, but it doesn't look like touching and one can't wait half the summer and all the fall for rains to come."

Toward the end of August Roddy wrote about the new baby: "There are many positive things that M.C. does. Watching and trying to catch the scarlet swan's feather that hangs over her crib. Seeing one from a distance. Recognizing Ann and perhaps me – certainly V.J. Her talk and smiles and searching for things to see."

By fall the household was more settled. Dorothy Perkins came every day to help with the housework and babies, while Ann typed the 100,000 words of *The Western Angler* twice – once for the U.S. market and once for the English. No photocopiers around then, and carbons would not do to present to a publisher. Ann was also serving on the School Board by this time. In a December 1938 letter to his mother, Roddy refers to "lots of work on the Western Angler still, mostly for the English edition. [No exclusively English edition was ever published, probably because of the Second World War.] There are lots of things in the air for next year, but there is no way of knowing yet how they will work out. I enclose a copy of the last letter I had from my New York agent ... I'm pretty pleased with the prospects for the Western Angler; I thought it might prove difficult to get a publisher interested in this and of course they may all shy off it at the last moment, but I have got quite a few strings to my bow and already, without even being published, the book seems to have done my reputation a surprising amount of good." The search for a publisher for *The Western Angler* ended eventually with a contract with The Derrydale Press of New York for their now almost-legendary edition of this book, which is considered a classic.

Years later Roddy said about writing *The Western Angler*: "The most concentrated piece of research I did was between the time I got married and the time I published *The Western Angler*. That was a deliberate thing. When I published *Panther*, there were a few comments – nothing I could really resent, but I remember a review by a very good outdoorsman. He said it was strange that the author didn't realize that the raven was a very rare bird on Vancouver Island. I thought: Goddam you —you say that to me and I've hunted and hunted on Vancouver Island and I've chased ravens endlessly, because every time you hear a raven in the bush you know there's a cougar kill there ... Well, I wanted to write *Return to the River* then and I thought I'm not going to let anybody take cheap shots at me. So I'm going to set myself up as an expert. It was that conscious that I published *Western Angler* before *Return to the River.*"

The December letter to Roddy's mother continued: "As soon as the river goes down a bit there should be steelhead in the Sandy Pool and I'm going to have a try for them; it will be my first real day's fishing since May. I do not expect to get very much more writing done before Christmas; there will be a bit of cleaning up on the Western Angler —almost 4 hours a day —and I've got several carpentering jobs I want to get done: a doll's bed for V.J. [The bed was my Christmas present —I still remember peeking through my fingers and seeing it under the tree as I was led through the living room to have breakfast *before* presents —and so well built it is with us yet], a new cupboard in the kitchen, jam cupboard and apple shelves in the basement [still there] and a new partitioned cutlery drawer in the pantry.

"Saunders [the new hired man who lived in the cottage just west of the house] is away on his holiday and a boy comes in twice a day to milk the cows, feed the chickens and split the wood. It's really wonderful to be free of all that and it makes all the difference in the world to the amount of work I can do. The only trouble is that I'm so busy with my work and so interested in it that I hate to take even a few hours of any day for gardening and things of that sort —and Saunders is definitely *not* a flower man! As a matter of fact, it's all pretty difficult just now, because the new perennial border [along the east edge of the lawn] is not ready and I'm trying to keep as much stuff as possible *out* of the old vegetable garden so as to have it ready for lawn whenever I can get the seed, with the result that there's no place to put anything. No doubt it will all straighten out in time, but it's a slow business."

In January 1939, the cow population increased to three —Tulip, her new calf, Heather, and Fern who had come to keep the children in milk while Tulip was dry. The good Jersey milk was credited particularly with Mary Charlotte's health and strength, and meant also that there was plenty of cream to sell. There were enough chickens to produce four or five dozen eggs a week for sale as well. The theory was that the farm would produce an income, but in the end it may just have paid for itself.

But there is no question that it fed the family very well and economically.

There is no need to write here of the turmoil in the world in the year 1939. It reached the farm and the family on the bank of the Campbell River and Roddy wrote of the impact in "If Armageddon's On," a philosophical discussion of the nature of war and reasons for it, published later in *Writings and Reflections*. Coming from a family with a strong army tradition meant that he gave little thought to the possibility of not volunteering (he signed up on September 2), but even at the time he recognized the possible effect on his career of a major interruption just as he was truly beginning to establish himself. As I read of the success he *did* achieve before the army finally took him, I cannot help imagining what might have happened if the world had not been otherwise occupied. Such basic factors as paper shortages, especially in England, undoubtedly took some of the impetus away – if the materials are not available to produce and transport books there are no sales, to say nothing of books and articles simply not written.

But in spite of the war, with Roddy waiting to be called for active service, the seasons in the house by the river rolled on. In February 1940, Roddy wrote his mother: "I had to leave this suddenly to go out and spray fruit trees because Reg was ready to start and George was busy. Then there was a Board of Trade meeting so that was the day. Then there was my birthday, and I needed to get a haircut, had to go up and see a man about some ploughing, then look at a road that should be put in for some settlers, then be on hand for Valerie Joan's great surprise for me – the cake with candles and snowdrops and crocuses and the very formal tea party with two little girls most daintily dressed in their best pale blue – V.J. behaving elegantly and primly all through, Mary Charlotte raising hell with the cake, her face, her dress but still showing quite clearly that she knew it was an occasion, something most special, and not being a bit more messy than her enthusiasm forced her to be. It was a lovely sunny day, and we sat in the study [a room on the west side of the house then] with late afternoon sun coming in at the windows and somehow making us a very complete family, with affairs of our own and growing traditions. It was all the better because I had managed to get away to the Sandy Pool for an hour between the settlers' road and the party and fish down from the head to the rocks with a big fly and the double handed rod." The Sandy Pool is now severed by a logging bridge. The big tree we sat under on the sand – rare for the banks of the fast-moving Campbell – was cut to make way for it, but back then it was reached by a trail that started at our house. Even when I was quite small, I was allowed to go along sometimes, a great privilege. I always rememher the whispery sound of my father's corduroy trousers as he strode along the trail.

The letter continues about the same crowded day: "Today the man came to plough and got the lawn and the orchard and the vegetable garden done in short order." There is reference to £500 to be sent from England and discussion of how to go about it in wartime. The money was a gift from family friends, apparently two wealthy older women who had made similar presents to other members of the family. Clearly it came as a surprise and was very much appreciated as there was also some question at the time about whether U.S. royalties could be accessed because of wartime currency restrictions. Roddy went on: "My new book [*Return to the River*, the life story of a Columbia River salmon] is going along nicely and I expect to hear soon if I will get the advance to go down to the Columbia." He also sold several short stories to the *Daily Express* in London.

A letter in March talked of more gardening: "We have a fine show of crocuses along the side of the drive – in the new and still unfinished bulb garden ... The whole of the strip that is eventually to be in bulbs is ploughed up now and I shall be growing carrots in most of it to give us a chance to cultivate the couch grass out. Then next year with any luck it will be all bulbs, with deciduous trees to shade them and perhaps perennial white clover to keep the weeds out. The lawn is to be put into Italian rye grass which will be ploughed under in July so that we can do the final levelling and preparing in August and sow the seed in September ... There's quite a lot of work to be done on the river end – I have to build cribbing and run a slope down to the top of it ... Making a place like this is a long slow business ... The new book goes along nicely, with interruptions. For the last week or so I've had a big collection of aquatic bugs in a soup plate on my desk so that I can watch them and get them into Chapter V ..."

In early June Roddy and Ann left the little girls in Seattle and made a research trip along the Columbia River. In later years Roddy described the circumstances: "I was on a spot eventually because I needed to go down around the Columbia and see exactly what was going on and I just hadn't got the money to do it, so I sent my agent six chapters and a synopsis and asked him to see if he could raise 500 bucks for this, and he conscientiously tried to and again they [Houghton Mifflin, publishers of *Panther*] wouldn't go for it and that's when [William] Morrow came into the picture and they produced the 500 bucks." Casually put, but this was actually a crucial turning point in Roddy's career. Money was extremely short and the publisher he thought he could count on wasn't interested. Was his determination to be a writer going to come to nothing? My mother told a story of my father polishing the silver, a most uncharacteristic chore for him, while waiting for news of a sale to arrive – it was very likely this one. To Mrs. Elmore [he always addressed his mother-in-law formally], Roddy wrote, "Getting the advance for the trip is a great relief to me and to the whole household I guess. I was just beginning to get a bit discouraged about the business of describing so much country and so many miles of stream that I had never seen. Now we've got not only an advance, but certain publication for the book ... Ann says it's something like security ... it doesn't feel bad at all." Nor did they realize then how important William Morrow would be as Roddy's publisher.

In a late June letter to his mother Roddy discussed various requests to take English children for the duration of the war and wondered about "the family's children," his cousins. Decie's two children were on their way to Seattle to spend the war with their American relatives, but Roddy had not heard of arrangements for others. He even speculated about renting "Uncle" Reg's house next door and hiring help if there were many children. In the end, there were none. The hired man was leaving to join the army, and Roddy continued to urge them to take him as well. His mother had had men from Dunkirk staying and Decie's whereabouts were vague, but she seemed not too worried. No doubt she was deliberately vague because of wartime censorship imposed to keep word of troop movements, etc., that might help the enemy getting out, even inadvertently – many of the envelopes still with the letters have been opened by the censors. Roddy's sisters were already in the service – Joan in a hospital; Valerie in the Army Territorial Services, originally cooking, but doing office work by this time.

In July a sick cow was a worry, Decie was safely back from Dunkirk (the first ship he boarded to cross the Channel was sunk and after two hours in the water he was picked up by another which was hit, but made it back) and the linoleum man came to lay linoleum on the pantry counters and floor. "Glen Trimble and Edward Dunn arrived and stayed with us until this morning. We enjoyed that very much because they are among our favourite people." This was perhaps the first of many visits from this couple who always remained among Ann and Roddy's closest friends. Roddy had fished for the first time in North America with Edward. Glen was slender and elegant and divorced, so, probably because of Edward's Catholicism, they never married, but each kept their own lovely house and garden in Seattle. Glen and Edward planned to come back that fall for shooting, but Roddy said: "... I should be called up by that time ... I'm writing down to find out if they've overlooked me or if they just don't want me." The answer was that they did not need any more officers at that point and that Roddy was too old to join in the lower ranks.

In early August a cow had died and been replaced, something was killing the chickens and the legacy had arrived from England, so the debts were paid with enough left for "*perhaps* the electricity." Ann's sister Mary was staying while she recovered from another goiter operation, and the flower border was a mass of bloom – a mixture of annuals and perennials, but the plan was to make it all perennials by the following year. The vegetable garden was "getting to its richest time, marrows and squashes and melons and tomatoes and peppers and cucumbers. Corn eight feet high and higher, lots and lots of beans, still some peas, celery coming along, cabbages, broccoli, brussels sprouts doing their part. There's so much here and it's all so nice: I wish you could be here for it, all of you."

In mid-August there is a long letter of praise for how the British people are standing up to the bombing. Ann and Roddy have registered for the services which was obligatory, although Ann would have been far down the list as a mother of children, but "it seems as though you have to be a friend of the prime minister ... to get called up." (With Hitler occupying Europe, the war was mainly in the air now and there was little current need for more troops on the ground). Roddy's mother had moved from Gloucestershire to a flat in London because the house in the country was impossible to heat due to wartime fuel shortages and the roof leaked badly. The bombing of London and the potential danger increasingly fills the letters, but the domestic news of children and garden are not forgotten and would, no doubt, have been more welcome than ever. The lawn was ready for seeding as soon as the fall rain came and the book progressed "pretty well." "Ann is busy with autumn canning and the typing of my book." Ann, in a letter to her mother, added, "I'm doing a 21-day diet – but badly – I'm going to insert a couple of days of the 'Fruit Regime for Stubborn Cases' starting tomorrow and something amazing *may* happen. We're sending off the first ten chapters of Roddy's book [*Return to the River*] tomorrow – the rest is yet to be written." A note in the margin says, "Nonsense, I am more than half-way through Chapter XII - R."

At last in mid-September Roddy reported to his mother: "We finally got the lawn seeded on Thursday after four summers of preparation ... It is a lovely rolling stretch that runs right down to the river, with a 150-foot perennial border along one side, a thick fir hedge behind that and a barbary hedge along the bank. Along the house side we have a post and rail fence running to the river and climbing roses planted along it, with a border in front of them that we use at present mainly for nursing.

"We also expect to get the electricity pretty soon now ... My book is going along slowly, badly interrupted this week by the lawn and I'm afraid due for further interruption in the near future because I have to run the Red Cross campaign for funds again this year." And in the next letter: "... the Red Cross campaign ... should finish up with $4000, though I shan't know until the end of the month because I am giving one big logging camp extra time to avoid conflicting with a war savings drive."

Ann wrote to her mother in October: "... above all things I think with thankfulness of my fat children who might have been in England and aren't."

And in October, Roddy wrote his mother: "I finished the second terrace under the balsam tree on the river bank yesterday – it was a big job with a fill of 4-5 feet on the river side which had to be cribbed up with planks. I'm covering the surface with sand now and will make a heavy table and some benches before next summer; then we shall have a really perfect combination there, full shade on one terrace and full sun on the other.

"My book is going very well ... the publisher has told me not to hurry because he can't bring it out before next spring anyway since the illustrations must be carefully done. I am probably doing too much research for it, but I've got the habit so deeply engrained now ... I read reams on every little point before I finally commit myself and of course that's one thing that's going to make it a good job ... the title of my new book. Well, I call it *Spring, The Life Story of a Columbia River Chinook Salmon*, but the publishers don't altogether like that." Roddy said later: "Morrow had an inspired editor named George Labaire. I had the book divided into sections and one of them was called *Return to the River* and he picked the title from the section and put it on top, and he advised me about several other little shifts and changes. He really was a great editor, I think."

Edward Dunn and Glen Trimble came for ruffed grouse shooting in mid-October. "... somehow it gets better every time they come." In the same letter Roddy reports that "Valerie's collar bone [broken when I fell out of bed in a temper several weeks earlier] is apparently all right now." He goes on to tell his mother of a children's adventure. "Both children take a daily bottle of milk over to Uncle Reg ... Today I had the cows in the house field [so generally called "Uncle Reg's field" that it was many years before I realized it belonged to us], which caused a little consternation: Mary decided it was too much for her [at two] and stayed at the gate, but V.J. started across, holding the bottle tight in her arms. The cows looked up, interestedly, and began to follow. She ran, they galloped after for a little, but in no time at all she was safely across. She came back by the road and I asked her why. 'The cows would have wanted my apple,' she said – Uncle Reg always gives them an apple for bringing the milk – so then I said, 'When the cows follow you like that it's best not to run.' 'Run?' she said. 'I didn't run, I just walked fast.' We talked a bit more and then I asked if she was happy going across with the milk. 'No,' she said. 'I was pretty miserable.' But she knew she had done a good job ..."

In a letter to Edward Dunn later Roddy described at length one last day of shooting for the season and then related the following: "Tell Glen that the models are all made and the children and I have had a lot of fun in the long winter evenings. The pretty domestic scene goes approximately this way:

Valerie: Will it be for me or Mary?

Mary: I want it. I want it.

Father: Curse the people. How do they expect a fellow to figure that out.

Father: Mary, leave that alone.

Father: No Mary, don't touch. Don't touch. Bad girl.

Father: Where in hell's B42, that curved piece. Have you had it Mary?

Father: You'll have to find it or we can't go on.

Valerie: Why not?

Father: Because – Hell, here it is. Damn you Mary, leave things alone. *(Exit Mary, crying)*

A little progress. Re-enter Mary.

Father: Mary. Don't touch.

Father: Valerie, stop jogging my arm, can't you see this is difficult.

Progress. Exit both children. Loud noises, from passage, of violence. Much progress. Much later father emerges wan but triumphant with completed model. Children fight, tear it apart. 'When will you fix it for us, Daddy?'

Just the same, they're on the mantelpiece now, three locomotives, untold tenders and flatcars, the splendid cruiser. We've had fun."

I remember the little wooden train kit – one of many delightful presents that Aunt Glen and Uncle Edward always brought – with great pleasure and have no recollection of the trials and tribulations involved in its making. It became part of the Christmas tree decorations, even though bits fell off now and then.

Letters for the rest of the year tell of a trip to Nanaimo to buy electric lamps and good progress on the book, with plans to try hard to get into the army when it is done. Roddy was concerned that trouble with his back or varicose veins might keep him out. "Canadian physical standards are very high indeed." Ann's brother Danny was in the U.S. navy at last (although the U.S. was not yet at war), after first being told he was too short. And the electricity finally arrived at the house. "... the favourite indoor sport is 'twitching' lights on and off — to father's terrific indignation as he broods about the monthly bill: my pet sport takes me outdoors — to look at the meter every so often and worry some more." In late November the book was off to New York and all the chores that had been put off were to be attended to "from making wooden lamp bases (some for Mrs. Elmore) to building a few more steps in the terraces. I also want to get a new start on a book ..."

In one letter Roddy described hearing the children and their friend Diana Hudson "reading off the willow pattern rhyme from the jugs — 'Two birds flying high, Little boat passing by, Apple tree with apples on it' and so on." He was reading the children *The Water Babies*. The water pump gives constant trouble and "the new oil stove [the old wood stove had been converted] isn't wholly satisfactory yet ..." The search goes on for a vacuum cleaner and washing machine, but they are expensive. Ann is making Christmas cards "from old prints of fish and birds and animals ... and having a gilt Christmas ... from the writing on the card to gilt nuts, gilt holly, a big gilt mirror over the fireplace [and the new little wooden train]." There is a trip to Nanaimo to the Dominion Government Biological Station "going over my book."

The last letter of 1940 to Roddy's mother tells of Christmas with Ann's mother and sister visiting and describes the day in detail. But, "One of my best Christmas presents came on the 24th — a letter from my New York publisher saying that their spring list will be out in a few days and they are making my book — it is called *Return to the River* — the main feature of their whole list, with two pages to itself. I knew they were pleased with the book but didn't realize it had impressed them so much as all that."

The first letter of 1941 continues in the same vein: "Exciting news of the new book continues to come along. It is to be illustrated 'freely and informally' by Charles de Feo, who is apparently hot stuff. And besides the regular edition at the usual price there is to be a special limited edition of 850 copies, which I have to sign. I expect the proofs along pretty soon and shall be busy with them. It all looks very propitious for a decent success." The rest of the letter describes a round of New Year's parties and a prospective trip to Victoria to "get a clear idea of what [the army] need and are looking for. If I'm not it I'll be glad enough to wait." The trip produced no encouragement, partly due to varicose veins, but also because there simply was no great need for men with Roddy's particular talents – the only way he could get in with the problem veins. The fact that the army had lost his original application was no great help either.

Roddy was already planning his "logger novel" and hoped for a decent contract so he could enlarge the cottage and get a couple to help on the place – the boy they had was not working out. "Ann finds the washing machine and vacuum cleaner a *tremendous* help and gets through the housework in no time at all – of course she just thinks up more things to do, but they are naturally more fun than routine tasks."

More news from New York in the next letter: "... about my future plans and they are most enthusiastic. I had made it fairly clear to them that I should have a hard time to get much done this year unless I can employ plenty of good labour on the farm, and they at once offered me a further advance on *Return to the River* or against my future work. I wrote ... yesterday ... that I want an advance of $65.00 a month." Roddy cancelled his contract with his London agent on the advice of his New York agent, who had heard Pinker was in financial trouble. The letter continued about "the two books for William Morrow – one is the logger book at last and the other will be a simple thing of specimen fishing days through the year ... I also have to do some research for the American Eagle book [often mentioned in notes through the years, but never written]. And now I am helping the local priest with a theological translation from the Belgian ... we slog through it painfully because I don't know theology very well and he doesn't know English very perfectly ... a Dutchman named Father Guerkes.

"Ann is busy painting the bathroom ... The bedroom I think is her next big job and I have to admit it's overdue even though I shudder to think of what things will be like while it is going on ... we can always go and sleep upstairs." Ann had sent dark fruit cakes to the English relatives for Christmas and a pound of butter and one of tea were sent to Roddy's mother each month as well.

William Morrow settled on an advance paid monthly for six months and thereafter depending on sales of *Return to the River*. The book was now to be held for the fall list to allow for proper promotion. Roddy's godfather, Lord Baden Powell, died. He told his mother he had already written to Lady Baden-Powell in East Africa. And the river was much too high for fishing.

"I wonder if you remember the Russell Richardsons – the deaf man and his wife of the Campbell River Timber Co., Gar Elmore's [Ann's sister-in-law] cousins ... They are going to be our next door neighbours, renting Reg's house on a long lease." His mother had restarted his subscription to the *Times* weekly – she used to send it to him in the logging camps – and "we would like to see again ... *The Countryman*, the little quarterly magazine published near Oxford. Ann particularly loves it." A report on the children said that "Valerie is quite a help about the house in lots of ways ... Once Ann came in from the garden and found that the two of them had washed and dried a whole big lot of dishes and silver, and done it properly too. I wish you could see Mary. She's the most positive, determined and aggressive little two-year-old you could find anywhere in the world."

In late February nineteen birch trees that were on sale because they had grown too big at the nursery arrived. "Most of them are in that strip of bulb garden on the right just inside the gate." A married couple had come to live in the cottage and help with the place, and the publishers had come up with three more book ideas for Roddy, making a total of five on the list with two already under way. Ann was making marmalade and would send some to England. Roddy wrote Mrs. Elmore: "Ann should have time to tell you all the details of domestic changes ... But I must tell one: we put our ¾ bed out in the cottage for our people and bought ourselves a Simmon's deepsleep mattress which I have mounted on plain boards on the same frame as before, now widened to 4'6" instead of 4'0". It is much more comfortable in every way."

In March Roddy wrote his mother: "Thayer Hobson, the president of William Morrow, my New York publishers, expects to be in Seattle next week and wants me to try to get down." A letter from one of the uncles, who seems to have been managing his mother's finances, suggesting that she could no longer afford the check she sent each month, as well as the fact that it seemed likely that the government was going to cut off the export of funds from Britain, prompted an assessment of Roddy's finances. "Things really look awfully good for us now, even though much is still in the future. To have a publisher actually wanting five books in two years must be something pretty like success in a writer's career, wouldn't you think? And when these proposals are made on the strength of a book not yet published it seems to me a pretty good argument of their confidence in one's ability – and they are expert professional judges of a pretty hard-headed type. No, I'm too nearly there now to turn back on writing as a career. [Undoubtedly the uncle was bringing up the old family suggestion that Roddy should get a job.] There doesn't seem much doubt that I have picked the right one and developed myself along it in the right way. If it does let me down in the end – well, that can happen with any job ... And out of the last year's work and happenings I've gained a strength and confidence in myself that I never had before." He did not need his mother's money.

The trip to Seattle was a great success. "Had lunch with my man and his very charming wife on Thursday ... We went into full details of the five books ... His enthusiasm by mail about *Return to the River* had worried me quite a lot, because I felt it might be a habit of the firm to be over enthusiastic with their new authors. But this is not the case at all. Hobson is an extremely shrewd and practical businessman. He says *Return* is one of the finest jobs of writing they have ever had, practically the only book they have ever known in which they felt there wasn't a thing that should be changed. He said ... that it is impossible to predict a big financial success for any book ... but he expects [*Return*] to be accepted quite quickly as an American classic.

"I explained my financial circumstances ... I said: 'I agreed to carry on until the end of July with my present advance of 75 a month. But after that I shall need something more like 150.' He said: 'Just so long as you have produced a reasonable amount of work that is nearly up to the standard of *Return* ... there shouldn't be the slightest difficulty' ... I have never known a publisher who was so co-operative and really helpful about one's work." This meeting was the beginning of a long and happy association with Thayer Hobson and William Morrow on both business and personal levels. Morrow was the initial publisher of all of Roddy's major books and, from their correspondence, it is evident Thayer and Roddy had more in common than matters literary. Thayer also lived on a small farm, and news of their chicken flocks often concluded the letters.

.6. More Books and Children (1941 – 1943)

The family was growing and so was the list of published books. The war hung heavy over the world, and the family, too, with Roddy's determination to serve. But the life of a young family with a successful young writer at its head has its own momentum. Toward the end of an April 1941 letter to his mother, Roddy wrote, after discussing the progress of the war: "The most important news on this home front I have kept to the end. Ann will be giving you a third grandchild about November 10th ... We had hoped to have them all about 2½ years apart ... but things really were uncertain then ... But now prospects seem to justify it, if not to demand it ... V.J. is already making extravagant plans for its care. It may complete the family – I'm not sure: Ann says she has a mystic feeling for the number five, and if we can feed them and keep them warm, why not?"

Help with the farming was impossible to keep. Ann wrote her mother: "The cows and chickens, of course, produce far more with Roddy's care and they only take him a half hour morning and evening. The garden takes him an hour between milking and supper and looks flawless (to me, not to him). I ride my bike more than ever and am full of health. I lose no weight, but I *always* wear gloves to garden."

More of children in Roddy's next letter to his mother: "We all went to church on Easter Sunday, Mary very good. She's a quick and smart little thing, perhaps more positively quick even than V.J. Talks magnificently with a wealth of long words that sound simply ridiculous when you turn round and see the size of the thing they are coming from."

And a May letter to her begins "Dearest [as they all do], I'm late again ... but I'm working very steadily now, almost all day and every day, and on top of that I am just finishing off the Canadian War Services Fund drive, of which I am local chairman, and just starting the Victory Loan Drive of which I am also local chairman. My logging novel is going pretty well as far as Ann and I can see. I have just finished Chapter X, which brings me up to about 40,000 words or somewhere near halfway. If I can keep control of it and get what I want to say through it may be a pretty good job of work." Roddy was still filling out War Office forms, and looking into treatment for his varicose veins.

"The children, as always, were delighted with your postcards ... They certainly give us lots of reason to be glad we have this place. They really do get the utmost out of everything – lawn and river and flowers and fields, chickens and cows and the rest. Every new batch of baby bantams is an adventure. They spot each migration of birds or butterflies even before we do ... Our dairy herd is doing nicely enough. The first of our home-raised heifers is due to freshen in about 10 days ... a fine big bag and heavy milk veins. That will give us four milkers and the little heifer born in February ... I badly need more barn space and hope to build a chicken house ... I'm going to have to do more about improving the fields too, if they are to produce crops to keep all these beasts fed properly." Roddy wished he could send his mother some of their good produce – "I hope they don't get you too short: I well remember last time, particularly at school when one didn't even get enough bread. War is a very senseless business ..."

At the end of May the book is up to Chapter 13 and the first eight are at the publisher's. As for the children: "The present great joy is the chickens in the kitchen. About this time we get sixty or seventy day old chicks to put under broody hens. This year there were no broody hens, or rather only one, so we have forty or fifty babies in a huge cardboard box in the kitchen. You can imagine the effect.

"Last week Heather had her first calf and she is milking up to 3½ gallons a day ... just right because our markets are coming to their biggest demand ... Mary Elmore is coming up tomorrow, to stay for only a few days I'm afraid, but it will be nice to have her, particularly when the border and the whole garden is looking its best. Right now we have big Russell lupines, peonies, several different irises, pyrethrum, aquilegia, Mrs. Sinkins, violas and heaven knows what else. But the real beauty of the thing is the colours spaced against the solid background of all shapes and shades of green. It's tremendously satisfying and I see plenty of it because I sit and write all day and every day in the glassed-in part of the porch, looking straight across the lawn to it ... I simply haven't been writing letters lately. That's one reason I like working away from my desk, out on the porch. I just take a pen and the book I am working on and go out there, leaving the unanswered letters piled up on my desk; and sometimes I keep away from the study for days on end so as not to see them. There's one wire basket on my desk I haven't looked into for months ... It's amazing what a difference this makes to the work I get done."

In June came "the first letter from my publisher about the logging novel. They are every bit as enthusiastic about it as they were about *Return to the River* and say flatly, 'It cannot be disputed that you are also a novelist ... what you are attempting here, and will unquestionably bring off, is supposed to be the most difficult operation a novelist can perform ...' I need hardly tell you that this is a great relief to me. I've also had word of ... a rather good Canadian publishing agreement for *Return* ..."

In the same letter Roddy says, after discussing the progress of the war, "Funny to think about what little troubles we used to bother about before this war – and still have to bother about for that matter. You should see me running around in circles when a cow is going to calve or is feeling sick or something. I've got one now with some sort of udder trouble ... But the new heifer is more than making up ... They are pretty beasts, feeding now in the field between this house and our old one, so that I can look out at them from where I am writing on the verandah."

More news of the publication of *Return to the River* in late June: "The limited edition will be published on Sept. 17th, the ordinary edition on Sept. 24th ... Yesterday I signed 250 of the title page sheets for the limited edition and expect to get 250 more tomorrow. A very dull job indeed ... My Victory Loan Campaign is over at last and has been a great success. Campbell River doubled its quota of $25,000 and now has five honour pennants flying alongside the big pledge flag.

"The garden is looking nice – the delphiniums are the best we have ever had and there's some lovely white phlox just coming into bloom now ... I am out on the porch working now and Ann is out fixing up cherries and making butter; Mary came out a few minutes ago with her face all plastered with black currant jam, so we sent her to wash it off and now they're both playing tag in their bare feet on the lawn."

The following week Roddy wrote: "Today is Sunday and poor Ann has had to go off to a Catholic picnic ... The children, of course, went off very happily; any picnic for them is a good and glorious thing. I got my hay cut early in the week and hope to get most of it carried tomorrow.

"My publishers have just given me a 100% increase in the monthly advance ... through till the end of January when it will come up for renewal and revision. Unfortunately a lot goes for taxes [big new ones for the war effort and both the U.S. and Canada took a share] before I ever see it, but it's pretty nice just the same and lets me get on with the job without worrying.

"I am going in to Buttle Lake on Tuesday to stay with the Reids until Friday. I have to come out because Buckie and Gar are coming up with Garby on Thursday night and will be here for about a week. It will be grand to have them and V.J. and Mary are very thrilled at the idea of having their cousin for a guest."

In mid-July Roddy wrote that the trip to Buttle Lake was so restful that he had since made great progress with the novel and was now up to Chapter 26. He had been asked in February to run as a Conservative candidate in the next election and refused on the grounds that "I am not a conservative." But now the Liberals and Conservatives were talking of running him as an independent. (In the end, the Conservatives nominated their own candidate and that was that.)

Valerie went to Seattle with Buckie and Gar to give the pregnant Ann a rest. Ann wrote her mother, "If she greets you and Mary with the vehemence she plans you will find yourselves flat on the floor." Roddy wrote his mother just before Valerie's return, "Mary Charlotte will be simply overjoyed to have her back after such a long separation. She got kind of depressed here alone with two old folks."

The old water wheel pump had been replaced by a gas pump and Roddy planned to get an electric one before the new year. "A thorough watering of our present lawn means 4000 gallons, which is a lot of water; but when you see a whole river running past you, you can't help thinking you ought to be able to get it up there some way."

By mid-August the novel was finished. "It is a big book, 25 chapters and 110,000 words, which is just about the same length as the whole two volumes of *The Western Angler* ... I have carried the vein injections as far as the local doctor is willing to go and shall be sending in my RCAF application ... The doctor here has written a letter to say that in his opinion my veins are not really varicose, but a natural physical characteristic; which may be a help [with getting into the armed services].

"I've had a report on Pinker's [his London agent] bankruptcy and am afraid now that there is no hope of collecting anything. His debts are 31,000 pounds and his assets 93, poor devil. I was lucky since he owed me only £12 or £15 at the time. Some writers must have been very hard hit indeed ... I have a new agent [in England], Hughes Massie, who works in close collaboration with my New York agent

"It's hot today. Ann is on the porch putting beans in bottles, V.J. is playing croquet on the lawn and M.C. is parading around with a parasol. Everyone very well indeed. Ann feels fine and has done so pretty well all along apart from the normal distresses ... We have, as usual, at this time of year, lots of visitors from all over the face of the earth. Alec Fisken was in for dinner the other day and said Pat and Donald [Decie's children who were spending the war in Seattle with the Fiskens, their aunt and uncle] were fine."

His mother asked Roddy why he referred to the novel as a "difficult operation." He replied: "It is of writing a novel about several main characters and going into the mind of each of them at different times – taking a single continuous story and using the point of view that will make it most effective at each given stage without breaking or slowing the continuity of the story. I have done it almost without thinking about it because that just seemed to me the way the book should be written. For one thing, I wanted to contrast two different characters all the way through. For another, there were some incidents better seen through one character's eyes, some better seen through those of another; this was important to what I had to say, so I just did it. I didn't realize it was extraordinary and I still don't think it is ... It isn't altogether remarkable that my first novel should be a fairly sound piece of work because I have been working towards it for a good many years now."

In September, "V.J. started school yesterday and spent her first full day there today, very happy about it. They are reserving the right to kick her out at the end of a week or so if they find they are too crowded, but I don't think that will happen. [I had turned five in April and was, according to the rules, too young to start school.] If it does we shall have to teach her at home, because the active little brain needs the fullest possible employment.

"I spent most of today straightening up the study and sorting a summer's mess of accumulated letters and papers into files or the fire. I have caught up on all my correspondence ... and am ready to start on the new book ... chances are excellent that these two last books, *Return* and the novel, will pretty well establish me. But books are uncertain and they may both have only moderate successes and still leave me a long way to go; that's fair enough too, because I am still young yet to get any sort of established position. But no matter what happens they will have done a great deal for me and will make the way easier for future books. And if the Air Force takes me and I have to stop writing for a year or two these books will make it easier for me when I get back – though if either of them is really successful I shall lose heavily through not being on hand to make the most of it." (Fifty-five years later new editions of both *Return to the River* and *Timber* are still being published.)

The school had allowed me to stay and Roddy reported that "V.J. has just gone off to school with young Joey Painter [a walk of a mile and a half], saying she is going to have to work very hard today because they are going to start writing in their books."

In late September Jesse Carmack, Morrow's west coast representative, came up from Seattle with Harry and Ada Hartman, whose bookstore Ann had worked in, to plan a publicity and autographing tour for the publication of *Return to the River*. "Ann is coming with me as far as Seattle [Roddy was continuing on to Portland as well] – it will be a couple of weeks short of when she will be having the baby and she is sure she will be feeling fine. She's feeling grand now and though it's kind of a novel idea to take a change just before the event, I think it is a very good one.

"Valerie Joan is still delighted with school ... and will probably develop into a model pupil like her mother. Whether she has any of her father's failings remains to be seen. Mary misses her quite a lot, but has adjusted ... and learns much of the day's work when V.J. comes home with it. This week we put on a big sports day for all the children of the district – more than a hundred and fifty of them – and it was a spectacular success. I've been doing a certain amount with children's games, chiefly boys' baseball, all through the summer."

Ed Dunn came for a little grouse shooting just before the trip to Seattle, which was a great success. Great reviews of *Return* were starting to come in even before that. J.R. de la Torre, writing in a Cleveland paper, said: "... nothing less than a masterpiece; and R.L. Haig-Brown, a trained ichthyologist who thinks as a scientist, feels as a humane and broadminded man, and writes like an angel." In England *The Field* reviewer said: "The author is obviously a trained naturalist and scientist," and stated the book was "of absorbing interest." A total of 10,000 copies had been printed and were expected to sell out before Christmas, and the book was on a New York best-seller list.

The Seattle trip involved many interviews and autographings. Mary Charlotte went with our parents; I stayed with the Painters. During the time in Seattle Roddy and Ann had dinner with Glen Trimble; Ann's family; Edward Dunn; and Mrs. McEwan, Decie's mother-in-law; and saw Decie's children, Pat and Donald, among others. There was more autographing in Vancouver and then back to Campbell River. Ann was having this baby in Campbell River because there was no way to pay a doctor in Seattle, since all U.S. earnings were required to be converted immediately to

Canadian currency and not taken back out of the country. The trip to Seattle was only possible because expenses were paid directly by the publisher.

On Saturday, November 15, 1941, Roddy wrote his mother: "Dearest, I have just cabled that your grandson, Alan Roderick, was born at 8 a.m. this morning. He's a fine boy, bright and cheerful and big (8lb. 6oz.) and Ann feels just fine about it. I took her to the hospital at about 1.30 this morning and when I left her at 3 o'clock or so things hadn't really started. So he came pretty quickly. They gave her less anaesthetic here than in Seattle, but that makes for speed and I don't think she looks any the worse for it.

"Everything here is going along very smoothly and well. *Return to the River* is being published in Sweden with a contract well above anything else I've had for translation rights – no word of England yet.

"The HB family ought to be satisfied with Alan Roderick at last. The North American branch of the dynasty looks like getting itself on a solid footing." Roddy obviously felt a lingering need to please all those English relatives one way or another – in this case, by producing a son! Ann and Alan came home on November 30 and Roddy wrote: "Alan weighs over 9 lbs now and seems splendidly well and healthy in every way. Poor V.J., happily starting off to school next morning, looked over at the cradle and suddenly realized she wouldn't see him all day, then burst into tears."

On December 12, the letter begins: "The war has hit us out here suddenly – poor Danny [Ann's brother] was killed last Sunday in that damnable raid on Pearl Harbor." Blackouts and air raid warning practices were immediate on Vancouver Island, and Roddy, as an Air Raid Police warden, had to patrol to see that the blackout was kept. There are letters of sympathy from Roddy to Mrs. Elmore and to Mary.

On the more cheerful side Roddy wrote his mother: "Your grandson is fine. He was christened last Sunday, only an hour or two after Pearl Harbour, Alan Roderick Edward Haig. The godparents are Edward Dunn, Willie HB. [Roddy's uncle who lived in Tite Street in London], Marjorie Quainton and Glen Kerry Trimble. The Edward is the necessary saint's name ... He's an awful hungry boy – already getting about one third more food than he is supposed to, but still hungry and a great one to yell about it. Ann is very well. Danny's death is a great loss for her, but she has taken it very calmly and philosophically...

"I've finished all the changes in my novel and got them away to New York, so you can expect the book in April or thereabouts. The title will be *Timber*, a novel of Pacific Coast loggers." The taxes were burdensome though – Roddy figured he had to earn £35 to get 20. Then there were Canadian taxes as well.

A page of the same letter is taken up with assessing the offspring: "They say in the hospital that [Alan] was one of the *longest* babies they have ever had ... so I guess he has a big frame to keep up. If he gets the Pope height and the Elmore weight he ought to be quite a boy ... Valerie Joan said to me today: 'You never do anything that's fun, daddy. You just sit at your desk and write and write every day. Why don't we go fishing or shooting when I'm home from school on Saturdays?' I'm going to try and see what I can do about that ... I read to them every night ... Mary is a very solidly built little thing and very pretty. Her hair is long, about down to her waist when it's loose and still curly at the ends ... They are good together and real friends, but this morning Ann heard the following discussion. It was over Mary wanting one of Valerie's handkerchiefs.

Valerie: Mother's don't use each others handkerchiefs.
Pushing Mary away.

Mary: I'll have to knock you down.

Valerie: Do you want to fight?

Tears on both sides.

It all sounds like a bit of dialogue from my logging book.

In the last letter of 1941 Roddy reported that his earnings were "creeping a little ahead" of his advances and that Alan Roderick was getting a stronger formula now, "though he still has an awful roar when he thinks he is being neglected. He's a cute baby and I do wish you could see him now, while he's still so small. By the time you do see him I suppose he'll be wearing trousers and being a damn nuisance to everybody. People keep telling us that boys are *much* more trouble than girls, but I think I can stand that so long as he keeps healthy and strong and makes life give him some satisfaction."

The letter went on to report that "Mrs. Elmore and Mary will be up for Christmas" and that "today I've been working on the new book, a juvenile about a boy going trapping for a winter." Then in a postscript dated December 18: "Mrs. Elmore just telephoned to say she had a cable from Honolulu as follows:

'Safe. Not as reported.'

and signed 'Danny Bruce'." It took a few more days to be really sure, but it must have been a happy Christmas. The story became, of course, a family classic – the short version is that Uncle Danny lent his dress shoes with his name in them to another man just before he went off that Sunday morning to spend the day at a friend's house on the beach. The other man was killed and identified as Danny and, in the confusion, it was some days before he even realized that he was listed as dead. Years later, when he came from Washington, D.C., where he'd retired after a navy career, to help celebrate my mother's eighty-second birthday, I asked him to tell the story. My poor aunt rolled her eyes at the prospect, but Danny is a great storyteller and the rest of us enjoyed the long version immensely.

January of 1942 was very cold. "Bright sun and clear days and nights with lots of skating. A corner of one of our fields was flooded and Ann and the children go there every day ... a lot of fun for everybody, though a worry for Father with pipes and pumps and lord knows what else to watch." *Timber* was due the next month and Collins was to publish *Return to the River* in England. Roddy, now district ARP [Air Raid Police] warden, probably chosen because of the army training he had had in England, said he was "more concerned about possible landing parties than about any straight forward air raids." The district covered about 8,000 square miles, and Roddy had about a dozen wardens to help patrol. He went on to say, "Your grandson is very well and much better behaved ... The girls love him and he loves them ... and quite beautiful in his mother's eyes – and mine for that matter ... I must say, though, that I didn't realize his arrival would create such a stir in the family. As Clarence [a Haig-Brown uncle] rightly points out, he is not even likely to retain his present position as head of the new generation, but I guess he is the real start of the new generation here." A heavy dose of English primogeniture, but fortunately for Alan the consequences of being the senior male member of a generation, such as inheriting family estates and being responsible for poor relatives, didn't happen. The Haig-Browns had never had any estates and the various relatives of both sexes had their own successful careers. It was partly to escape such archaic customs that many people came to North America – and it certainly worked in our part of the family.

By the end of January the new hired couple had left because her mother was dying, and it was decided to sell off the cows and not have help any longer. Export of English publishing income was cut off and finances were tight – Roddy said he was paying half his earnings in income tax, partly because of double taxation in the U.S. and Canada. (This was corrected by an agreement a few months later.) But what was ultimately the most significant news of that winter was that Roddy had been named magistrate for the area. In a February letter to Thayer Hobson at Morrow he wrote: "I have become a Stipendiary Magistrate for the Counties of Nanaimo and Vancouver – not for financial reasons; the immediate sum is probably a slight loss [because of time taken from writing] rather than a gain there – but for literary and, I hope, humanitarian reasons. The job really should give me a lot of new knowledge about how people act and why, and how this part of the world operates. And it doesn't take up too much time; I go down and hold court three or four times in a normal month and maybe settle the odd case out of court. So far I've found it every bit as interesting as I hoped, and I don't think we'll either of us ever be sorry about it."

On the back of the carbon copy of one of the many letters my mother typed for my father I found a daily schedule she made in early 1942 that may have been an effort to answer the question "Where does all the time go?" It lists the routine tasks of the day structured around meals and the baby's bottles. Monday, Wednesday and Friday mornings were for washing and Tuesday, Thursday and Saturday were cleaning days. Two afternoon hours were designated "Type," children's supper was at 6:30 followed by reading and bed and "our dinner," then two hours for "mending, letters, knitting, reading." It certainly all got done, but probably not with the hoped-for precision!

The ARP took a great deal of time as the winter went on and there were also the Victory Bond and Red Cross drives again, leaving frustratingly little time for writing. In a letter to Thayer Hobson, Roddy admired the production of *Timber* and was amused by the copy "with the little Minute Man [American militiaman of the Revolutionary War used as a symbol to sell Victory bonds], which I shall prize." *Timber* had good reviews, including Joseph Henry Jackson in *The New Republic*: "... neither a nature novel nor a propaganda story about labor. Nor ... a romantic novel. Mr. Haig-Brown has made it all of these things and at the same time a novel of a trade so closely bound up with the earth that things happening within its scope partake of the earth's own violence and strength." It had sold 3664 copies by the end of its first month in print, which made finances a little less worrisome. It had even "crept on to the edge of *The N.Y. Herald Tribune* best seller list" by May.

The farm was settling into a new regime. In the letter to Thayer, Roddy said: "Don't worry too much about the cows. So far as I can see I'm not going to be allowed to get by with selling them all. Ann says I can damn well keep one of them and milk it myself, and that, goddamn it, is what I guess I'll have to do. If I do that and somehow find the means to get an electric water pump in place of the infernal gas-machine we have now we should get along fine." To his mother a week or two later he said: "I'm doing the milking now as we have no help and Valerie and Mary just love to go out with me, feed the chickens, collect the eggs, talk to the cow and so on. Sometimes they even get up and come out for the before-breakfast milking. I kind of like doing it myself except that it makes one more thing at a busy time; having them come out makes it about worth while though, because they can learn and see so much." The letter also says, "Ann ... means to handle the vegetable garden this year pretty much on her own – it seems like an awful lot ... I took one day to check over the perennial border and felt guilty all day but got something done."

By April Roddy told his mother: "We are not finding it too bad without help. It means we have a little money to spend on clothes and such things, which is nice, and the farm still produces a lot without too much trouble. Ann spends part of every afternoon in the vegetable garden and that is enough to keep it in fair shape. I milk first thing in the morning, attend to my various jobs all day until six o'clock, then milk again, collect the eggs, feed the dogs, get the oil and wood and spend the rest of the time till dinner on the border, the wild garden or some other outside stuff." He also described Valerie "fishing with a stick, a piece of string and a flower tied on for a fly – it looks pretty as anything floating down the river, and one day a fish is going to come up and take hold of it." (The fish were smarter than that.) To Mrs. Elmore he wrote of Mary keeping up with Valerie and her school friends: "Mary holds her own, as she always has, always will, by a solid determination of character that brooks no interference with her rights as she sees them. She can say 'I won't' with a weight of conviction quite unrelated to mere physical prowess."

The ARP job took more time than ever; "full time work as far as I can see" and it didn't pay "even expenses," Roddy wrote his mother. "The trouble is the family has still got to eat and the only way they can keep on doing so is through the writing." Roddy hoped to try the army again when he finished the current book. Alan was six months old – "really beautiful and a most attractive person in nearly all his moods. He is most talkative and loves to laugh ..." Alan was beginning to work on teeth and Mary said to him: "You've got no teeth, boy, only the pink of teeth." But: "It's hard to realize that you have never seen Mary C. and maddening too." His mother had made a new will for which Roddy congratulated her and said: "Will tell V.J. that she will one day have charge of the family pearls."

A dry summer brought worries about the possibility of incendiary bombs from the Japanese, who had raided the Aleutian Islands, but "the children are all brown as berries and naughty as summer children always are ... Alan loves the dogs, and loves to be carried around outdoors above almost anything." When a friend came to get casting instruction on the lawn, "Alan sat in his pram and cheered the whole time, then held the rod afterwards as though he really knew something about it."

In mid-summer Roddy came home from a ten-day ARP course to find a letter from the British consulate in Seattle asking him to join their staff. An investigative trip proved that Roddy was younger than they thought and would be eligible for the U.S. draft, and had no independent income. The job, "in the good old way of the British government is one where you are expected to make quite a fancy little show on a salary of about £50 per month." It had been assumed that Roddy's book royalties would provide the necessary extra income, but such was not the case. The possibility of leaving made both Ann and Roddy realize how very much they loved Above Tide now and how they would hate to leave it, even for the pleasures of Seattle.

The war news, both family and general, took up a lot of the letters, which were fewer than before because of lack of time. In spite of it all, his mother had sent a few pounds to Thomas Thorp, an English second-hand book dealer with whom my father dealt for many years. "... the books have started to arrive. It's really wonderful to have them, because we enjoy that more than almost anything – Thorp's catalogues sort of take the place of movies and all that sort of entertainment so far as we are concerned, and it's far more profitable and worthwhile entertainment than any other I know. The library has really outgrown the study now and we often talk of adding to the room."

In September the boys' trapping book (*Starbuck Valley Winter*) based on Roddy's experiences in the Nimpkish was finally done, and Roddy said, "I shall be starting on another book at once, but I shall try and see where I can get with a recruiting sergeant fairly soon. I want to write a group of short fishing articles, almost stories really, and I have a new novel pretty well planned." The book so casually described as "short fishing articles" became *A River Never Sleeps*.

"The judicial work goes along nicely. I am just back from trying the Monday morning drunk and disorderlies, but occasionally there is an interesting case and interesting things are always happening. Last week a K.C. [King's Counsel] who was Attorney General of the province until the last election appeared for a defendant; rather awe-inspiring and quite a strain – he lost his case. It'll take a very fancy lawyer to rattle me from now on though."

The longest letter in some time, now that the book was finished, continued: "Alan's in here with me now, crawling all over hell while Ann is picking plums. We think he's a grand baby and I really think he must be because everyone simply raves over him – they come especially to see him, the real fans that is, such as Marjorie Meredith and June Painter." An added note from Ann told of the girls looking fine for winter in gray flannel suits and navy blue coats. "Of course, they think they would really be more fetching in something pale lavender with a little cat fur around the neck. I remember having the same feeling about the navy blue coats Mother got for me." (Perhaps that is why our mother rarely dressed us in anything navy blue. I have the same reaction to brown, which was the more usual color for coats and skirts and shoes and hats in my childhood.) And, reporting on the garden: "Our fruit is below normal, and I'm in a bit of a panic at the moment about getting all my three hundred bottles filled, but I shall make it somehow. A new friend the other day was telling me how lucky I was to have so many large bottles all the same and I told her how you bought me twelve dozen of the very best to start my collection."

In October, Roddy wrote: "I've finished up a lot of carpentering ... a grand new flight of front steps ... the old ones were steep and awkward and they had just about fallen 'to parts', as the children put it. The cupboards and improvements in our room are all painted ... Now the only completely unrenovated room in the house is the attic. With Alan getting out of babyhood it's almost time to do something there." New York was "absolutely delighted" with *Starbuck Valley Winter* which was to be published in the fall of 1943. He planned to fish the Sandy Pool next day to fill the last of Ann's empty bottles. Roddy had been made a judge of the juvenile court as well as magistrate, and found "the work more and more interesting." It is probable that he was able to bring some sympathy from his own experience of resisting authority and being "not amenable to discipline" to his understanding of the young who appeared before him in his new capacity.

By December Alan had moved upstairs to his own room and "Ann and I have our refinished room to ourselves at last. The colours are ivory and coral and chartreuse, every single thing square and built in." Mary and I now shared the guest room until the "attic" or third bedroom upstairs, which had been Mary's alone, could be refurbished; and Alan was in the original baby's room, which had been mine until then. *Return* was out in England and doing well, Roddy had been on another tour of his ARP territory in the police boat, and Ann's mother had been up for American Thanksgiving.

Just before Christmas, "Ann and V.J. and M.C. are out at an early Christmas party and Alan is in the study with me. He has just learned how to climb half way up the bookcases." An early January letter describes a cheerful family Christmas: "V.J. and Mary had a bike and a wagon respectively for their 'big' presents — V.J. a little upset because she doesn't know how to ride the bike yet — and Alan got many things which he has since discarded in favour of his old friends the pots and pans ... The Brayshaws [Tom and Becky] came up just before New Year and stayed for four or five days. I went up the river two or three times with Tommy and we had some really beautiful steelhead fishing — lots of bright clean fish up to 14 or 15 pounds and taking the fly just about as well as they took minnow or prawn ... At Christmas time I made a pair of mahogany lamps for the living room and a big low coffee table." There is suddenly a "possibility that I may get on with the army examiners and work at fitting men into jobs they can handle best."

In early February of 1943 Roddy reported two feet of snow and cold down to 12 below zero. "It burst four pipes for me, froze nearly everything else up solid and ruined the copper coil in the stove that heats our water. This last was the worst trouble because you simply can't replace the stuff these days; we put in a coil of ¾" galvanized pipe yesterday ... The snow meant breaking trail for the cow to get water, to say nothing of chopping holes in the ice ..."

About the same time Roddy wrote Thayer Hobson: "I just plain like Morrow's; I suppose you'll be telling me that's not the right attitude for an author to have towards a publishing house, but I can't always be fitting in with your ideas ... I'm not as far ahead with *A River Never Sleeps* as I had hoped to be. I can't help wondering what you will think of that book. The thing that put it into my mind was repeated questioning by other fishermen ... 'Why don't you ever write a book about fishing — you know, catching fish, hooking them and playing them and getting them out on the bank. You must have had plenty of experiences that way, but you always go scientific on us'... The plan isn't as tight as I'd like it to be and the writing is digressive in spots, but that's the way it comes out and I daresay that's the way it should come out."

The first edition of *Return* in England, 5000 copies, had practically sold out and Roddy had at last been accepted by the army (although there was no vacancy in Personnel Selection where he was to serve). "I shall hate having to give up the magistrate's work, but I'm pretty sure I can come back to it after the war; it's almost as bad having to desert the farm, but a lot of people have had to do that." And the parcels to various family members containing Ann's rich, dark Christmas fruit cake made it across the wartime Atlantic yet again.

In March Ann and Roddy took Alan to Seattle while Roddy was on a ten-day fire-fighting course there for the ARP. Alan was shown off to all the Seattle friends with great success, even though he was the age to take apart their living rooms. Mary and I had stayed home with Ann's friend Nellie White and all had gone well. We hadn't even come down with expected chicken pox, although we did later. I remember being told that we couldn't help with our usual chore of feeding the chickens because the chickens might catch the pox – I guess we must actually have been considered not well enough, but that was the sort of gentle tease we regularly got from our father.

A report on the three children reads: "Valerie is still doing *very* well in school. She reads beautifully ... tonight she was reading aloud to Mary some stories I wrote for her [published in a 1980 limited edition as *Alison's Fishing Birds*] and practically acting out the dialogue ... Mary is 'quainter', if you know what I mean. She uses huge words most correctly and expresses herself in the most vivid and unusual phrases – really sharp about things that make you sit up in your chair sometimes and say to your self: 'Damned if that isn't the way it ought to be said.' Alan's conversational efforts are very limited – he laughs instead and he can laugh in a hundred different ways and degrees."

At the end of March Roddy had an appointment in Nanaimo with an Ottawa army man: "Presumably the man from Ottawa wants to see exactly where he will put me and what he thinks I am fit to do." Roddy met with "the three majors of the Directorate of Personnel Services" and "the man from Ottawa said they want me very soon." In late June 1943, a letter from Ann to Roddy's mother says: "Roddy has finally just got himself off to the army." It was just as well it took that long because it gave Roddy time to get fifteen chapters of *A River Never Sleeps* finished, finally locate a small electric pump and install it and 130 feet of pipe to the river, as well as getting the garden cleaned up and a dozen other last minute things done. Ann had time to get the vegetables well under way and learn to milk the cow. Roddy was asked to run as a coalition Liberal-Conservative candidate for the Dominion Parliament, but was glad to be able to say no "with a clear conscience. I can't swallow the whole line of any one particular party."

·7· Ann's War (1943 – 1946)

Life in the house by the river certainly didn't come to a halt because Roddy was finally in the army, although it might have. In an attempt to keep him home when the war first broke out in 1939, my mother told me, she had threatened to go back to Seattle if Roddy joined the army. But there was no question of Ann abandoning the farm for the duration now. Nor, in the end, would there have been if Roddy had gone in 1939.

For the first several months Roddy was stationed in various parts of British Columbia – mainly Victoria, Nanaimo and Vernon, so he was occasionally able to come home on leave, but his work as a personnel officer was heavy and his letters limited to two or three a week. He was also finishing *A River Never Sleeps* in his spare time. Ann did her best to send a letter every one of the four days a week that mail left Campbell River. Her letters were usually one full, single-spaced typewritten page and are dense with details. I remember the sound of her very speedy typing lulling us to sleep upstairs on what seems, in retrospect, a nightly basis. I must often have been listening to these letters being typed, as well as book manuscripts. Ann kept a carbon copy of each letter and it is these that we still have. There are also carbons of business letters she wrote for Roddy, others written to her mother or friends and, often, the weekly feed order for the cow and chickens to Buckerfield's in nearby Courtenay.

Ann set the scene in one of her occasional letters to Roddy's mother in June of 1943. She said, "I used to think I was very busy around here, but until Roddy went, I hadn't half started. Heather, the cow, and I are the best of friends, though she did put her foot in two gallons of milk this morning. And we've hatched out two lots of baby chicks. We are very old-fashioned in that respect and have them with hens instead of in brooders so they're not much trouble. I have the housekeeping down to an incredibly simple standard, so it's not bad, though I do everything myself except the ironing. Valerie [just 7] and Mary [just 5] are wonderful. They mind Alan [18 months] and set the table and hang out the clothes and bring them in and sort them and straighten things up. All their straightening can't quite keep up with Alan, who is in to everything and upsetting everything, then going good-naturedly on to something else as soon as he is removed from one source of trouble. His work this morning has been to run around the house outside turning on the garden taps. Yesterday we turned off the electric pump, but that makes it rather inconvenient inside the house."

A typical letter to Roddy, who at this point was at Officer's Training Camp at Gordon Head near Victoria – he was taken into the army to be a personnel officer, but training camp with its spit and polish, courses in map reading, firearms, truck driving and other basic army lore came first – begins: "Darling Heart, Since I wrote to you on Sunday morning, my great whirl of activity seems to have slowed down. Your letter took me all morning, then in the afternoon I wrote to Marian ... , Sue Haws ... , Goddard and to your mother. Then I weeded the herb garden almost all, and in the evening I cut the half of the lawn I didn't cut last week. Monday morning, I cleaned up the kitchen (sort of) and then hoed the old raspberries. And after lunch I astonished myself by going very sound asleep. Oh yes, that was because Dr. Agnew had called very early to say that Edna [Lansdowne] had had her baby – all fine – and it was a boy. I let Joyce know and he let Ed [Lansdowne] know. When I finally woke up, I went swimming with the children. We had our first lunch on the beach. Afterward we lay on the lawn and all three children ran around naked and very beautiful. Then I cut the other half of the lawn. When I was reading to the children, Mrs. Abbie came along ... Just as she left, Uncle Reg [Pidcock] arrived back from ten days up at the lake. I showed him my vegetable garden and he was simply astonished. [Uncle Reg was a prodigious gardener himself – his raspberries were legendary.] I also got him to look at the lawnmower, but to no avail. He thinks it's very stiff because the revolving blades scrape so against the stationary blade ... Reg went off again today – to Courtenay. After he left, I hoed the squashes and the new raspberries; there's a hot west wind blowing and today everything I touched, and it was a lot, has faded right into the dirt. I also put crosspieces with holes in them and wires to hold the old raspberries up. I'm watering the lawn every night, but it's turning [brown] anyway. I find that after two hours the pump motor is pretty warm, though not uncomfortable. I don't know whether it's because of that or because of turning the electric pump off mornings to keep Alan out of it." This hardly sounds like the slowing down Ann refers to in the beginning of this breathless paragraph.

The next paragraph started: "This morning, I got up very early, because of Alan, and took him milking while the girls slept; then I washed but I'm ashamed to say wasted the advantage of my early start by finishing *Waverley* [Sir Walter Scott] while the tubs filled ... I forgot to tell you that Monday morning, while I was feeding the chickens, Heather sort of scraped her hoof against the gutter and broke about an inch off it ... There's nothing in the book about it, so I guess it's alright, but it seemed alarming. I mailed you the towels and hangers ... And in the third paragraph, "Of course, I'm stewing about the hay. From what Nellie said Alf should have cut it yesterday, first of all ... Tom Hudson told me tonight that he cut his own hay today ..." A letter from Roddy assured Ann that the pump was fine, told her how to adjust the lawnmower, and that the cow's broken hoof was nothing to worry about. He also urged her not to worry about the hay which eventually got cut after a welcome rain and was safely stowed in the barn before the next rain, with Ann and friend Nellie White doing much of the work.

Adversities such as war are always noted for inspiring people to new heights, but I still find it remarkable that a young woman with three small children, who had, ten years before, been very much a city girl working in a first class bookstore with no experience of country life at all, should have taken charge of the complicated business of running a small farm so very firmly. But then my mother was considered by many to be a remarkable woman, for her brains, her energy and her organizational ability. It is obvious from the letters that her inspiration to keep the place running smoothly came from her love for Roddy, and the enormous importance to both of them of what they had already created at Above Tide in the seven years they had lived there. The letters also told of the children, often with direct quotes from them, although not as frequently as one might imagine – an indication that, for Ann and Roddy, their relationship with each other was paramount. The children were important, but intellectually, emotionally and physically their absorption with each other was intense.

I was able to write letters and Mary, not yet at school, tried, but found it better to dictate what she wanted to say and have Ann type it. Ann wrote of reading to the children at bedtime, which our father had usually done. We had solved the problem of sleeping in warm upstairs rooms in summer by moving to the porch which ran along the east side of the house. Mary and I slept in the two matching sleeping bags Roddy had been so pleased to buy in 1933 as part of the preparations for marriage. I remember the feel of going to bed out there – there was a wonderful heavily scented honeysuckle in June. In one letter Ann mentioned her disgust at the sentimental story of *Little Lord Fauntleroy*, but said she was too far into it to stop. (I liked it so much I read it again at least once.) She was glad to move on to Roddy's *Silver*, which I distinctly remember hearing out on the porch in the dusk of summer nights. It seemed to bring my absent father closer.

In July, Ann wrote of finishing work on the tomato plants at twenty minutes to eleven one night, one clue as to how she got everything done. Of the children she wrote: "Dear Valerie ... vacuumed the study and living room and swept the kitchen, hall and bedroom, so things are pretty nice. I shined beyond belief your copper ashtray and I've got water lilies in a silver bowl here on the desk. [Making Roddy's study perfect for him even when he wasn't there must have eased her longing a little.] Valerie does wonders voluntarily, and becomes steadily more disobedient to direct orders. She is just as bad as Alan about turning the tap on and the sprinkler. I want to spank her, but don't quite do it – partly, of course, because I can't catch her ... Mary has been fussing for a week about the dress known as the school uniform ... and today she put it on and said, 'Do you know why I wanted this so much? Because Daddy's wearing a uniform, too.'"

Ann sent magazines, and mail that seemed to require a direct answer from Roddy. The magazines usually went with comments on articles and included the *Saturday Evening Post*, *Life*, *The Saturday Review of Literature*, *The New Republic*, *The New Yorker*, and the *Atlantic Monthly*, though not every issue of every one, partly because of time and partly because friends were used to having them passed on. *The New Yorker* was still going on to the Hudsons decades later.

There are details of finances (still obviously very tight in spite of army pay, partly because officers bought their own uniforms, including a great coat that cost $150); a complicated exchange about winding up the magistrate's business account; and lots of reports on the condition of the garden and the animals; and news of various friends and neighbors who turned up to visit, or to either help or be helped on an almost-daily basis. Uncle Reg was always around to fix whatever needed fixing or help worry about the cow or the dogs. Nellie White, who grew up on a northern Alberta farm, shared garden and farm chores, partly for pay and partly by barter for the use of vegetable garden space and the washing machine. I remember her and her three children well – they lived not far down the road, and Nellie remains in my memory as lively and talkative and lots of fun.

Our only neighbors up the river then were a family of girls with the older two the ages of Mary and me. I remember their blonde hair and beautiful blue eyes, perhaps because of the contrast with our own dark hair and brown eyes – whatever you have yourself always seems ordinary. Their father came and went on an irregular basis leaving their mother often in need of help with the crises of life alone with small children, and our mother seemed always available. Immediately down the river, still renting Uncle Reg's house were the Richardsons, who sometimes invited Ann to play bridge – a welcome break from chores and children, no doubt. The first year Roddy was away they gave a dinner party for her birthday. Uncle Reg had built another house next door to his rented one after his barn where he had an apartment had burned to the ground the winter before. A barn full of hay goes quickly and the awesome spectacle made a vivid impression on me. There were lots of visits to and from the Hudsons – Mavis Hudson and Edna Lansdowne had baby boys in the Campbell River hospital at the same time that summer. We had picnics and tea parties on the Hudsons' beach at the mouth of the river, especially for Diana's birthday in July. News of various other friends punctuated the letters regularly – in a town as small as Campbell River in 1943 everyone you met on an errand "downtown" was a friend and their doings important to Roddy.

Roddy made it through training camp without having to spend an extra month – he had worried that he would fail map-reading because of all the mathematics. He came home for a couple of glorious days in July "wearing battle dress, looked very tough and talked much of his chances of getting overseas," wrote Ann to her mother. I found him both fascinating and slightly frightening in uniform. Edna Lansdowne and the new baby were staying until they could get back to Alert Bay. Roddy returned to begin work as an Army Examiner (or, as Ann explained to her mother, what the U.S. army called a Classification and Assignment Officer). In either army the job was to interview incoming recruits and try to settle on a place for them that would best use their training and talents.

Ann reported that I made my first communion with all due ceremony and only a few tears over breakfast in the priest's dining room afterwards when Father in his austere black suit teased me and said I was to have no breakfast when I was last to be served. I don't remember the tears, but I do remember the bacon. The harvest began with berries and the first vegetables, I had my tonsils out and Roddy wrote that there might be a time when Ann didn't hear from him for some weeks. She replied: "It was so good to hear that you will be in Nanaimo. But please don't write me any more nonsense about not worrying if I don't hear from you. If you ever get to go overseas you'll damn well know it and you'll damn well tell me and I'll damn well worry. You don't have to say which ship you are sailing in what day to get over the general idea." Roddy was already deep in his job as an Army Examiner and receiving considerable praise for the quality of his work.

By late fall the copious harvest was in bottles (beans, tomatoes, corn, plums, peaches, berries and occasional gifts of fish or venison) or, for the apples, in rows on slatted shelves in the basement, and the potatoes (884 pounds) and carrots in a cool corner of the dirt-floored basement away from the wood and coal furnace. As with summer fruit, what wasn't needed for the family was sold. Ann had managed a visit to Roddy in Nanaimo where he was now stationed and he had had a couple of weekend leaves. Money was still tight, but Ann was planning the redecoration of the kitchen now that the harvest was nearly over. Alan was beginning to talk in almost-recognizable words. Ann had hoped to have Mary go to school a year early, as I had done, but the school said no, so she was teaching her grade one using the old correspondence school papers of a friend's child. And, continuing the lifelong pleasurable task of arranging and cataloguing the books, Ann "made more room in the closet, put Greek and Latin and law in and made room outside for some new ones which I listed first ... I meant to paint the floor, but the Hudsons came in for tea."

Tenants came and went in the cottage as wartime jobs shifted people about. Any housing was in demand and the rent money was no doubt welcome. Visits from professional gardening and nursery-owning friends occasioned much talk of garden and tree planting in Ann's letters – the gradual move away from a perennial border toward rhododendrons and azaleas was beginning. One letter lists all the little chores waiting Roddy's next leave – when he came they did a lot of work on the flower garden. A man named McClure was working on fencing to hold the sheep Ann was planning to buy in the spring, as well as building new steps. Ann mentions that friends think "Mary especially is the sweetest child they've ever seen in their lives. McClure also adores Mary." The boys' novel, *Starbuck Valley Winter*, about two young men spending a winter on a trap line, was published with, among others, "a most excellent review ... from the New York Times." Written by A.T. Eaton, the review said: "The book is full of the feeling of out-of-doors; the scent of pine and fir; the motion of swift dark rivers; the life of wild animals ... the author manages to put before us Don's problems and ambitions, his pride in being independent, his determination, his adventures and his triumphs ... A book that boys will enjoy and ... should not miss."

For the first time we were to celebrate Christmas in Seattle, where Roddy would join the family (though there was an awful moment when it seemed he might not). In early December Ann wrote of addressing about a hundred cards she had made from old prints of birds, and making Christmas cakes and puddings. We were in Seattle for about a month and, as I remember, we travelled to Victoria by train and on to Seattle by boat. It may have been on that trip that our father boarded the train in Nanaimo to visit and stayed until the train was *actually moving* before he swung off the step, to our great amazement. I don't remember much of the Christmas celebration, but I'm sure it is blended in with other visits there – my impressions are mostly of bigness and glamour – my grandmother and my mother's friends all seemed to live in huge, fancy houses, their children were terribly sophisticated, the cathedral we went to was enormous and the stores were glittering. I thought Seattle was wonderful!

Ann's letter to her mother once we were home said: "The lovely party is over and we've quite settled in. In some ways it was quite the loveliest visit we've ever had with you. I know the little girls will remember it with the same feeling I have about the epic trip to St. Catharines [Ontario, when my mother was four and they went to visit her maternal grandparents]." Roddy had returned earlier to Nanaimo and on the way home by boat and bus we paused overnight there and our parents had dinner with Roddy's fellow officer Gus Seton Thompson, "whom Roddy's been dying to have me meet." Ann's letter goes on: "Got home to find the house warm as toast, the bedding all aired, and about a week's supply of groceries in the kitchen, all done by dear Uncle Reg."

Ann plunged right back in to the routine as soon as she got home. Painting the kitchen was first, and before long Heather calved with much attendant fuss and worry as she did not seem to be recovering properly. By February Ann was weeding the perennial border and Uncle Reg was spraying the fruit trees. Roddy's captaincy was official and he was soon home on his annual two week leave, which was shortened to ten days because he was transferring to Vernon. In a letter to his editor Thayer Hobson at Morrow during the leave, he wrote, "the job is really large and completely fills each day and every day of each week, Sundays and all.

I've been amazingly lucky to hit anything so satisfying and all-consuming; I can't get over the scope and freedom I'm given ... I was in the army once before [in 1926], you know, but it wasn't a damn bit like this." He went on to ask what Thayer thought of *A River Never Sleeps*, now complete, and agreed it was wise to delay publication until the end of the war was in sight.

In early March Ann canvassed for the Red Cross all one long day while the children stayed with Nellie White. The events of the day filled a couple of letters with up-to-the-minute news of neighbors, combined with worry over the children sliding down the garage roof, and Roddy's seeming to have a touch of flu. The flu soon proved to be catarrhal jaundice and Roddy was in Vernon Military Hospital on a non-fat diet for the rest of the month. There seemed to be general agreement that the jaundice was brought on partly by overwork and the resulting exhaustion. Roddy enjoyed the chance to read a lot, but was too tired to take advantage of the time to write – though he was attending to some army business and report-writing toward the end of his stay, and he did write me a letter about staying off the garage roof. Ann's good news for the month was that she could successfully ride Alan on the back of her bicycle and that Mary was learning to ride hers so the whole family would soon be on wheels – gas rationing and the difficulty of repairs made the car no longer operational. There was a continuing dialogue about plans for a new study after the war as well as some thoughts on Roddy's part in very cautious language about what their life would be like after the war – which he summed up by saying he hoped he would make more money. He probably didn't want to tempt fate by making too many large predictions. Ann was building a savings account with army pay to provide security and they both agreed most strongly that the place by the Campbell River was the base for the life they wanted to live. No more thoughts of staying only ten years.

From Vernon Roddy was to go to Harrison Hot Springs in the Fraser Valley near Vancouver to convalesce further, but a special assignment to Ottawa that had been talked about came through and he was allowed instead to spend the first two weeks of April 1944 at home. Then it was off to Ottawa by train to begin a major examination of the personnel system of the Royal Canadian Mounted Police. This was Roddy's first trip east of the British Columbia interior (he had crossed the U.S. by train once, when he first arrived in 1926) and he wrote detailed letters of his extensive travels, often by air, all during the time he was with the RCMP, partly as notes for a possible book. He was based in Ottawa and stayed at the Lord Elgin Hotel, but visited RCMP detachments from the

Maritimes to the Arctic Ocean and took great pleasure in getting to know his country better. If anything, Ann wrote more letters than ever. One, on April 30, begins "Here's the old farm and garden daily" – cow troubles, new baby chicks, lots of rotted cow manure carried across the road from the barn to the birch trees and constant weeding everywhere. She was planning to plant a grapevine outside and let it grow into the glassed-in part of the front porch. (She later did and it still produces wonderful Concord grapes each summer.) The cottage was to have new tenants, but the previous one had left her furniture and belongings behind, thinking she would return, and, in addition to everything else, Ann had to pack and ship these to Vancouver and get the little house repainted before it could be occupied. Nellie White helped.

In May Ann was planning to have the house painted but there was great difficulty getting a decent color of brown paint in wartime. The children delighted in postcards their father sent – "Alan ... insists on sleeping with his cards. They would make a nice collection, but he loves them so, it seems better to let him hold them to pieces." Ann asked Roddy to get her books in French when he was in Quebec.

On the first weekend in June, Ann had fourteen little girls to celebrate Mary's birthday in the study while the mothers had tea in the living room to celebrate Mavis Hudson's birthday – an annual celebration Mary and Mavis shared whenever they could. On that same weekend Roddy went to New York to meet with his publisher and agent. He wrote five long pages about the details when he got back to the Windsor Hotel in Montreal, where he was based at the time. He had spent the first morning with his publisher, Thayer Hobson, and the people at Morrow, and then gone on to lunch with his agent, Ivan von Auw, at Harold Ober Associates whom he had not met before. There he also met Ober, who usually handled his magazine articles, while von Auw dealt with the books. He liked them both a great deal and revelled in the pleasure of good food and good book talk. From there it was back to Morrow where there was a party for the opening of new offices at which he met, along with numerous salespeople and others, Charles de Feo, who had illustrated *Return to the River*. De Feo gave him the originals of the frontispiece and three illustrations from *Return* (which hung in our hall for many years) and was looking forward to illustrating *A River Never Sleeps*. Roddy spent the weekend at the Hobsons' house in Connecticut where he thoroughly enjoyed the company and the food, but said that he much preferred the setting at Campbell River, although he described their old New England farmhouse in great detail. He then spent another productive day in New York coupled with some sightseeing, mainly Rockefeller Center, before going back to work.

Roddy was soon on his way west to visit prairie RCMP detachments. He arrived in Regina the day before the first ever Co-operative Commonwealth Federation – later New Democratic Party – government was elected; he and Ann remarked to each other on the event with pleasure. Although their families were mainly either Conservative or Republican, Roddy and Ann quickly developed personal philosophies through reading and experience, such as Roddy's in the logging camps of the Depression era, that favored the left side of the political spectrum. In early July, Roddy managed to get home for a few days. When he left, Ann went to Vancouver with him for a glamorous overnight stay in the big city, leaving us with friends. Then Roddy went to the Arctic and Ann went back to farming and children.

Ann wrote through the summer of the slow but steady progress on the house painting with the help of old Mr. Bunting (his son Allan ran the grocery store where we shopped). A decent shade of brown had at last been arrived at by mixing two others. The children spent the days in the river; friends came and went, including some from Seattle in spite of the difficulties of wartime travel; the cow wandered; the water system was cranky; and the harvest burgeoned. Ann ordered Lewis Mumford's *The Condition of Man* and the poetry of Rainer Maria Rilke from Morrow – later letters show that they were both reading Rilke. And Roddy sent Hugh MacLennan's *Barometer Rising* with much praise for it. There were other books, and beautiful nightgowns when he could shop in the big cities. (I remember white, chartreuse with brown velvet trim, and black lace, sometimes with matching peignoirs.) The army pay made it possible to do more than just improve the house! Negotiations concluded, after much discussion, over selling the old Ford car and putting the money aside for a new one after the war.

In early August, on a day as busy as all the others, two long-awaited black lambs arrived to join the cows and chickens. They were named Plum and Cherry and were the beginning of a flock that numbered up to a dozen at times. They kept the grass trimmed (and sometimes, when they got out, the roses, too, if the deer didn't) and provided lamb for the freezer and black wool for the sweaters the Cowichan Indians of southern Vancouver Island knit, with Tom Hudson doing the shearing each year. I remember what seemed an unending job of trying to keep those sheep fenced in and the letters serve to confirm that memory. If they didn't get through the fence wire, they went around when the river level dropped. Of course, sometimes someone left a gate open, but *never* us, of course. If we didn't already know, we learned the importance of closing farm gates. Fast. And how stupid sheep are – where one goes, the rest follow, especially if there are a lot of children whooping and hollering after them.

By the beginning of September, Ann described Roddy's RCMP personnel work to her mother thus: "His report's been accepted at a very formal luncheon given by the Commissioner of the RCMP for him and his superior colonel and general and this week he's giving a training course in personnel work to the Mounties he picked for the job – so it's not going to be one more beautiful report pigeonholed. In spite of many kind offers from them [including heading the RCMP personnel service], he's going back to the army – and, hold your breath – being stationed in Victoria. He's disappointed not to get overseas [not enough seniority], but is counting heavily on the Pacific war. He'll be home for two weeks (they haven't forgotten the jaundice) in a few days." Roddy himself described his success as a "triumph" – strong word for him. In Ann's mother's reply, she said: "Must say I am glad Rod has stuck to the Army – Rod in an R.C.M.P. uniform would have been too, too devastating."

School started and Mary finally joined me there, in grade one in spite of Ann's teaching – the school wouldn't recognize it. After what must have been a very good two weeks leave, Roddy was posted to Vernon instead of Victoria and Ann went on with her work. The girls, who had moved to the guest room when Alan came upstairs from the crib in our parents' bedroom, were getting a proper bedroom, all pink and blue, overlooking the river. (We got switched back again to the other end of the hall after a couple of years – too much thumping about over our parents' bedroom early in the morning.) The guest room would be available again for guests; and they came soon – Roddy's cousin Celia Brice and her husband, who were moving from Winnipeg following his retirement. They eventually settled in Duncan, but stayed with us for several weeks.

In late September, Mamie Maloney, a newspaperwoman who had recently moved to Campbell River with her husband, Teddy Boggs, an accountant for a logging company, wrote in her *Vancouver Sun* column "In One Ear" about Ann. "How DOES she do it!", the piece began. Mamie went on: "When you drop in unexpectedly ... Ann may be scrubbing floors, milking cows, perched up on the topmost pear tree, feeding chickens or shooing the sheep out of the vegetable garden, but the minute a guest appears Ann drops everything, slips into a clean frock, smears on some lipstick and proceeds to while away the rest of the day entertaining you as if she had a flock of servants looking after all those chores you guiltily realize you are keeping her from. 'It's all a matter of attitude,' Ann explained ... 'Work is something you can always do ...' So Ann proceeds to whip up a luncheon for her unexpected callers and serves it up in front of the fireplace in a manner that makes you think you're eating in the Savoy or the Waldorf Astoria."

On sending the column to her mother, Ann wrote: "I'm everlastingly grateful to you for the ability to be glad to see people and wine or dine them according to the hour, without letting the entertainment eclipse the guests in my attention. It's one of the many gifts you've given." The same letter is filled with details of household decorating, especially the new bedroom for the girls, and arrangements to have her mother's sewing machine sent up from Seattle. A Seattle friend kept us supplied with dresses her daughter had outgrown, and Ann says there have been so many this year that "I've only bought underwear and socks, and everlasting shoes, to replace the ones they make out of cardboard, damn their everlasting black profiteering souls."

A month later Ann wrote, after the machine arrived: "I've just been having a sewing orgy ... The children can't believe that Mother invites them to bring forth their split pajama pants and torn pillow cases instead of screaming to blue heaven when a little thing is overlooked and becomes a long thing. And Alan comes running from wherever he is, screaming with laughter because it's like a motorboat."

In another letter to her mother Ann wrote: "Three weeks ago Roddy came up with his corporal on the way to a camp north of here. Just for fun they decided to give me the M test, which is their preliminary test to ascertain officer material, general information, mechanical aptitude, etc. It has 211 points, over 180 is officer material and high marks in certain parts – mathematics, recognition of tools, calls for special training in that area. Roddy had told me so often about a brigade major who made 209 that I knew it was phenomenal. So of course, I took their little test and hit it for 202 – tools and all – to the corporal's complete flabbergastedness; but Roddy insisted loyally when he got his breath, that he wasn't a bit surprised. Then they went north. By the time they got back three days later, I had convinced myself that I had more to offer the war effort than anybody that was in it, and since I couldn't be a WAC, I should park the children on you and Mary and work the graveyard shift at Boeing's which you know has been my secret ambition for years. Roddy, whether out of his wonderful wife-managing technique or sincerity, I know not, said that he guessed the idea had something; so, of course, from then on, I steadily gave it up."

Roddy was very reluctant to have been sent back to Vernon – being away had made my father abundantly conscious, if he wasn't already, that home in Campbell River sharing his life with Ann was the only thing that made sense for him. His persistent struggle to get into the army may make that seem contradictory, but that was done from a sense of duty born of upbringing, and, on a personal level, devotion to his mother and sisters. The constant progress Ann made with the place always impressed him enormously when he came home. The routine of interviewing men was broken for Roddy by some fishing and for both of them by a weekend in Vancouver in November after Roddy returned from a brief trip back to the Directorate of Personnel Selection in Ottawa. He had leave for Christmas, when Ann's mother and sister Mary came up from Seattle, and by then it seemed he would probably be going overseas at last. Roddy was home for New Year's as well, which they celebrated at an elegant party at the Painters.

The early months of 1945 were punctuated with fairly frequent leaves for Roddy as he moved around B.C. interviewing men, with the overseas assignment on-again/off-again amid threats of an unwanted desk job in Ottawa. In February, Ann and Roddy met in Vancouver and she wrote her mother: "Roddy and I had the usual luxurious fun. He got me a nice silly little hat, we saw a phewy movie, had tea at Shaughnessy Golf and Country Club, which was very nice, dinner at the Allied Officers Club, which wasn't, and talk and talk and talk, of course." And bought the *Encyclopedia Brittanica*, a necessity in any well-equipped household. We used it often – it has all the rules for playing croquet properly, for example.

By mid-March Roddy was at last on his way overseas. Ann was spraying fruit trees, coping with the water system, a leaky septic tank, lambing sheep (two pairs of twins) and a calving cow. Heather remained thin and sickly after her calf, called Primrose, was born and required all sorts of special treatment, usually time and labor intensive. Both Uncle Reg and Tom Hudson were often on hand to help, as was Helen Butters, a friend who had come to live with us for a while. The most exciting spring visitor of 1945 was Ann's brother Danny who was at last home from sea duty in the Pacific. He was followed by Harry and Ada Hartman and their children on a visit I remember well, if only because the water pump stopped working and we all had stomach flu. It seemed as if everyone who came went to work in the garden in some way – one more way of keeping up with it all. Ann also planted one field to alfalfa which meant a great deal of preparation, including spreading three hundred pounds of lime.

Roddy's assignment to England was only for a couple of months. The work was concerned with interviewing men, often in hospitals, about their rehabilitation and return to civilian life – the reverse of the work he had been doing in Canada. Of course, Roddy saw much of his mother in

London and other family whenever he could, especially his Uncle Decie. He was able, too, to see his sister Valerie, who had some leave from the army; and his Haig-Brown aunts, Rosie and Alice, who lived in Oxford and of whom he was very fond; and godfather Uncle Clarence at Godalming near Charterhouse, which he visited. His sister Joan was in Europe as an ambulance driver. The letters back and forth discuss the progress of the war freely now as the end nears. When VE Day finally came in May, Roddy was visiting his old tutor, Dr. Davies, at Headbourne Worthy near Winchester and, after Churchill's speech, he and the friend he was with rang the bells of Dr. Davies church for him. "The Bells," the story of that day, was first published in *The New Yorker*, and later in *Writings and Reflections*.

Roddy also shopped steadily for books, as he had always done, in London and Oxford and at Thorp's in Guildford, Surrey, whose catalogue was a fixture in his and Ann's book-buying life. He bought fiction (Saki, Eudora Welty, Henry Williamson), poetry, erotica (English, French and German, and the *Kama Sutra*), criticism (Arthur Koestler) and gardening (Gertrude Jekyll) and fishing books (titles not mentioned in the letters) with emphasis on good editions from the Nonesuch Press and, once, so they would own *one*, a Kelmscott Press edition of William Morris' *The Sundering Flood*. Some fifty books are described and there may have been more. There were meetings, too, with his English agent, Hughes Massie, and the English publishers of his books. Sales and prospects were good and plans for after the war copious. Collins' edition of *Starbuck Valley Winter* had sold 6500 copies and their services edition of *Return to the River*, 14,800. Black's planned a new edition of *Silver*.

Roddy told Ann that, more than ever, being in England made him realize how much he was now a Canadian. The house, the garden, the river and the fields in Campbell River meant everything to him in terms of place, and Ann meant everything in terms of his emotional life. Their ever-increasing need and desire for each other, even after a decade of marriage, was a strong theme in all the letters. Many contain paragraphs fantasizing what they would do when they were together again. Roddy often describes attractive women, but always concludes that Ann is the one who knows his needs best. He said that his shopping for books made him feel very close because he was buying the books as much for Ann as for himself. He thought of the pleasure they would have in reading and discussing the books together, especially the erotica – risqué or even banned then, but now easily available, often under A for Anonymous in bookstore walls of paperback fiction, though some would more likely be found in an "adult" bookstore. He wrote, too, of the gardens and trees he saw around the hospitals, which were often in people's country houses, or from the trains. Oaks, copper beeches and birches were compared with the ones they had planted or hoped to put in after the war.

From Above Tide in mid-June, just before Roddy left England, Ann wrote simply, "Poor Heather is dead." The cow had gown weaker and weaker since calving and one morning when she could no longer get up and her eyes were rolling back in her head, Ann had to ask Uncle Reg to shoot her. Reg and Tom Hudson did an autopsy and found a darning needle grown into her heart – the obvious cause of all her troubles. How it got there no one knew. But her calf, Primrose, another golden Jersey, was with us for many years.

Roddy got a couple of days' leave at the end of June when he first got home, and then went back to Vernon to organize personnel services for the Pacific Command, which was to fight the Japanese. During July, the books he bought in England arrived regularly in the mail, and, mixed with the daily details, Ann expressed her delight over them. They thought Roddy might have to depart with troops for the Pacific without further leave. Ann wrote: "I am burning with the idee fixee of seeing you – somehow, anyhow." Roddy replied: "That is something I am feeling too, most strongly and all the time. I think it's going to be all right. I think I am going to get home to satisfy that feeling for a week, perhaps two ... " Ann quoted his words in a letter to her mother.

Roddy did get leave in early August, and, while he was home, the war in the Pacific ended. In a letter to Mrs. Elmore, he described those August days: "The weather is simply perfect. The children are brown and beautiful and healthy. We spend the biggest part of each day in the river, up at the Sandy Pool or across behind the big rocks on the far side – the little rubber inflatable boat is a godsend in all this and the children simply love it. Ann and I went up quite a way above the Quinsam the other day and rode down, getting thoroughly wet from the broken water but enjoying it immensely." We children thought that was very dramatic as we waited for them on the wing dam at our house; our mother stopping all her work to "play" added to the drama. The big new swing and climbing rope that had been put up on a February leave got a lot of use that summer, too.

Roddy returned to Vernon and the summer season ended for Ann with a flourish of visitors, including her brother Bucky with Gar and the children. Roddy was almost immediately sent to Camp Borden in Ontario, to his annoyance, but there was little for him to do there, so, after a brief stint in Ottawa, he was back on the coast at Victoria working with prisoners of war from Japan on their way home to Britain.

The one good thing about Roddy's trip east was that he had been able to call on Toronto publishers. His books so far had been distributed in Canada by either the British or U.S. publishers and he very much wanted to be published in Canada. As a result of these meetings, William Collins and Sons became his Canadian publishers for many years. By now he was straining at the harness of the army, but there was little he could do – he had joined late and it was expected that he would be needed until the following June. But both he and Ann were making plans for that time – Roddy by making notes for future books, Ann by thinking about relinquishing some of her work on the place. She said in one letter that much of her hard work had been a deliberate method of getting by without Roddy, but "I've come so close to putting the work on the place above everything else in my ideas and affections. I won't love the place as a means of self expression and a way of getting praise and esteem; it's only a place you got to put your wife and children in." In another letter, after resolving not to and still getting into a political argument during a bridge game, Ann said, "I know I'm too vehement. Come home and tie me down." He used to do it, too. He would say, "Oh, Annie," in a slightly pained tone. No one else ever called her that and neither did he except at such times, or, she said, when he wanted something.

The fall was as bountiful as ever, and on a day when everything wasn't happening at once, Ann described it thus: "I am wanting you this week to see the place transfigured as it has never been ... smoke from Blodel's [logging] slash [burning] gives that unreal red light – and everything, everything has come to fruition. I stand under the prune tree with the yellow wooden bowl and the grass is so green and the fruit hangs like fantastic grapes in giant clusters; the Gravenstein apples are bright red and at perfection. All of every day I've been canning. I pick a bucket full of ears of corn, then cut down the stalks and Primrose comes running for them. I take the corn relish recipe and go around picking just what I need – onions, a small cabbage, green peppers ... I painted the kitchen woodwork shiny white and the counter is spread with tomatoes and pears almost ripe. And the white hens lay six eggs every day and even the cat and kitten cooperate by bringing many rats and mice to display under the kitchen window. And the children go about in all their new fall clothes – fluffy pyjamas, overalls with all the buttons and shiny brown shoes. I've never felt such a throbbing, pulsing life in the place."

By mid-November, after another session in Vernon, Roddy was stationed in Nanaimo as head of the main B.C. sortation unit for discharging men, which made him seem almost home. Leave was more frequent and plans for postwar building were moving along quickly. Ann had talked with a contractor about changes to be made in the roofline so that bathrooms could be added upstairs, and kitchen and study remodelling plans. They finally decided to add a whole new room to the east side of the house for the study, partly because, as Ann put it in a letter to her mother in January, " —the year end take from the publishers was quite phenomenally large and anyhow, himself wants it." In the same letter, Ann wrote: "For Christmas Roddy gave me a white silk jersey sort of tailored negligee with a sheer night gown banded with satin and slippers all to match, all made to his order and my size and most becoming."

Their letters to each other are filled with little sketches for windows and cupboards, or reports on inquiries one or other of them had made about materials – still not readily available and expensive when they were. Roddy set himself up a desk in his room at Nanaimo to begin serious writing, but the flow of letters to Ann did not slow. Neither, I'm sure, did hers to him, but she either stopped keeping carbons or they are lost. Ann and the children went to Seattle for her sister Mary's wedding which was postponed when the groom could not get there in time. (The wedding, for which Ann and Alan returned, did take place a few weeks later, but the marriage did not last.) Roddy was scheduled for discharge in mid-April and for minor surgery for leg veins and hemorrhoids just before that, but in mid-March he was having trouble with his back and there was a good surgeon stationed in Nanaimo for ten days, so he went into hospital for the surgery and to have the back trouble diagnosed.

The surgery went perfectly well, but the back trouble proved serious. The only cheerful note at this point was that Roddy had finally become a major. He had actually been given the rank before he went overseas, but had to drop back to captain to go to England, then be given it again when he returned, but dropped back again when the war ended. He had even been promised the rank of lieutenant-colonel if he stayed in the peacetime army to continue his much-praised work in personnel, but there was no question of doing that.

The back problem was traced to a damaged disc and Roddy was transferred to Vancouver Military Hospital. The prescribed treatment was three weeks in bed with fifteen-pound weights on each leg to stretch the spine and allow the disc to heal, and an operation if that did not work. This took most of April —I remember hoping against hope that he would be home for my tenth birthday on April 21. At the end of the month Roddy was discharged from the army and sent next door to Shaughnessy Veterans' Hospital for follow-up physiotherapy. The operation was deemed unnecessary, but would probably have to be done eventually. Roddy was able to go out to visit friends and shop between treatments, and he took advantage of the opportunities to look for tools and a wheelbarrow, to buy Alan a baseball mitt and, as always, to haunt the bookstores. He also bought a heat lamp for his back. His last letter to Ann is dated May 19, 1946. He expected to be home in a day or two and he was. It may have been late for my birthday, but there couldn't have been a lovelier time of year to be finally home.

At last the years of waiting were ended – three years of waiting to get into the army and three more waiting to get out. Neither Above Tide nor Ann and Roddy's love had paused, but both had changed and grown.

During the previous few weeks in the hospital Roddy had almost completed reading the proofs of *A River Never Sleeps* and written a commissioned article for *Maclean's* magazine on cougars. The next job was revising the text of the 1939 Derrydale limited edition of *The Western Angler* to update it for a Morrow trade edition. New illustrations were provided by Tommy Brayshaw after Roddy discovered his skill as an artist when they were working together during the war. He had seen him doing pen sketches of fish on hotel stationery and knew that this was the person to illustrate the new edition.

Ann wrote her mother on May 30, 1946, "Roddy is home and it's simply bliss. The children are good all the time, the broken things are getting fixed and the alteration work is starting up again ... tonight, after a gigantic cleanup [of the children's rooms] he's starting army discipline on order in their bedrooms. Pray that it works." It did, kind of. We would go upstairs on Saturday morning sometime after breakfast, riot around a lot, tease each other, eventually pull things together when we got bored with the silliness, and then invite Daddy up to inspect, usually about lunchtime when we got hungry.

Most of the story of the next few years can be gleaned from Roddy's letters to his mother again. At the end of May, he wrote: "It's wonderful to be home again and Ann has everything here in most beautiful shape – children well and happy and full of life, a great big vegetable garden growing splendidly, cows and sheep and chickens all doing what they should be doing. We are having some difficulty about our additions and improvements to the house – *much* more expensive than it should be, all materials almost impossibly hard to get, labour hard to get and of doubtful quality when you do get it." But by late June the new study was framed and the other work was moving along. "The new roof is a blue green [asphalt shingles] color and we have cut away the eaves to make the house look lower and neater – which it does."

In early July the doctors were satisfied that all was well with his back and Roddy was told to "go ahead and try it out ... I've done exactly that and everything has been fine." And, in other news, "We had a really bad earthquake ... It knocked down most of the chimneys between here and Union Bay [40 miles south] ... It was a terrifying business and our house shook as though it would surely collapse ... some crockery broken, including a favourite big plate and a good tray, most of the books off the top shelves, almost a fire in the kitchen when the stove pipe fell off, and a baddish crack at the base of the living room chimney." That earthquake was the strongest I have ever been in and the memory remains vivid. It happened quite early on a Sunday morning. Ada Hartman and her children were visiting (Harry had died the previous year at forty-seven, a great sorrow to Ann, who had so loved her years in his store) and we all filed out of the house through the kitchen, just as the stove pipe crashed apart, and sat on the ground. The trees shook as if the wind were blowing, and there, as astonishing as the quake itself, was our father – outdoors in his pyjamas. He must have been still in bed with the heat lamp on his bad back – a regular morning routine. The quake delayed the building of the new study chimney – the mason was far too busy fixing damaged chimneys.

But the building went ahead. "... we have to scrounge and scrounge. Yesterday we tore down the old water tower and will be using a lot of the siding on the walls (outside) of the new study ... We have plumbers in today, getting pipes up into the future new bathroom, but I'm not sure when we'll get fittings ... The children all three sleep out in tents and love it. I'm ready to add on to their swings and rope ladders and horizontal bars – I got a discarded scramble net and have the makings of a very good see-saw." Doug Smith (Roddy's immediate boss in the army) came from Victoria with his wife and their two children, and the Jensens with their three daughters were coming from Seattle – "they are a *very* lively family indeed." True – and it was the *most* fun when they came. Mary Jensen and Betty MacDonald (who also came to visit) were sisters. Betty is best known for writing *The Egg and I*, but Mary also wrote. One book, *The Doctor Wears Three Faces*, told, in terms as funny as her sister's famous book, of the life of a doctor's wife. My sister Mary and I usually spent part of our visits to Seattle with the Jensens.

In early August "Edward Dunn came up to bring me my new Labrador pup, Lancer's granddaughter ... I think she'll make a thoroughly good [hunting] dog. She picked up a three-day-old chick from a box in the kitchen yesterday and carried it safe and sound to the living room, where she laid it gently on the floor." The little dog was named Linnet because she was small like the bird of that name and became a wonderful children's dog, especially for Alan. Forget hunting. Edward was Alan's godfather and when they took him fishing "Alan kept up as we walked, took an interest in everything ... He talks a lot, but always manages to be interesting and to the point. I certainly hope he will keep on this way, because it makes him a very pleasant companion." He has.

Roddy told his mother that he was also busy with magistrate's and juvenile court work which he had resumed as soon as he returned from the army, "but I'm trying to keep that ... to two half days a week." It seems as if Roddy was always trying to keep the time on the bench to a minimum, but Campbell River kept growing and so did the job. Aside from his strong commitment to what he saw as an important duty once he was asked to do it, he enjoyed the work and did it well. Over the years very few of his decisions were ever appealed and, of those that were, very few were overturned. He frustrated some by what seemed to them the restraint of his decisions and was considered to be "soft on Indians." Alan tells of meeting quite a few people who told him that the worst part of appearing before his father was not the sentence, but the scolding. As his daughter, I can well-imagine the pained, sorrowful look on his face as he gently, but firmly, told a defendant to think about the consequences of his actions and suggested that he perhaps take a little more responsibility for them.

Roddy continued urging his mother to come out for a good long visit the next summer. A major event of that first postwar summer was the arrival of a long-desired canoe, described in a letter to Ed Dunn as: "a big freight canoe (17' long, 45" beam)." That blue Peterborough canoe was the center of many summer days on the river. The years on the Nimpkish had made our father a fine canoe man. I now marvel at the way he could stand in the stern and pole up through rapids – setting the pole, thrusting hard and positioning the canoe so that it held steady in the flow until he set the pole again. I was the bow paddler most of the time and considered it a great honor. (Alan used the canoe before he was married to Vickie Assu to visit her at Cape Mudge on Quadra Island across Discovery Passage from Campbell River. We both still sorrow over our father giving it to two wandering guys in the seventies who had lost theirs in an accident.)

By October Roddy wrote his mother that he hoped "to be moved into the new study by the end of next week. They've also finished the upstairs bedrooms and as soon as the plumbing fixtures arrive we can finish off the bathrooms." Both the work on the bench and the publishing of books were going at a great pace. "*A River Never Sleeps* is supposed to come out in New York this month [finished in 1943, but held until now] ... The new edition of *Panther* is out and expected to do very well. There's a new Canadian edition of *Starbuck*, a pocket book (Canadian) of *Timber* and a pocket book (American) of *Starbuck* to come." About the same time, in a letter to Mrs. Partridge, the mother of Dickie P., whom *Silver* is dedicated to, Roddy wrote: "I'm just back from a week's trip up north after ducks and geese, but I don't shoot and fish nearly as much as I used to. It's a good thing really because I see things more keenly and clearly when I do get out, but a shade embarrassing at times because my public is everlastingly flocking in here, expecting to find the old master with rod or gun in hand and finding him instead seated before a blank sheet of paper with a swarm of children on the hearth."

By December, from the new study, Roddy wrote that he was finishing the revision of *The Western Angler*, doing "a couple of articles for sporting magazines ... three texts for Standard Oil advertising (descriptions of Canadian beauty spots) and getting a start on my new book [the sequel *to Starbuck Valley Winter*]. *A River Never Sleeps* seems to be doing very well so far. I've had a lot of letters about it, some from quite famous people, and the few reviews I have seen so far have been extraordinarily good – much better than I had hoped." In January 1947, he sent his mother several reviews, including ones from the *New York Herald Tribune* and the *New York Times*, and conceded that they "are really very good." *The New Yorker* said: "The writing has lots of charm and some touches here and there of Thoreau." Appreciation of *River* has only grown over the years since its publication and it will probably still be available in some form a hundred years from now.

Ann had a trip on her own in January by bus and ferry to visit Tommy and Becky Brayshaw in their new house at the head of the Fraser Valley near Hope. In her thank-you letter on her return she said she "found everything well. They didn't think they could run the house just as well without me as with me though." She had seen some of Tommy's drawings for the new *Western Angler* edition and included an urgent message from Roddy to him to "send what you have now" to Morrow. And she reported that she bought a sectional sofa for the new study in Vancouver and "am having corduroy slipcovers made in a deep rose beige," chosen to match the shade of faded old red book bindings on the shelves. Curtains were to be twill – "lots of rose beige and less of a pale yellow beige ... rugs are out of the question both in supply and in price."

The flood of mail about *A River Never Sleeps* went on, slowing progress on *Saltwater Summer*, but by early April when the family was leaving for an Easter trip to Seattle – by bus and boat since cars were not yet much available – it was almost done. *Saltwater Summer* tells of the two boys in *Starbuck Valley Winter* fishing a boat bought with the trap-line money. Although it has long been out of print, it is still mentioned with enormous pleasure by those who read it. For some it is one of only a few books they have found worth reading; for others it got them started reading books or, at the very least, Haig-Brown books. The reviews when it came out that fall were excellent. "Haig-Brown writes skilfully and with authority ... ," said A.M. Jordon of *Horn Book* and R.A. Brown in the *New York Times* said: "The action is fast, the description is detailed and interesting, and the character development adds to the worth of the story. The plot is both dramatic and plausible." The book also contained one of the earliest public criticisms of the harsh treatment received by citizens of Japanese origin during the recent war. In other news, the children had had measles; and an English cousin, Valentine Bartelot, who was immigrating to Canada, had arrived safely to stay until she went to work as a caterer.

The Seattle trip was a great success as always – a lot of book promotion work for Roddy and "we went out to dinner every night – superb dinners and charming people." The success of *River* was also renewing sales of *Return*. "I'm still getting good reviews of *A River* and one of the best of all will be in *The Atlantic Monthly* next month." Ann's sister Mary was starting a landscaping business in Seattle after working for a San Francisco seed company during the war. Her brother Bucky was working for a logging company near Seattle after spending the war in a Seattle shipyard. Danny was remaining in the navy and heading for Guam for two years. At the end of the letter Roddy said to his mother, "It will be wonderful if you can arrange to get here about next June. I think we should surely have a car by then and all our alterations *should* be finished. You will also have a new grandchild to see, aged about nine months. Ann is expecting a baby sometime in October."

In May, Roddy wrote of travelling three hours by police boat, accompanied by Ann, to hold court on Stuart Island in Bute Inlet on the B.C. mainland. This trip reflected his feeling that the courts served the people in that he went to the eastern edge of his district to sit rather than have all the people involved travel to Campbell River. I imagine he would have liked to do this more often.

Work in both gardens went on steadily. Ann had continued with the vegetable garden and Roddy was working on the lawn, and the perennial and rose borders. Farm chores were split. Later in May Roddy wrote: "We had a very charming visitor this week – Eddie de Rothschild of the banking family and the famous Exbury gardens near Southampton, where his father, Lionel de R. developed so many wonderful rhododendrons ... Very simple and straight forward, full of enthusiasm for everything he saw ... We went fishing, of course ..." And, undoubtedly, talked of rhododendrons.

In June, Roddy's mother sent blue booties for the baby, followed soon by pink ones. Roddy reported: "We are having a big garden party here next Wednesday for the Parent-Teachers' Association (Ann is president), and my border and the van Fleet roses are looking just about their best." He was at work on a new adult novel "– we call it 'The Wildman Novel' so far." Work went ahead on the remodelling again with the help of a Veterans' Land Act loan. Fixtures, except for the bathtub, were still awaited for the upstairs and now the kitchen was underway, though the first-ever refrigerator – no more icebox and cooler – and a dishwasher were nowhere in sight. There would be a new front door and entrance hall on the south side of the house, too. No more traffic through the kitchen. And the earthquake-damaged living room chimney was being rebuilt at last.

Roddy went to Vancouver to speak to the Canadian Librarians Association, mainly about *Saltwater Summer*, and *Starbuck Valley* was awarded a medal by the Canadian Association of Children's Librarians as the best juvenile published in Canada in 1946. (It had first been published in the U.S. in 1943.) He had recently given other talks on the United Nations and selective logging. His reputation as a speaker on a variety of subjects was growing, although he was never terribly enthusiastic about making speeches. He preferred writing what he had to say, but knew speaking to the right audiences could sometimes carry more weight. And he had a hard time saying no.

He flew into Buttle Lake to fish and got trapped by bad weather in July, so he made the twenty-eight-mile journey out on foot to be at Mary's first communion on time – and in his wet clothes. Seattle friends, Cebert Baillargeon and Edward Dunn, came to fish and hunt grouse, respectively. The grouse hunting was a return to an annual prewar tradition which went on almost without interruption for many years.

In September Ann was due to go to Seattle to await the baby's birth in the comfort of her mother's house, just as she had done for Mary and me. Shortly before she left, she ordered a black ram to join her increasing flock of sheep. And, she slipped on wet grass and broke her ankle. So it was off to Seattle with Mary for company, school lessons in a suitcase, and Ann's leg in a cast.

As in any absence, Ann and Roddy wrote frequently to each other. Roddy's letters to Ann cover sixty foolscap pages over five weeks, and now that he is the one at Above Tide, read almost like Ann's to him during the war. The tale of endless, crowded days, full of chores, children, visitors and other interruptions of one kind or another rolls cheerfully on, interspersed with the business of writing the novel.

When Ann broke her ankle, the plan to have a housekeeper while she was away and for a while after she came back was moved up and Mrs. Brazier and her nine-year-old son, Bobby, came to stay during the week. After Ann had left, when they went home on the weekends I filled in as housekeeper. Roddy thought that Alan was pretty happy playing with Bobby, but that I missed Ann a lot. He was delighted with Mrs. B. – "She is really nice and *devoted* to the children."

A major crisis of that fall of 1947 was caused by a plan to complete the final stages of the B.C. Power Commission's John Hart hydroelectric dam while shutting the Campbell River off completely during the salmon spawning season. Roddy went to work immediately he got word of the plan and finally succeeded in getting a minimal flow guaranteed, thus saving the tyee salmon run that had made Campbell River so famous. He and Ann had already had a personal battle with a construction crew over the building of the road to the dam through one corner of the field to the west of the house. The work started while Roddy was still in the army and I remember our mother going out to confront the bulldozer as it marched through the corner of our field without warning of any kind. Eventually, after a lawyer wrote letters, a settlement was achieved.

Roddy had made a short trip to Vancouver just after seeing Ann off to Seattle and he reported to her: "The Vancouver papers made a big play of the Tyee issue. Torchy [Andersen] had a lovely editorial after making headlines out of the story. Everyone I saw in Vancouver spoke about it. Lee Straight had a story in Friday's *Province* headlined, rather optimistically, 'Haig-Brown is Salmon Saviour'." The Campbell spring salmon run did survive that assault, but not without considerable concern until the rains came (which brought silt, causing new worries).

On the first weekend Ann was away Roddy went out to dinner with some admirers at Painter's Lodge and returned with them to find that "Valerie had the curtains drawn and the fire lighted and acted the perfect hostess until she took herself to bed at 10:30 – she had Alan asleep when we got home." He reported that he found the guests "a little boring – anti-negro, anti-semitic, anti-labour and damn little to contribute anywhere. But I was nice to them." But the next day "started beautifully. When Valerie finally came down we all three went to work to clear out the nursery [the now-vacant old study next to Ann and Roddy's bedroom] and clean up the basement. Did a pretty good job too. Mrs. B. will wash the nursery floor and we'll be ready to paint. Then the trouble started." Here begins a long, complicated story of a woman who arrived with two friends to complain that two other friends had been roughed up by the police at the dance the previous night. Sorting this out took some time over the next several days. There were no lawyers or social services in Campbell River in those days, and, as the magistrate, Roddy often found himself settling disputes of one kind or another (usually marital) informally. In this particular case, the police asked to have the magistrate from Quadra Island hear the case because they thought Roddy "might have heard too much from 'my friends.'" Was Roddy just a touch annoyed, perhaps, at the inference that his judicial impartiality had been so easily compromised?

The same day he went on with a short trip up the river in the canoe. And then Roddy continues: "There are endless things that should be done – border, vegetable garden, nursery and so on. I did hang the [new upstairs] bathroom curtains today, on oak strips, but should have painted the strips first, I see now. The curtains look beautiful." There is more in a discussion that had been going on for a couple of years about buying a small tractor. And finally: "I've got to stop ... It's 12:30, Joanie [Painter] and a flying boyfriend were just in ... Much love to you all, not forgetting Mary C."

Another typical day began with a trip to court. Then George Nichols, who had been renting the cottage for some time, was worried about his wife, Lucille, so Roddy went over to see her and lend her his heat lamp for her shoulder. Then came Herb Barclay (Mrs. Painter's brother and a lawyer) to discuss wills and such. He stayed to lunch. After lunch, as Roddy got down to work, some fisheries biologists showed up to discuss the plight of the salmon in the low river. Then it was supper time and after supper Uncle Reg, now having great difficulty with his eyesight, came in to have his mail read. He still had a car and we often used it to do his or our own errands. The children's excitement for the day was a small, but real – complete with the fire engine – chemical fire in the boys' cloakroom at school. And during the morning Roddy had dropped in on Con Reid who had lived for many years at Buttle Lake and had recently been declared to have died in 1938 by a Vancouver newspaper. At Reid's request Roddy had written to the paper resurrecting him. When Roddy went to tell him the letter was written "he pulled out his bottle and made me have a drink with him – 'you don't get a chance to have a drink with a dead man every day.'" Sometime during the day there would have been farm chores, too.

As the time went on Roddy managed to paint the doors of the new study and weather strip them to keep the rain out, make wooden letter file boxes for the shelves beside his desk – the old wire ones didn't look well – and paint the nursery floor. A small bulldozer was hired to make the driveway complete a circle instead of stopping just west of the house at the garage end of the cottage, smooth a road down to the vegetable garden by the river, and take advantage of the low river to deepen the pool below the dam for swimming. "The children loved the bulldozer, of course. Alan and Bobby got to sit in the seat with the motor running while Mr. Wilkes had his lunch." And, of course, there were troubles with the pump. Ann reported that "Mary's lessons go well and steadily. Her behaviour is just enough short of angelic to be credible."

Ann inquired if she had told Roddy that she "sat at the phone [at his desk] one day and wept because the five-stage outline [for the new novel, *On the Highest Hill*], all on one page, that was lying there was so beautiful." Roddy replied: "I didn't know you had seen the five stages. I want to know what you think of early stages like that. The pattern is still getting clearer in my mind, but I'm not sure how I'm going to work the emphases to get the most out of it and none of the exact detail is clear, though I think I'm solving the problem of the degree of intelligence and education the man must have – it has been a tough decision."

One afternoon Roddy took a trip up the river in the canoe with a notebook to look at the fish and the temporarily visible riverbed. "Practically nothing was unexpected – always, at a place where fish have come from, I found a nice depression in the bottom or a good sheltering rock." And, after leaving the canoe and walking from the Sandy Pool, he found, at the top of the Upper Island Pool, "the tyees – probably 150 or 200 of them." Other parts of the river held other kinds of salmon as well as cutthroat trout and an occasional steelhead.

The same letter goes on to worry about my shoes which were "right worn out." Roddy ordered *two* new pairs. "That's pure experiment, but I'd like to know (a) how a good pair would stand up and (b) what having two pairs at a time would do for us." Ann was "horrified" about the worn out shoes because they were only a month old, and said I *must* get rubbers for the new shoes, as I had been told to do. "And keep the new shoes dry, clean and alternated." She agrees that the "principle about 2 pairs is absolutely right if one could ever afford it." There was always some conflict about how the money was spent – Ann felt that Roddy kept her rather short of housekeeping money, but always had enough for his own extravagances. Her comment about affording two pairs of shoes obviously contained a veiled complaint. Alan remembers that when you went somewhere with our father you got a proper restaurant dinner, but with our mother you got a hamburger.

Another letter asks Ann if she wants more reading material and mentions Joseph Shearing's *So Evil My Love* and Toynbee's *A Study of History*. "*The Saturday Review of Literature* has a new section, My Current Reading – they write to famous people and ask what they are reading. Justice Douglas is the first, and the top book on his list is *A River Never Sleeps*." (Douglas was Associate Justice of the U.S. Supreme Court at the time.)

After reading of the endlessly interrupted days, Ann wrote, "I am now determined ... to run some really effective interference for you. I have two ideas. One old one – get Miss Boffy to put us on the list for an extension phone in the kitchen no matter how hopeless it seems now. If a buzzer doesn't come easily with a phone we could put one in ourselves. The other is to have a set time of day when, whenever we got our choice, we could tell people to come in." The extension phone came fairly soon and a separate buzzer was added. The idea was to take calls in the kitchen and buzz the study only when necessary, and the system worked fairly well. I can remember really intense periods of screening when the end of a book was in sight or page proofs were needed back in New York yesterday. We also had a rule never to say that our father was fishing on the rare occasions when he was, because so many people thought he fished constantly. In fact, the actual occasions were less frequent than even a conservative estimate might arrive at. The idea of confining the visitors to a set time never did really work, although it may have eased a busy day now and then.

Roddy's letter on October 6 said, "Your telegram of this evening has the family in an appropriate state of expectancy." Ann was going to have labor induced the next day. The rest of the letter tells of being up most of the previous night to listen to the troubles, mainly marital, of a friend staying for a couple of days until her mother left the hospital and they could go home to Comox. Roddy also related the story of Mrs. Brazier's recent desertion by her husband and mentioned that the clothesline broke twice that day, both times with a full load. Another thing to fix. Mrs. Brazier was turning a bumper crop of quinces into juice and canning it for Ann to make jelly with later.

On October 7, 1947, still in the cast, Ann delivered Evelyn Celia, called Celie in the family, named for a Haig-Brown aunt (who actually spelled her name Coelia, but after much debate it was decided to drop the "o"). On October 8, Roddy's letter began: "Mary telephoned just before suppertime last night that you were ½ an hour out of the delivery room and fine, with a daughter. Mary C. came along right after that with the weight – over eight pounds – such a gigantic baby. Valerie was much impressed by it all and is delighted at the outcome. I think she prefers a girl. On the whole I think I'm for it too. Given absolute choice I would have said 'Boy'. But there's a long gap between this one and Alan so from Alan's point of view little is lost. And there's damn little one can do to prevent this little number being the baby of the family, which is a far better spot for a girl than a boy. I want to see her very much. Is she black? Valerie wants red hair. I told her not bloody likely." Ann's letter of the same date told the details of the delivery.

The pattern of gardening, writing, court and chores mixed with lots of visitors, sometimes with troubles, sometimes purely social, went on until Ann came home in early November. The children roller-skated around and around the basement where a cement floor had recently been poured; Roddy listened to the baseball games and went to PTA meetings for Ann, and Board of Trade and Fish and Game as well; friends brought meat, mainly venison, and even fish enough to keep the grocery bill admirably low; some dogs chased the sheep; and a load of coal arrived for the fireplace in the new study. Roddy cut my hair because I was off to spend the weekend with a friend. The novel was "progressing, though not on paper. I think I'm going to get the right start though and keep it working all through." He painted the study floor gray and helped Alan build a boat. Lin had puppies. One was kept and became – Puppy.

In one of her last letters from Seattle Ann sent a clipping from the newspaper column "Mirror of Your Mind." In answer to the question of whether marrying the right person would make you happy, consulting psychologist Lawrence Gould replied that it would not make you any happier than you have it in you to be, and went on to explain that some spouses feel unhappy because they harbor secret feelings of unworthiness and see their mates as far superior to them. Ann said: "Read me acting bitchy or cranky. I *know* it is a feeling of inadequacy. That's why words of praise for routine tasks are such an avid hunger, to be assuaged by any means." Roddy answered firmly, "This is a cooperative affair, all the way through – around the house, with the children, outside on the place, in bed, in the library. Without either one of us it would probably still work, in a sort of a way, but it wouldn't grow any more and it wouldn't be the same or nearly as good. I could never in the world have figured out a house, or a household like this on my own. You should realize how much of it is your own if only because it ran so well for you when I was away. You should remember all the bits and pieces you've shaped and fitted together almost entirely on your own – the kitchen, the bedroom, the sheep to keep the orchard civilised, the – oh hell, you name them ... You don't seem to realize how definitely it takes two to make a family for a writer ... Very few women would have consented to raise a family at all under the conditions you've had to take on, much less have directly aided and abetted the hazardous proceeding ... And I only write through you. This will be fourteen years we have been married, eighteen that we've known each other. I might have been writing anyway, but it would have been immensely different."

In October, Roddy wrote his mother, "Ann had an 8 lb., 7 oz. baby girl." There had, no doubt, been a telegram to her at the time of the birth. Her visit began to seem definite after a year of procrastination. Roddy hoped that she would arrive in early spring and said, "The novel should be done by the time you get here and I expect to be working on another non-fiction book – much like *A River Never Sleeps*, but *without* fish." He was sending her the new CARE food parcels ordered from a central depot, an important item in those first postwar years when the people of Europe were still short of food, and wanted her opinion of them. (These letters to his mother are still kept in a heavy cardboard box from one of those parcels. If the contents were as solid and good as the box itself, they were a success.) His sister Val was working for his publisher, Collins, in London, and Joan was in Somerset, where she lived for many years, working with horses. Val went to Oxford to study social work before long and eventually became the Director of Probation Services at Holloway Prison in London. On the domestic side, "... Celia is fat and growing fast. The new dishwasher and automatic clothes washer [a combination arrangement in which you lifted tubs in and out according to desired function] is installed and working at last. The carefully planned new kitchen already works beautifully."

To his publisher Thayer Hobson, Roddy wrote of his pleasure at finally seeing *The Western Angler* in its new form. "It's certainly a load off my mind to have it available again after so long ... I'm sweating along with the novel, rather better than I have been. It's a pretty ambitious little book, as planned, but the writing of it is very touchy. I'm liable to send along a few chapters ahead of time, to check on whether I'm in the ditch-digger class as a novelist. But I'll dig the ditch to the end in any case ... The working title is *On the Highest Hill.* And there are six part titles: The Alder Flat, The First Valley, The Big Lake, The Narrow Valley, The Gully, The Highest Hill. I'm sure you'll change the title." Roddy's story of a man's travels deeper and deeper into the wilderness as he searches ever deeper into himself in a struggle to find meaning in life was once described by a friend as "there but for Ann goes Roddy," a play on a popular song title, "There But for You Go I."

After Christmas Roddy wrote, "... the children, except Celia, are happily back at school. C. is a fine baby and is doing very well. She'll be crawling by the time you get here, I suppose, but she certainly loves to be held and played with now. In fact she gets pretty angry if someone isn't doing it most of the time. Ann is busy painting the new hall – there's still a good bit to be done after the alterations, especially in the kitchen – shelves and cupboards have so much surface."

In late February, Roddy wrote to thank his mother "for the birthday wishes – do you realize I'm 40! – and for *Horizon* ... Much interested to know of the English *River Never Sleeps* I haven't seen it yet. I shall be seeing Billy Collins [his Canadian publisher] in Victoria about March 19. Jess Carmack, Morrow's West Coast man, arrives here tomorrow to stay the weekend and talk over my novel. It is going along quite nicely, but I shall be glad of someone to look over it. We really keep awfully busy here – between children and writing and magistrating and visitors and emergencies you won't have a very restful summer I'm afraid."

In mid-April "a last minute note" said, "Present arrangements are that [cousin] Valentine and Rosella [her sister, who had also emigrated from England] will meet your plane on arrival at Vancouver and will see that you are looked after until your plane leaves for here at 3 p.m." Roddy met his mother at the Comox airport – the nearest at that time – on April 25, 1948, in a taxi. Still no car. I remember him saying, with amusement, that one of the first things Grandmother did was look at his pipe to see if it was a good English Dunhill. She may have had one for him in her luggage.

Of course, there is a gap here in the letters, but I remember my grandmother's visit with nothing but pleasure. She went for daily walks and it was our delight to go with her when we were home from school. She always had time to talk and she often went along with whatever we were doing, perhaps watching us swim in the river or exploring the riverbank with us. Celie, no doubt, spent as much time as an active baby would on her knee. I remember her, too, writing letters in her room. She stayed until mid-October, so she was with us for her sixty-eighth birthday on October 3rd and Celie's first on October 7th. She cabled her safe arrival back in England on October 18.

Roddy wrote his mother the day after she left. "It was sad to leave you there in Nanaimo. We watched the boat on her way out ... All the children miss you a lot. The constant comment is: 'It's so dull around here without Grandmother.' But Mary occasionally is in tears about it. And Celie occasionally says her word for grandmother and looks around as though she expected you to appear from somewhere.

"We haven't heard anything from Mrs. Elmore and Mary or from Marian and Keith [Fisken], but hope very much that all the meetings went off as planned. I had a letter from Dr. [Reg] Kinsman today saying how much he enjoyed seeing you on the way through Vancouver. [Dr. Kinsman was a Vancouver pediatrician and gifted amateur pianist who had a summer house near Campbell River and was an old friend. He probably saw Roddy's mother from the ferry from Nanaimo to the train for Seattle.] Our routine goes on much as ever, though without quite so many visitors, I think – more children, fewer adults. I was in court this afternoon on a rather long case with lawyers and all the trimmings and have another equally bad to come up on Friday. I finished Part V of my book last night and am now on Part VI, the last. May still have it done by the end of the month. It will be a great relief to be free to start on something else, though it's always a let down too. It's nice to be able to write knowing how easily you'll be able to picture everything and fill in the details for yourself. All love to yourself from Ann and me and Valerie, Mary, Alan, Celie. Your very loving son, Rod."

By the end of October Roddy had been on a short duck-hunting trip by boat with Ed Dunn, and two Campbell River friends. "Lots and lots of widgeon and some high and difficult flighting shots at mallards ... have finished wiring up those trees that you and I worked on last summer and yesterday we all, including Celie, went over and cleaned up the barn field with a gigantic bonfire. This afternoon I got a good start on Ann's kitchen cupboards ... she's hoping to get the whole room painted by Christmas. I've heard from both Ivan and Thayer in New York about Part V of *On the Highest Hill* and they think it is very fine indeed."

In early January of 1949, Roddy wrote of Christmas and the weather and his work. He had completed the alterations to the new book over the holidays "only three days later than I said. So I think they will have plenty of time to get the book out by April. I think the alterations improve the book quite a lot ... We've had extremely cold weather, but very little snow, ever since December 1st. There has been plenty of good skating and Ann and the children have made the most of it. Even I tried it out yesterday. We had a fine Christmas with Mrs. Elmore and Mary both here and lots of parties. Everything very much organized and supervised by Valerie Joan. Celie enjoyed it lots. Got much too tired, of course, ... but finished up none the worse and delighted with her new toys. The finish of it all for her was the children's party, on the Thursday after Christmas, when twenty children filled the house and yelled their heads off all afternoon. Celie thought that a shade too much."

By February the book proofs were done, it was still very cold and the first lambs had arrived. "We don't seem to be getting much closer to the new car yet ... the place we are getting the car from will get only one a month which may be any model from a truck to a limousine. It's a nuisance, but we've waited so long now that I don't feel like trying to do anything else about it. A couple of weeks ago I had to go to Vancouver to speak and I should be in Victoria today for another of those cabinet meetings on clearing Lower Campbell Lake [removing the trees and stumps along the flooded shoreline behind the new John Hart Dam], but I bogged off that. There are so many things one is expected to do and I want a little peace at the moment to get a start on a new book."

By early March the weather was a little warmer and most of the snow was gone. "We've had a particularly bad lambing season so far – only three left out of nine born. Of the others, one was killed by ravens, a set of three (triplets) all died, and another ewe lay on her two the first night. There are still four more to have their lambs and we are hoping they will do better."

To Edward Dunn Roddy wrote his thanks for a new pair of waders, mentioned the sheep troubles and, in news of the children: "Alan is happily bottle-feeding a lamb now. He and the girls have suddenly taken to tying flies with great enthusiasm. Results a bit scrappy so far, but it won't take them long to pass my very moderate skill." He mentions hearing that a mutual friend has a new boat and wonders if he could be persuaded to come on the duck-hunting excursions. "I must say I'm afraid anything better than the scatter-brained way we organize things now might easily detract from it all, but I imagine we could reduce George to our haphazard level in time." And finally, "Ann and I are on the point of leaving for a weekend in Victoria, to the great disgust of all the children."

To his mother Roddy reported that they "had a beautiful time in Victoria." The main purpose of the trip was for a routine check on his back by an army medical board, but Roddy went round the bookstores, and made a radio broadcast and Ann did a little shopping. "Then we visited friends, going out to teas and dinners and meeting them for lunch. All very pleasant and a nice change, as was staying in the Empress Hotel [still the grand centrepiece of Victoria's harbour front – her mother had stayed there on visits in the twenties] and trying out a new restaurant or two."

In mid-March Ann wrote to Roddy's mother: "Darling, My mother just rang up from Seattle to see if I was dead or anything because she hadn't heard for so long. I actually had the flu twice, but you will have noticed it wasn't fatal." Ann then thanks for cooking and garden books Roddy's mother sent and reports on Celie finally being able to walk around outside as the winter ends: "... she goes everywhere much too fast. She says (among other things) porridge, lunch, Kitty jumped, bath, hot, bed, dance-dance (with that she turns her fat little self around and around) ... As it gets to spring and outdoors time I miss you more than ever. We will be a sadly out-of-kilter family sitting under the walnut tree this summer." Roddy described Celie about the same time as "a bright laughing little girl at least 99% of the time. In the other 1% she puts on scolding tantrums that disappear almost immediately but sound like the end of the world for their brief moment."

Finally, in April: "The biggest news is that we have the new car at last. A very handsome, very pale grey, the whole car extremely modern... seats with plenty of room for three people on each ... everyone tells us that the Chevrolet has a much better post-war record than any of them." At last the end of bicycles, taxis and borrowed cars. An earlier letter said the car cost £600 (about $1800) or three times what Ann had paid for the Ford in 1933. "We made our first trip, the whole family, two days after it arrived – down to Parksville [about one hundred miles south on Vancouver Island], where I had to go to a magistrate's conference. Ann and the children picnicked on the beach and we were home again before dark."

In early May *On the Highest Hill* had been out for a few days and there had been some good advance reviews in literary trade papers. "The book is Morrow's main fiction item for this spring." But overall, the reviews were mixed. Ann Schakne in the *New York Times* wrote: "There is magnificence of spirit in a magnificent setting and for that spirit the reader feels pity, terror and awe, but never foolish regret." But J.H. Jackson in the *Herald Tribune* said: "The theme here is sound enough; the difficulty is that the conflict is realized only on the simpler levels. Like Colin himself the author is least successful when dealing with people ..."

Mary and I had gone to Seattle on the first of several annual Easter visits (I was getting my teeth straightened there). Mother drove us to Victoria in the new car and we took the CPR ferry. "The girls got back from a wonderful 10 days in Seattle and I met them in Victoria. Delighted about everything except the reception given them by the Canadian customs. No serious trouble, but the woman just wasn't kind to them at all, they said." Indeed, she wasn't! She made us *open* wrapped presents we had been given to bring to the family! We burst into tears all over Daddy when we met him in the lobby of the Empress Hotel and for years I tried not to get in a line with a woman customs officer.

In May Ann wrote her mother a five-page letter (much longer than the usual) which hopped from one crisis story to another after thanking her mother for the presents she had sent back with Mary and me. "I've decided the reason I achieve so many domestic crises is that I keep the raw materials always on hand." She doesn't say so, but a close reading indicates that the children are most of the raw material. For one, Alan had been given a probably rotten goose egg that needed a broody hen to hatch it. The Catholic Women's League president and the local priest were not getting along. "They had a knockdown, dragout at a meeting at our house, which left everyone concerned limp as a rag for days; so at the next meeting when I felt another round coming on I led the meeting in a request to Father to say a rosary with us." Later, when Father sought Ann's advice about what to do next, "I gave him a capsule version of the Sermon on the Mount and Helene Deutsch's *Psychology of Women* and told him I'd think about it."

After having the PTA speaker stay the night, there was "a weekend with four children besides ours, and a weekend with an amusing engineering couple from whom Roddy borrows books and vice versa. Much 'How peaceful it is here' talk. Ha-ha. The Communist Union sponsored a sports day to which I sent the children to get the mob of ten or so that was here off my hands ... all the children in town were there, and Valerie won the running races and the high jump. An hour before the Stingers (book people) came a truck skidded slightly ... and crashed into a tree in front of our driveway. Driver not hurt, but dazed, was being picked out when they arrived. An hour later the sawmill caught fire and about ten of us went – the biggest fire I've ever seen."

The next day the Brayshaws came to stay; the same day as the PTA nominating committee meeting. The following morning a Seattle friend and his uncle stopped by for breakfast about the same time the men arrived to rewire all the electric motors to run on the new 60-cycle electricity instead of 25. None of the electric motors – frige, oil-stove fan, water pump, radio, washing machine – worked properly for several days.

"Sunday morning, ghastly sight, we found that Roddy had backed into the door of the Brayshaw's car when he 'just touched it' backing out of the garage the night before. The *most* embarrassing hour there's ever been in this house, until Tommy got down and was shown it. None of the H-B's could believe that *Daddy* had done it, and he couldn't believe that a car could be so soft ..."

The entire next page is taken up with a detailed and hilarious account of "the riot" of getting me ready for my first formal dance. (I remember the dance in the old community hall very well, but not the chaos preceding it.) "The eighth grade was invited to the High School graduation dance and there's been days of talk about dresses and etc., etc. ... [Valerie] says the thing she likes about racing is the terrible keyed-up excitement beforehand – Roddy says that's what most boys at school can't stand – and she had the same feeling about the dance. She designed her own dress from ideas in Vogue [I'd forgotten this, too] ... White pique with fitted bodice and full skirt, puff sleeves ... She wore her hair straight to the horror of the little numbers at school ... Mother's gold shoes and single pearls ... I had to help with a dinner for the graduates, but as soon as I got back the riot began. Valerie got the dress on over the appropriate length petticoat, devised somehow or other. Of course she wore Aunt Mary's adorable nylon underwear [first ever bra, white, with matching panties]. Father paced up and down in dinner jacket beaming while I argued against hair being pinned back (successfully). Alan kept shouting what were the boys going to wear. Nylons? A great full skirt? Pearls? Mary had a brain wave about a slightly motheaten jacket Grandmother left here long ago, and kept insisting Wear the coat, wear the coat. Celie was so excited she had to be gotten out of her crib and rushed up and down the hall in her long nightgown, shooting a toy gun and yelling, 'Nylon, nylon, coat, coat the coat.'

"... at a quarter to nine, the *boy* came. This a great triumph, most of the eighth grade went by itself. [I asked him because I *thought* I would be the only one without a date – it was years before I did such a bold thing again.] We took them and burst with pride all evening. Valerie and boy took a long time getting courage to dance ... Valerie then managed to find a boy from over on the island she met last summer [he found me and became *the* boy all through high school] and kept her two swains happily competing until one o'clock ... The nice thing was that she didn't look a day over thirteen for once in her life."

Roddy described the same and other events to his mother a little more offhandedly. *Life* was calling for advice on photographing the Columbia River salmon run; he was writing a fishing article and hoping to start a new book. In the garden the daffodils were in bloom; a new camellia, Mme. Sarmont, had been planted by the front steps; and a new cherry on the grave of Cherry, the sheep. There were also new floribunda roses for the border – Elsie Poulson, Karen Poulson, Pinnochio, Red Ruffles and others. I "won the races for girls under 18, under 16 and under 14" at a May 24th sports day. The annual PTA garden party was on Mary's birthday, June 2, "but her big day is Saturday, when Ann is taking all the children down to a gymkhana at Comox." The next big garden event was Beth Painter's wedding in mid-June: "Valerie had a wonderful time as a bridesmaid ... The garden looked fine ... the border right at its best with peonies, iris, aquilegia and lupins all in fullest bloom."

In book news: "It hasn't been officially announced yet, but I've been told that *Saltwater Summer* has won the Governor General's Award for the best juvenile published in Canada during 1948. It's quite good to get that after *Starbuck Valley* got the 1946 award – it was called the C.L.A. award then, but it was the same general idea."

Roddy, Ann and Celie went to Seattle in late June for a week. "I made my talk at the Fly Fishers' Club dinner – a very fancy affair with eleven state game commissioners and all the top fish and wildlife service men from the federal government there – and also made my usual rounds of the bookshops ... *On the Highest Hill* seems to be selling quite well in spite of doubtful reviews ... seems clear that it's not going to be a best-seller. Just one more of my steady, dependable old jobs." Perhaps this is why Roddy never wrote another adult novel. He may also have been discouraged by criticism of his ability to handle dialogue – he was enormously sensitive to criticism, not a good condition for a writer.

In mid-July of what still may be the busiest summer on record, Roddy wrote: "Mary Jensen and her three very vivid daughters were up with us for a few days. The Todds [with four children] and the Quaintons and Joanna Eckstein will all be here from Seattle. And the summer visitors 'in passing' are here already. You will remember how it is." And a week later, "Lord Alanbrooke, the wartime chief of staff and Churchill's right hand man was here and I took him out for a couple of days to look for big fish. We didn't find any, but he's very keen about birds and we had a wonderful time anyway." As I remember, he particularly wanted to see hummingbirds. A typical mix of visitors – friends, of course; people who had read the books and wanted to meet the writer or fish with him (few got to do that because there was so little time), others who had been told by mutual friends that they simply must go to Above Tide. Sometimes admirers just left a note or a gift in the rural route mailbox at the end of the driveway. A few took a photograph from a distance and sent it later. Most people were welcome and interesting – though there were those who just came to fill the gap before the tide changed and it was time to go fishing. Not quite so welcome.

An August letter of Roddy's to Edward Dunn, mainly about fall grouse hunting prospects, had an addition from Ann reporting to the godfather: "Alan made his First Communion July 17 with a seemingly proper understanding and an appropriately devout demeanour." To his mother, Roddy wrote: "We've been fairly busy ... Jo Eckstein, a Seattle friend, was here for a week and the Todds, also from Seattle. Earle Birney, the poet, was here for a day with his family; Doug Alcorn, the psychiatrist [an army personnel friend]; Dr. [Norman] MacKenzie, the president of the university [of B.C.]; the Al Schwabackers from San Francisco, distant connections of Jo's; Jack Mead, the ex-Deputy Commissioner of the RCMP; the Denman's from Seattle and so on. I've been to Buttle Lake twice, once with Ann. Both cats have had kittens, Lin has had pups and Primrose has had a calf. And I have been unusually busy in court. The girls are now away at their Guide camp." In spite of it all, he also reported that he was "making fair progress with the book [a collection of essays on the various aspects of his life, except fishing]."

Another letter two weeks later has a visitor list just as long. One from Ann in late September reported on the harvest. "This year has yielded such a harvest as never was. I have the frozen food locker [space rented at a place down the road – the world was not yet full of home freezers] and the basement cupboard overflowing, and we're still eating all the ripe tomatoes we can from the ones ripening in the house. I'm still making bits of jelly from quinces and crabapples and green tomato and onion pickle, though everything in the garden has been finally frozen stiff." And typing "a large piece of Roddy's book." Ann's news of the children told that "Dee" as she called herself "really belongs to the other children more than to me. None of them ever say 'Do we have to take care of Dee?' but 'Can't we take Delie with us?' She does everything Alan suggests, which sometimes gives him a chance to be naughty by remote control."

Another letter to Edward from Roddy – that fall's grouse hunting was delayed by a fire closure in the woods – asked if he could find "Roger Tory Peterson's *Field Guide to Western Birds* ... and bring a copy up with you. Also, though this may be harder, a copy of the 35 cent *How to Know the Birds*. I have the $2.00 edition and want to see the other." The hunting trip did happen and was a great success as always.

In late September Roddy wrote to his mother "Your man, Borradaile, was here for a couple of days and we went into a lot of details about the possibilities of filming *Pool and Rapid*." Roddy described Osmond

William Haig-Brown of Charterhouse, Roddy's paternal grandfather.

Alfred Pope, Roddy's maternal grandfather, at Wrackleford in Dorset.

Roddy's mother, Violet Mary Pope, formally posed in a Dorset studio.

Alan Haig-Brown, poet, journalist, teacher, soldier and sportsman.

Roddy's father, Alan Roderick, officer of the Middlesex Regiment.

The wedding portrait of Alan Haig-Brown and Violet Pope, married in 1907 in Dorchester. The bridesmaids are probably two of Violet's three sisters.

Grandfather Pope's country house, Wrackleford. Roddy and his father (left) and mother (right) spent summer holidays here on the edge of a little trout stream.

Roddy's father posed his son with gun and dog by the Wrackleford garden wall.

Roddy, at seven, in one of a series of formal portraits taken each Christmas.

As did all English schoolboys, Roddy (right front) played team sports, in this case, football. This team played for Twyford, the school he attended from 1918 to 1921.

A self portrait of Roddy, aged 18, at his first logging job in 1927, in the woods of Washington State north of Seattle near Lake Cavanaugh.

One of the great trees on the lawn at Wrackleford, fallen in a winter storm, provided a seat for Roddy, his mother, his Uncle Decie and his sister Valerie in 1930.

Annetta Maud Wright, Ann's mother, probably at the time of her marriage.

Baby Ann in Seattle in 1908, looking just a little bit apprehensive.

Ann with her father, Bruce Elmore, a much-loved Seattle doctor.

Ann, right, with her sister Mary and her brother Bruce in their party finery.

Ann, left front, in her first year of high school at Seattle's Forest Ridge Convent. Gertrude Dunn, Edward's sister, is third from left in the front row.

Ann in her Campfire Girl uniform laughs with her little brother Danny.

The family house on Federal Avenue in Seattle where Ann lived until she married.

Ann in 1933 – the picture for which Roddy bought "a little leather frame."

Roddy in 1933. These two portraits were taken just after they were engaged.

Ann on her wedding day, January 20, 1934, at her mother's house.

Ann on the wedding trip to California, sitting on the running board of the Ford bought with her earnings.

Walking the cougar kitten Ann and Roddy tried to raise at Campbell River in 1934.

Baby Valerie Joan with Ann in a Campbell River garden in the fall of 1936.

Becky Brayshaw with Roddy, some fine fish and one of the long series of black Labradors. Tom and Becky Brayshaw were frequent visitors at Above Tide.

A solemn V.J. examines her father's camera in this summer 1937 photo. One of the bantam hens scratches under the kitchen window behind them.

Roddy's mother and cousin Agatha at the Campbell's Sandy Pool in 1937.

Above Tide in 1937. Roddy often wrote in the windowed corner of the front porch.

Gardening was always an important part of Ann and Roddy's life at Above Tide.

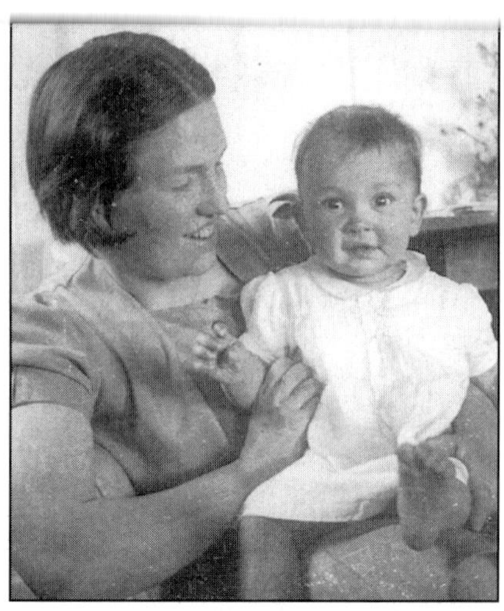

Ann with Mary Charlotte in 1938. Roddy commented on the "positive things" she did.

Mother and daughter V.J. on the back steps, perhaps on the way to church on Sunday.

The new cribbing along the river bank in 1940. The fence divides the rose garden along the lawn and the orchard. The skiff on the beach was called "Tyee."

Roderick Langmere Haig-Brown with his son Alan Roderick in the living room in early 1942. "We think he's a grand baby," wrote Roddy to his mother.

The ever-cheerful baby Alan goes along to harvest the summer fruit.

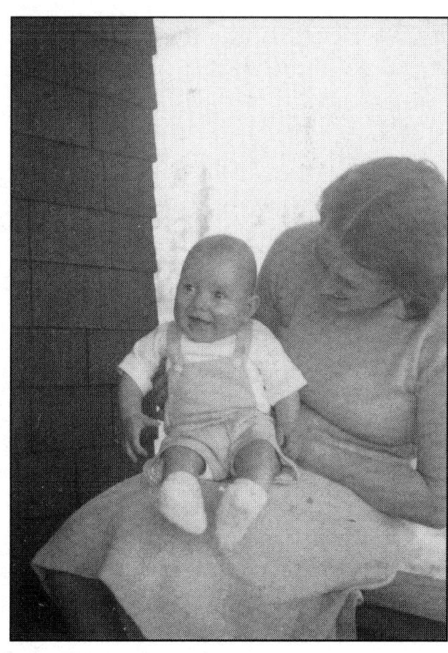

Ann with her son in 1942. "He has an awful roar when he thinks he's neglected."

Two sisters take very seriously the job of posing with their baby brother, who had been christened Alan Roderick Edward, with two godfathers and two godmothers.

Roddy finally got into the army in June of 1943 as a personnel officer, after having tried every possible way of joining he could imagine from the time the war started.

Ann and Alan in one of a pair of photographs taken for Roddy in 1943.

Valerie and Mary in the photograph their father carried during the war.

The Jersey cow heads into the barn to be milked by Ann or Roddy - a twice-daily chore they both enjoyed doing for the peaceful moment it meant.

Valerie Joan in a white dress with blue lace bodice at Above Tide.

Alan Roderick wearing the sailor suit that was a small boy's proper formal wear.

Mary Charlotte wears white with red scallop trim in her portrait taken in front of the turquoise curtains in the living room. The bench she sits on was made by Roddy.

Pausing after "the riot" of getting Valerie ready for her first formal dance.

The canoe arrived the summer Roddy came home from the war.

A little brown summer boy squints into the sun from high on a log.

Alan feeding the orphaned fawn we raised and then released on a quiet island the following fall.

Alan steadies the dog as he and Roddy pose on the wintry lawn. The dog is clearly not yet an eager hunter and, in fact, neither Roddy nor Alan hunted very much.

Roddy at his desk in the new study wearing a yellow sweater that Ann knit. The bird-watching binoculars were always on the desk, but the pipe went when Roddy stopped smoking.

Roddy "on the bench" as a Stipendiary Magistrate for the Counties of Nanaimo and Vancouver. He was later made a judge of the provincial court and served until 1975.

Washed and brushed – the children, that is – Roddy always looked neat - the Measure of the Year *family poses for a photographer with the black sheep of the family.*

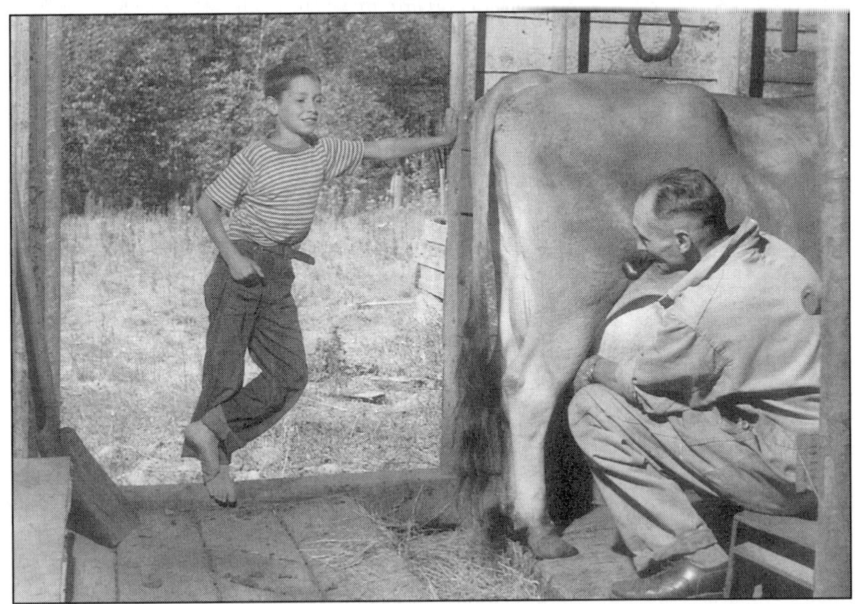

Milking time was a good time for long conversations with our father. Roddy thought Alan an interesting talker when he was little and Alan continues in that vein.

The big blue Peterborough canoe slides easily through the Line Fence Pool on one of the seemingly endless sparkling summer afternoons we spent on the river with our father.

A summer dinner on the terrace outside the study in the early fifties. Roddy had made the table and benches years before, but welcomed a proper chair for his bad back.

In 1952 the family group posed on the occasion of Roddy receiving an honorary doctorate at the University of British Columbia. His robe is red with a blue velvet lining.

Ann, Alan and Mary in the study at the party before the Campbell River premiere of the NFB film Country Magistrate, *which featured Roddy.*

Lady Olave Baden-Powell gives Mary the Girl Guides' left-handed greeting during an inspection on the lawn at Above Tide.

Late snow and spring lambs in the orchard between the house and the river. The black sheep did a wonderful job of keeping the surroundings tidy for many years.

Heavy winter snows kept Roddy busy shoveling the roof during the fifties. The "new" study with its corner windows took the place of the front porch as the family and the book collection grew.

The family at home for Thanksgiving weekend in 1956 when Gretchen Harlow was living with us.

Roddy smiles fondly at Mary who looks equally pleased at her high school graduation. Roddy was a superb dancer and made a school gym seem an elegant ballroom.

Roddy in presentation buckskin fishing in northern Saskatchewan.

Roddy enjoys a fishing day with his good friend Van Egan, who took this shot.

A bearded Roddy, on the occasion of British Columbia's Centennial in 1958, bounces a quizzical first grandchild, Ann Luja, on his knee in the summer sun.

Dunc Marshall presents Roddy with "a very fine marble desk set with two Parker 51 pens" as the Fish and Game Club makes him an honorary member in 1959.

Wearing his city gray flannel at the speaker's lectern at a banquet or meeting became a more and more familiar setting for Roddy as his public profile rapidly increased.

Newly married Mary and Bernie Bowker walking the path Roddy mowed through Uncle Reg's field from the church to their wedding reception on the lawn in 1960.

Fishing occasions were not frequent and often for the benefit of a photographer.

Roddy listens thoughtfully at his desk in the study in 1965, books ever at hand.

By the daughter of the Big Fir soon after the big tree blew down in a southeaster.

This looks like the classic fisherman's pose describing the big one that got away, but Roddy often gestured in this open-handed way, and he is probably just conversing.

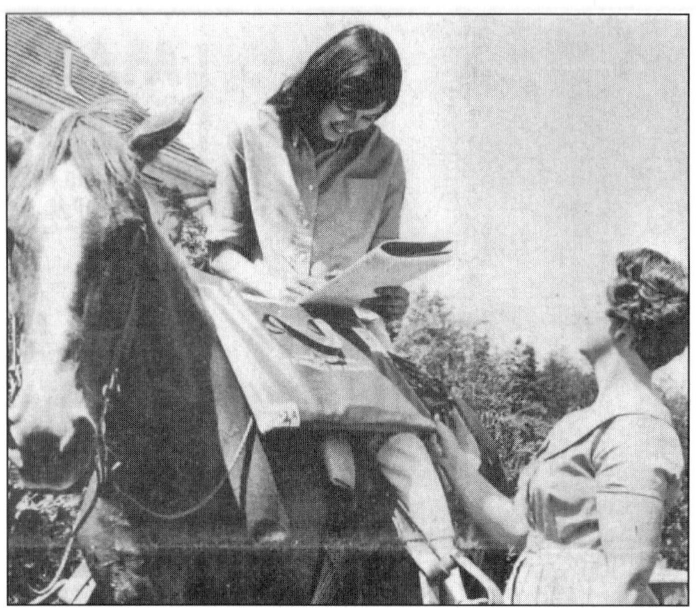

In 1966 Celie combined her passion for horses and her job as a collector of federal government census statistics. She is talking with Barbara Finch.

Once again Roddy put on the elegant honorary degree recipient's robes when Celie received her Bachelor of Arts degree from UBC in the spring of 1968.

This portrait of Roddy taken on a trip to New York was one of Ann's favorites. He posed willingly enough for the camera, but didn't always enjoy it as he does here.

Ann and Roddy share a joke at the kitchen table in 1976 over a lunch of Ann's hearty soup, which was always served in the big Chinese bowls.
(courtesy of Christopher Springmann)

Roddy and Glen Trimble pause for lunch during the annual fall grouse-shooting weekend - one of the longest-standing traditions of Above Tide. Tana, the dog, waits and hopes.

Alan, Ann, Celie, Valerie and Mary at the Adams River in 1978 during the sockeye run, when a park there was dedicated to Roddy for his work on salmon enhancement.

The study terrace in full summer splendor. Ann gradually filled the terrace with potted plants in the style of the Italian gardens she enjoyed so much when she visited.

Ann hated having her picture taken so there are not many good ones in existence, but this one, taken for the church directory, pleased her so she got prints for each of us.

Borradaile, who had called Roddy's mother in London to locate him, thus: "He has been in charge of photography on some very fine films – *Elephant Boy*, *Saunders of the River*, *The Overlanders*, etc. etc." The same letter told of the losses in royalties caused by a major devaluation of the English pound. A later letter said he had written a script for the film, "but the book is not really a good one and I am so far away from it that I don't want to waste time on it when I might be doing something new." The movie didn't happen, but the Borradailes became good friends, and in 1952 Borradaile did film *Country Magistrate* for the National Film Board, which pressed us all into service playing ourselves.

Roddy made a quick, but exhausting, publicity tour to Seattle in October. Celie had her second birthday which was such a success that "from time to time since she has suggested that another birthday is about due." The new book was "going quite nicely and should be a fair job when it's done. The title ..., at least for the time being, is *No Want of Wonder*. Haven't heard what New York thinks, but my agent is delighted with the first ten or twelve chapters." The working title for the book was from G.K. Chesterton: "The world will never starve for want of wonders; but only for want of wonder."

In November, Ann and Roddy went to Vancouver for Young Canada's Book Week, where Roddy made a speech to a librarians' gathering "against censorship, which caused a little flutter and did three radio jobs the next day, autographed in a bookshop or two, and spent hours having photographs taken by a man who wants to make a series of Canadian artists, writers and musicians." They also had tickets to the Monte Carlo Ballet, "a little extra dividend." Files from that time contain a carbon copy of answers to a questionnaire, probably for a radio interview. The questions went back with the original but a couple of answers to what were mostly routine biographical ones are fun. "Fishing and not going anywhere," perhaps answered a question about spare time. The final answer reads: "I have a great reputation as a conservationist. This is based chiefly on the fact that I have worked and written at various times in favour of such unexceptionable objects as sustained-yield cutting of timber, preservation of watersheds, maintenance of breeding stocks of fish and game. I have rarely been successful in achieving anything except a reputation by these activities."

In late November a very long letter to Ivan von Auw responded to the devastating news that William Morrow did not want *No Want of Wonder*. Consolation came from Ivan's own enthusiasm and Roddy speculated that they may have thought the book was going to be an almanac or book of days. He had discussed a *fishing* almanac with them. But he didn't want to leave Morrow and was planning a juvenile and a fishing book for them for the following year. Other possible publishers for *No Want of Wonder* from whom Roddy had received written general inquiries included "de la Torre Bueno of E.P. Dutton ... Harrison Platt of Bobbs Merrill ... and Alfred Knopf. And I have heard that Joe Lippincott is interested." Roddy went on to discuss finances: "We have nothing else but books and royalties, to be perfectly frank." He still hesitated to take up Ivan's suggestion that he write more magazine articles – he preferred books. In the end he wrote: "The main problem is to find enough enthusiasm to finish *No Want of Wonder* properly, then get on with the next books. If two books in one year won't buy me out [of any debt against royalties with Morrow] I had better go back to [working in] the woods."

To his mother he wrote: "Unfortunately New York doesn't like my book too well – essays, they say, don't sell worth a darn – but they'll get over that in the end. It's not about fishing, but about almost everything else we do, from milking cows to magistrating, from splitting wood to writing books." Alan's mid-November birthday brought a Meccano kit and he was especially delighted "because he and Mary play together a lot with hers and now he can contribute." Christmas would be quiet "because Mrs. Elmore and Mary are going to Arizona to be with Bucky and Gar and I have to keep steadily on with the book."

By early January snow was the dominant factor. "We've had a lot of fun with the snow, though a lot of work too. Getting a Christmas tree was a minor problem, since anything approaching Christmas tree size was practically flattened. Since then we've had a lot more – there's between 4 and 5 feet on the ground now – and we've given up trying to get the car out to the road. Roofs have been the worst worry – the chicken house actually started to collapse. The children, at intervals of shovelling, have been busily bob-sledding on the steep hills. They are delighted because the opening of school has been indefinitely postponed. All except Valerie, who worries about her Latin [which I did by correspondence and the mail would have been held up]." That must have been the year we could eventually slide from the top of the new study roof to the ground as the shovelled snow piled up over several weeks. Alan and his friends tobogganed off the chicken house roof so much that, by the end of January, Roddy said, "the chickens don't even mind any more."

A January letter to Uncle Edward told of Alan "busily hunting blue jays with bow and arrow to give the juncos and towhees and song sparrows a chance at the feeder. I'm afraid he's getting a little discouraged though; he says: 'I'm going to plant the arrows around in the snow so they'll perch on them and spike themselves.' Occasionally he considers dipping the arrows in poison, but he'd still have to hit them ... this damn snow has effectively used all my time since Christmas and really cut my chances of taking time out for steelhead to almost nil. Three trumpeter swans flew quite low over the house one day when I was shovelling snow; there are rewards for virtue."

On February 1, Roddy wrote his mother: "... a little more snow all the time, but we seem to be getting along all right – all the animals still alive and kicking, all the buildings still standing, no pipes burst; fuel supplies going down very fast, of course ... meanwhile we are keeping warm, at least inside the house. In many ways the snow is very pleasant – clean and dry and quiet ... some beautifully sunny days. I went fishing ... got a 14-pounder yesterday, but the line freezes in the rings of the rod and makes things fairly difficult. Finished the book last Friday and hope to get the last of it away before I leave for the magistrate's conference in Vancouver." And that, sadly, is the last letter Roddy wrote his mother. She died of a heart attack a few days later at sixty-nine.

The news of our grandmother's death came by mail. Mary and I had gone downtown with our father, and, as we often did, we had picked up the mail from the rural route box at the gate on the way out, perhaps hoping for royalty checks to put in the bank. The rest of the mail was put aside to read later. On the way back from our errands, we stopped at the frozen food lockers and I went in to get what was wanted. When I came out, my father was sitting behind the steering wheel, blue airmail letter in hand, in tears – I think the only time I ever saw him cry.

·9·
The Early Fifties (1950 – 1953)

The hard winter of 1949-50 – hard with snow, with rejection, and with Roddy's mother dying – turned to spring and snowmelt, and Morrow's acceptance of the new book after all, to be called *Measure of the Year*. But there was a shift in Roddy's work brought on partly by a desire to be less dependent on Morrow. Instead of taking a monthly check from them, which meant he sometimes owed them money and vice versa, Roddy would move toward taking royalties only as they were earned. It also meant that he felt both the need and the freedom to take other work.

In March, Roddy wrote Tom Mahony, now his editor at Morrow: "I have recently sent forward to Ivan von Auw a sample 15 days of the proposed Almanac. It ... seems to come out rather better than expected. A good part of the rest of the book is safely planned. You will notice that in these 15 days the theme of trying to catch tyee salmon on the fly in freshwater carries fairly steadily through ... A sharply different theme for each and every day would be almost impossible – and, I think, duller." The almanac idea soon evolved into essays which became the four fisherman's seasons books over the years. *Fisherman's Spring* was completed by fall.

In July Roddy was writing to his agent, Ivan von Auw, to discuss arrangements for a film to be made with MPO Productions of New York. "I received a letter from Judd Pollock and the MPO check a day or two after writing you. Have answered Pollock's letter and now expect Madison here in mid-August, at which point I hope we can develop a story line. The check means we can carry on without Morrow payments through September. I ... hope to do the Unforgettable outline next week."

The "Unforgettable" was a proposal for *Reader's Digest*, which paid very well. Over the years Roddy wrote three potential stories for their unforgettable character series, but none were accepted because he refused to make the requested changes, stating that they would make the stories too sweet or mushy. The three were about his father, Uncle Reg, and Nellie White. The latter two were eventually published elsewhere and, when I collected my father's articles for publication in book form after he died, the publishers placed the article about his father with – *Reader's Digest*. I could almost see the wry grin of amusement on my father's face.

To Jess Carmack, Morrow's west coast representative, Roddy wrote that fall: "We had hoped so much to see you during the summer, and it has been a wonderful summer. I'm glad you think more of the book's [*Measure of the Year*] chances than New York seems to. They've got a defeatist attitude and they're clutching at the book's nature stuff instead of emphasising its more general qualities. The juvenile I'm supposed to do in the rest of the year is about Mounted Police; I haven't figured it out yet. I have been doing short stuff, including a movie about wildfowl migration. Strangely, the more you do, the easier and better the ideas seem to come."

To Ivan, in late October, Roddy wrote: "Larry Madison is here with me now and we leave on Wednesday for another week's work on the duck film ... I expect to leave for Washington to do the bald eagle research, etc. immediately on getting back here." The film with Larry Madison was called *Out of the North* and the narration included some fine free verse on migrating birds. Both Roddy and Edward Dunn appeared in the film along with the Labrador retrievers of the day.

A month later, a letter to Thayer Hobson began: "It was grand to find your letter waiting when we got home and know that you like the look of *Fisherman's Spring*. I think it is a decent piece of work and quite unlike the mass of fishing stuff now being published ... Ann and I have just spent a very successful three weeks down in Washington State, mainly searching out a location for the bald eagle book. I think I have found something pretty grand – the open Pacific Coast of the Olympic Peninsula ... We were also in Seattle for a short while and found *Measure of the Year* having what seems a far quicker and wider success than any of my previous books ... if it is in any way reflected through the rest of the country we shall have to take *another* look at future writing plans."

But to Ivan von Auw he wrote: "My enthusiasm for Morrow's enthusiasm for *Fisherman's Spring* is somewhat tempered by the fact that it pushes me farther than ever back towards the line they seem to want – fish, nature and juveniles. Some of it is O.K., but it is terribly limited and limiting. I'll have to run in a book with a little more scope sooner or later or I'll be tabbed for the rest of my life." Writing again at the end of December, Roddy discussed the future at length. "I'm glad we are so well agreed about what I should do, or try to do. *Measure of the Year* seems to be selling at least as well as any book I have written, and judging by my mail and the early reviews it is touching a wider and more enthusiastic public." R.L. Neuberger in the *New York Times* said: "Mere mention of the name Roderick L. Haig-Brown makes the pulse of a salmon fisherman beat faster ... Now Mr. Haig-Brown, writing an autobiographical book about himself and his family, shows that he knows something of the human species, too."

"Immediate financial prospects are not too bad. There is the 'advance' from Collins Canada still to come [the book was already published so the advance was long overdue], which should take care of January. And I am writing a bulletin for the Dominion Fisheries people at a price of $500 which will carry on from there ... I am not too well satisfied with the way things are at Collins Canada since Sweeney left. They were disgracefully slow in getting *Measure* on the market and their edition up here is a pretty disgraceful job ... I am getting a very slow start with the juvenile, but still hope to do it fast once I get going. At the first opportunity I shall try to slip in something short for magazine sales. I very much want to do some more for *The New Yorker*."

Early in 1951 Roddy was writing to Tommy Brayshaw about the bulletin for the Dominion government because Brayshaw was to do the illustrations. "The thing will be simply done ... Main emphasis will be on salmon life histories, especially sockeye. I shall go fairly heavily on migrations, spawning and so on, and perhaps especially on diatom-shrimp-herring-salmon-human cycle. Something on the fishing industry ... Something on menaces – predators, fishermen, logging, pollution, dams ... Something briefly on the safeguards ... The probable title will be *Canada's Pacific Salmon* ... The river has been high and I haven't been fishing at all. We had a good Christmas and New Year with Mary and Mrs. Elmore up here. Love to Becky and all good things to you both for 1951."

Later in January Ann wrote in a covering letter to go with the now-complete manuscript for Tommy: "I dragged Roddy to Seattle for a one-night stand last week – a very high-powered dinner party at the Baillargeons – worth the trouble to me, but Roddy's not sure. We got home literally minutes before the snow started. Reg Kinsman is here, Roddy is going out [fishing] with him later. He hasn't caught anything yet."

In February Roddy wrote to Stan Read, a UBC English professor and good fishing friend, replying to his critique of *Measure of the Year*: "You are an admirable person to write such a long and excellent letter. I believe every word of it, of course, and give the full professional weight of your position to every word, what's more." Following a page-long discussion of the details, Roddy said: "Ann and I have every intention of coming down to hear [pianist] Solomon on Feb. 16th and to see you all."

In March Roddy was doing some preliminary work on the script for *Out of the North* and wrote to Larry Madison, replying to a suggestion that he attempt to incorporate some thoughts of God's mysterious ways concerning the migratory instincts of waterfowl: "The February letter did stop me for a moment ... The risks, of course, are enormous. Ever since Joyce Kilmer wrote about God and Trees the very idea of such associations has been scaring serious writers silly. On the other hand, to a writer nothing is impossible; so my second thought was to hang on and let it come (this after making a few deliberate attempts and scaring my own self silly each time). What I got in the end is herewith ... I think the point comes clearly through in sum, and the mood is good, or will be with the pictures putting it there. Enjoyed the clips, though I'm afraid one of them looks more like a commando raid than a duck hunt. That guy would wear that hat.

"Spent last week in bed with the damned herniated disc, which has effectively gummed up a lot of work ... We shall be doing more on the migration around April 25. I'm glad you are giving the duck film everything. Don't be afraid to say what you think of this God-stuff. It isn't the only way it can be done."

In April Roddy was writing to Stuart Keate, editor of *The Victoria Times*, who was doing a profile of him for *Maclean's* magazine. "For a short while, especially when doing the research for *The Western Angler*, I became too deeply involved in fishing and fish. I did not like it. Ever since, I have tried to keep the thing in its place, as the supreme sport, but definitely a sport, an interlude to, if at times an expansion of, other living.

"I should like, or think I should like, to escape from all the bruising contentions of conservation fights, magistrate's work, controversial issues of all kinds. I never shall, of course, and it probably wouldn't be good for me if I could ... I should like to draw away into reading and thinking and writing.

"You ask about experiences on the bench, with myself as a hero or a Solomon. I don't think there are any, and I doubt if there should be any.

A judge or a magistrate has to sit and listen and try to understand. If he takes time out to be witty or quotably wise, dramatically benevolent or spectacularly tough, he probably won't have time to understand – too busy admiring himself. Mostly on the bench I just sit and sweat blood trying to keep up.

"I hate to be such lousy copy after all the trouble you have taken. But at least I've got a spectacular wife. Put a little more of her into that middle part. Hope you have a good trip east ... tell the CBC they ought to pay writers a hell of a lot more; we got to eat too."

In April of 1951, Ann wrote to Grace Richardson, who had lived next door in Uncle Reg's house for so long. When her husband died, she had moved to California to be near relatives. Old friends Dr. Bathurst Hall and his wife, Dorothy, had bought the house and Ann described extensive renovation plans for the house both she and Grace had lived in. About the family, Ann said: "We are all very well, though Alan has a greenstick fracture of his right arm, just about healed up. We got a new garden tractor yesterday and expect to do great things with it, though at present we're all a little scared of it. It also has a snowplow." The tractor was a small one that you walked behind and did service in the garden for many years.

In June Roddy wrote to Letcher Lambuth in Seattle, a fishing friend and maker of fine rods, who had invited him on a trip. "I am terribly sorry to have been so slow in answering your fine invitation. My uncertainty is entirely over the hearings on Buttle Lake and Strathcona Park. Our side is pressing for a date in August. The dam builders want 'the second or third week in July.' I have to be present to argue at the hearings and I also have to be available for consultation with the various organizations concerned in the time immediately before ... This fight has been dragging on for nearly a year now, and I can't possibly leave it at the last moment."

Stu Keate's *Maclean's* article had appeared in June. Roddy wrote him: "I've just seen the article and think it is fine. Ann also approves. I think the cuts, being the more personal parts, are really better out; but that's from the point of view of the patient. My one real criticism is your libel of our good B.C. brant geese; they being honest, hardy northerners, come through the winter fat and sassy, while the soft playboys that flutter off to California come back thin and played out. What a moral is there.

"The Battle of Buttle Lake goes on with great vigor. We have recently won the support of the Auto Courts and Resorts Association of Vancouver Island, and expect to get the Ratepayers of the Island ... I spoke to the ACCVI convention here last night, with what effect I don't know. Down in the States the Wilderness Society is taking quite an interest in it all ... The important thing will be to have the press well represented and ensure that expert testimony is given publicly there by Parks Division men who know the score. It is fairly evident that the government is hoping for a small and quiet hearing."

Buttle Lake was in the heart of B.C.'s Strathcona Park and to dam the headwaters of the Campbell River and destroy a provincial park was a terrible thing. But until a few voices on Vancouver Island were raised, the B.C. Power Commission was going to go right ahead. Buttle is a long narrow lake with steep sides and raising it even a little would drown all the creek mouths and little beaches, to say nothing of creating a need to log the lovely virgin timber along the lakeshore. But the few voices became many and the long battle was joined and fought out over the next several years.

The following month a letter went to Craig Ballantyne of *The Montreal Standard* who was sending a writer-photographer team to "do" the family of *Measure of the Year* for *Weekend Magazine*. "I shall be home in the latter part of August and will do my best to cooperate with Messrs. Willcock and Jacques, even to drinking some of their whiskey. I can't answer for my family; some of them allege I have exploited them too much already and they will stand for no more publicity. Unfortunately they are below whiskey-drinking age, otherwise I would feel sure we could overpersuade them." The team did come and we did stand, protesting, to have many photographs taken. Mother rushed about with a hairbrush and clean clothes and kept us all looking far tidier than usual.

In August Roddy wrote Ivan (in the midst of the *Weekend* photography) that he had "done half a dozen broadcasts for the CBC and they now want me to do two further series, as well as a Wednesday night show which I am working on this week. There have already been suggestions about publication of these, though I don't know just how they would work out. I am selling only first Canadian broadcast rights. [He did gather the scripts in book manuscript form, but they were never published.] I expect Madison here shortly to finish off the duck film and will let you know when that is done ... I don't like all this interference with my regular work but it seems to come my way and does help to keep things going."

Fisherman's Spring was published to the usual positive reviews that went with all the fishing books. It consisted of relatively short essays on fishing and fishing-related topics – probably short because the book evolved from the almanac idea that was to have consisted of single days. Haydn Pearson in the *New York Times* wrote: "By the time he has turned a dozen pages in this very pleasant and informative book, the reader appreciates that Roderick Haig-Brown is much more than an expert fisherman. This is a book for everyone who delights in the out-of-doors ... a little gem among fishing books."

Mary Weiler, an artist friend who lived on Cortes Island and came to stay whenever she was going to have a baby to be near the hospital, had just visited. She painted a beautiful original paper doll for Celie and Ann wrote thanking her and suggesting a commission. "The fact that you've put your talent into as charming a toy as the paper dolls, makes me ask if you'd accept a serious commission to do a mural on plywood to go back of the farm on the mantel." Mary did accept and the mural took its place above the English lead farm animals, originally sent by our grandmother, but added to in Christmas stockings when they became available in Canada. The mural eventually migrated to the upstairs stairway and the farm to the bookshelves in the upstairs hall, lovingly arranged and re-arranged over the years by both children and grandchildren. The letter concludes: "This is a nice, grey quiet day in the midst of the August madness, but it looks like going mad again any minute."

The fall was taken up with more film work. Roddy and Larry Madison spent most of September cutting the ten thousand feet of film already shot. After more filming, the finished result was to be ready for Roddy to write the narration early in the new year. A National Film Board crew was also completing filming for *Country Magistrate*, a short film designed to show potential immigrants about justice in Canada. Local people played the fictional parts and we played ourselves. A premiere, complete with searchlight, was held in Campbell River. We found the repetitiveness of filming a bore after a while, but the fancy gathering, with our father in black tie and the RCMP in red coats, to show off the finished product was exciting. The only sad note was Celie in tears when she found that her big part had ended up on the cutting room floor. I remember that the regular feature film that followed our big moment was *The Man in the White Suit* with Alec Guinness. There must have been food and drink, but I have no recollection of any of that.

In October Roddy asked Ivan if he had "anything more definite on the Pan-American Airways preparation. It will be quite difficult to fit that into the rest of my work, to say nothing of my domestic arrangements." The purpose of the trip was to write a booklet on Chilean and Argentinean trout fishing for the airline, which was opening new routes to those countries. The trip produced the booklet, several articles and *Fisherman's Winter* (somewhat to the annoyance of fans who would have liked a book on northern winter fishing). My father also developed a great fondness for the Chilean countryside, its people and its wine.

For reasons we never could understand, Pan-American Airways sent our father off to Chile a couple of days before Christmas, where he stayed until early March. Ann and the children drove Roddy to Nanaimo to catch the ferry for Vancouver, and, when they returned, Ann reported: "... everything was fine and the black striped T-shirt heartbreakingly on the bed where you had left it. It took Alan only about an hour to say surprisedly: 'I miss Daddy already.' Thor [my high-school steady] said: 'It seems very empty here,' when he came to take Valerie to a movie."

Ann's first few letters to Roddy list Christmas cards received and tell of the progress of a plan to keep up with the mail as it came in. Ann would answer the backlog of non-urgent mail that had piled up in the last few months before Roddy got back, and then there would be a hope of keeping up with things on a daily basis in the future. There wasn't much gardening, but the animals still demanded care. In the week before Christmas Ann had to drive to Courtenay to pick up the feed order from Buckerfield's because it missed the freight truck. "... it was a southeaster to end all such. The waves were just like the [open] ocean. Dear little car didn't mind at all though. I hit no holes in the road. I'm getting to know them. During the evening Mrs. Simmons [who lived just up the river by the Sandy Pool] called so shaken because their huge cedar had crashed into the river narrowly missing the house. It is stranded this morning in the middle of the river, head down in front of our swimming place. Do you think it will stay there forever?" (It didn't – it floated on down just before Roddy returned, to our great disappointment because we had so much wanted him to see it.)

The oil stove wasn't working properly, making the rush to "force food out of it in time for movie and Guides" exhausting. Ann was relieved that Thor was off to Vancouver for Christmas. "Valerie acts so soupy, though she's a fabulous furnace man in this gruesome weather with the other children yelling at her because it's not warm enough, though it seem's so to me." The furnace was still run on wood and coal and I got quite skilled at keeping it going. In a letter I reported to my father: "The furnace is fine except when I sleep too long and let it go out. I discovered a wonderful way of starting. Just use heaps of paper and no kindling."

We had expected to have a very dull holiday season without our father, who always enjoyed Christmas, especially the ceremonious dinner, but at the last moment, Ann's mother and sister Mary did come up from Seattle. Ann made the long and difficult drive to Victoria to pick them up from the ferry in heavy snow with inadequate chains because the local garage had misplaced ours. On Christmas Day after dinner the family joined the Painters for their after-dinner tree. (Ours was always in the morning.) One of the weekly talks that Roddy had done for the CBC happened to fall on Christmas Day. "Mother and Mary C. and I listened in the car because the Painter's radio wasn't very good and poor little Mary wept and wept. It didn't seem like actual you to me, but all the others loved it. Mary Elmore didn't even go with us for fear of missing it, and she adored it." The same post-Christmas letter concluded: "But the big thing today was the mail," and described Ann's reaction to Roddy's first letters and then went on: "Now here's the wonderful thing. You have a letter from Norman MacKenzie saying that the Senate at the University 'would like to confer an honorary degree upon you, if that meets your approval, at the next Congregation of the University, on the fifteenth or sixteenth of May ... I would particularly like you to give a short address of not more than twenty minutes ... after the fashion of one of the charming chapters of *Measure of the Year* would be admirable, because I have rarely read a better philosophy more simply or more soundly expressed.' It was on the radio and several were talking about it, but the letter just came. Also the [Vancouver] *Province* picked up your remark about the wilderness's fate being in the hands of old men who have lost their sense of wonder, if indeed etc. and put it approvingly at the end of Dec. 23's editorials. So much for your hope that it wouldn't be noticed. And Lady Baden-Powell sent most beautiful things ..." This last was because she sent a few mementoes of their godfather to each of her husband's twenty-odd godchildren after he died. Roddy's treasures included a gold watch chain (which became a charm bracelet that went twice around our mother's wrist), a pen holder and some salmon flies.

At the end of December a letter from "the bank in England" announced that they had "disposed of your holdings" (perhaps part of his mother's estate) and were sending some $3500. Roddy replied that that sum would take care of the Veteran's loan for remodelling the house and the car loan as well. Other business concerned turning over his part of the arrangements for the annual British Columbia Natural Resources Conference which it was now clear Roddy would miss. Ann concluded the letter, "You can come home any time now. Every advantage of having you here is surpassingly clear to me. I love you."

New Year's week was bitterly cold. The family heard the next CBC talk "sitting in the kitchen on New Year's night and loved it." Ann drove her mother to Victoria and put her on the Seattle boat, worrying because she was getting very absent-minded. Her sister Mary had already gone back. The hearings concerning damming Buttle Lake continued to wind their way through the courts in a manner that is now all too familiar to conservationists. On January 18 there would be an appeal concerning the jurisdiction of the commissioner who had heard the original arguments. Local rumor had it that there would be no expansion of the pulp mill unless Buttle Lake was dammed, and an alternative suggestion of a dam at Upper Campbell outside Strathcona Park was considered too expensive. Ann was reading D.H. Lawrence short stories, still catching up on the mail and typing "the RCMP juvenile."

In mid-January the lights went out as Ann typed her letter, but, being an accomplished touch typist, she finished anyway. But the next morning she wrote: "As the children were just leaving for the bus, a phone call from the school said no school. The blank out last night was something connected with their heating plant. You could hear the roar almost going in waves up the road as the news was shouted out to the children already waiting for the bus. Alan melted away, called at noon from Simmy's [his friend Alan Simmons lived just up the river], and came home at 5.00. He had been on a hike, collected fir cones and had a thoroughly happy day." A later letter tells of mail, visitors, driving children to drama club, Guides, Boy's Club [gymnastics], basketball, etc., and a woman who called regularly on Sunday to say she didn't want to appear in court on Monday. Another magistrate from nearby would have been covering for Roddy, but the woman should have been calling the police station anyway. Celie, now five, suggested "that we should get a shade for the front door to pull down and one side could say Haig-Brown Out and the other Celie taking nap. Quiet please."

On January 20, 1952, Ann wrote: "Yes, it is January 20 – the eighteenth January 20th – and it doesn't seem like yesterday. It seems to me that we have filled eighteen years and grown in them and made, if not the most, an awful lot of them. Those beloved children – this dear house." The rest of the page is filled with details of correspondence. Ann had promised herself that, once she had caught up with the mail, she could paint and a week later she wrote: "I'm sitting smugly in the most beautiful kitchen you ever saw ... It's the most *satisfying* clean-up and paint-up I've ever done, because it all went to carry out already made plans, nothing had to be changed, just brought up to scratch." The weather continued alternating among various kinds of awful, but Ann and the children went one night to see *Show Boat*. "That Ava Gardner," she wrote. "You should see her. And my favorite Fish-gotta-swim song." The cow didn't calve which meant continuing to buy milk and upsetting the household budget, the study roof leaked, Thor came too often. But, "last night Mary said, 'I often hear Valerie telling her friends something using great big intellectual words and it sounds sort of familiar and I realize she's telling one of your exact stories.' Valerie said, 'Of course, I love the way you tell things.' I was flattered beyond words." Roddy's Aunt Rosie sent the fourth volume of Churchill's history, and a woman wrote that Colin's sister or teacher should have guided him into the forestry service in *On the Highest Hill*, and thus saved him from his tragic end.

In early February Ann wrote Edward Dunn: "Roddy is having a completely marvellous time, and is thrilled with Chile. Of course, wherever there are brown trout there are Englishmen young and old who went to Charterhouse, to Lancing or saw Alan Haig-Brown play for the Corinthians; but there are also, to Roddy's surprise, Americans who swear by *The Western Angler*, etc."

Ann's painting and decorating moved to the front hall, where she worked on devising the best way to mount bird prints from a Wilson portfolio on the walls. "The color I have for walls is teal green and heavenly. My plan to get a cotton rug is postponed until March because I'm too afraid of running out of money what with the washing machine breaking, the dentist, etc." And at the end: "The children are all so nice and considerate and polite to me that I can hardly believe it and am constantly touched beyond words. I sometimes slightly think I have a favorite child, that is, until I'm alone with one of the others."

On February 10, after the death of King George the Sixth, Ann wrote: "All of this week, and I suppose, next week, too is the King. Did it seem bad to you to be away? ... Canada's proclamation of the 'high and mighty princess, Elizabeth Alexandra Mary' was the first in the Commonwealth and we heard it as it was read ... There are still no commercial programs, and people seem to talk of nothing else. Alan said after the proclamation trumpets: 'If I could just blow one of those notes, I'd be perfectly happy.' And Celie said, after two days of listening to the radio and understanding perfectly: 'I hope God *does* save the Queen.'"

The dog, Lin, was in heat. "Alan carefully shut her in the basement —but with Val [the other —male —dog]. So then we let her out. Val barks at all the dogs that come and they bark back and paw the ground. In the excitement, the *rabbit* killed a chicken. Val got so excited that he tried to mount the chicken twice. We made him stop, the chicken was still walking around but groggy; then the rabbit started jumping it over and over again. I put it in a box but it got out and finally died from exhaustion."

The Catholic Women's League met at the house. Alan and his friends killed a coon to both his and Ann's horror. Ann said she "still didn't know what I should have said. You will have to adopt an attitude for us." Roddy was asked to speak at the annual dinner of the Neurological Surgeons of North America in Victoria in June. "Honorarium and expenses." Ann was reading Galsworthy's *Modern Comedy.* "Our old opinion that the second volume wasn't up to *The Forsyte Saga* is much revised in my mind." And she was painting the living room yellow.

In her last letter Ann arranged to meet Roddy in Seattle when he returned in mid-March. She also reported that a friend told her to get the latest *Harper's Bazaar* because it had pictures of Chilean people. She "felt gypped because there was only a picture of a woman and her daughter. But the next day came a letter from you about Augustin Edwards and the two people [in the picture] were his wife and the daughter that was with her father when you stayed." Augustin Edwards was the publisher of *El Mercurio*, the major Chilean newspaper of the day, and head of Chile's largest bank. He had been captain of the Chilean ski team and was a great fisherman. When he heard that Roddy was in the country, he tracked him down and insisted he stay at his lodge near Petrohue.

We were, of course, more than a little pleased to have our father home and the rhythm of our lives re-established. We were used to him being available most of the time. If you rushed in from school to tell of a triumph or complain of a teacher's injustice, it was very often Daddy who would be there to listen. Our father usually seemed interested in our concerns (although he often took the teacher's side) and we interrupted his writing fairly freely. He even interrupted himself at times. A water fight with the garden hoses could bring him out to aid the losers by providing an extra hose or just to laugh at the mayhem.

In mid-May the University of British Columbia conferred an honorary Doctor of Laws degree on Roddy. We all went to Vancouver to see our father, in elegant red robes lined with deep blue velvet, receive his hood and give the Convocation address, entitled "Power and People." Then we continued on to Seattle to visit our grandmother for a few days – one of a very few trips we ever made as a family. Not long after we got back to Campbell River, Lady Olave Baden-Powell arrived to stay for a week while she took a break from a North American tour as World Chief Guide. Mary and I were both Girl Guides and we were thus doubly impressed to have her with us. She was, I suppose not very surprisingly, a bit like our English grandmother. A young woman secretary was with her and we went for walks with one or both of them, just as we had with Grandmother.

That summer I won the B.C. Junior Track and Field championship, due in no small part, I am sure, to the constant support and encouragement of my father. He came to the major meets whenever he could – I remember especially a Caledonian Games in Stanley Park in Vancouver where the bagpipes and drums and Highland dancers added immeasurably to the excitement of the day.

In January of 1953, our parents went east together, leaving us with Helen Butters, our mother's friend who had stayed for a while during the war. Roddy had speaking engagements with flyfishers in Boston and New York, and the trip also gave him a chance to meet with publishers in Toronto and New York, as well as with the people at Ober. We were all quite furious with them for deserting us; I documented this endlessly in letters I wrote almost daily to Thor, who was now going to school in Vancouver. By the end of January the tone of the letters picked up with a call from our parents saying they were in Twin Falls, Idaho, and would be home the following Tuesday. "I talked to Daddy and of course burst into tears. He said be good till Tuesday and then be as bad as you like." They were delivering a new car for a Vancouver dealer. I remember them saying they picked motels by choosing ones with TV aerials – they proved to be the newest and therefore most comfortable. We missed our parents most at the family dinner table. "Writing to you and reading your letters are the only real pleasures I have in life. When Daddy and Mummy come back I hope supper gets to be another one. There is no reason it won't except when someone has to tear off to somewhere." The hour over family supper at the kitchen table was always lively. We all brought whatever we were reading to the table, but rarely read much. Conversation could be about the events of that day, but it was just as likely to be about politics or philosophy (with sometimes hot and heavy discussion between our parents), or shared laughter over a *New Yorker* cartoon or our father's teasing. He was very good at teasing. We all learned from him the art of repartee that played on one another's mistakes or failings, although we didn't always exercise the restraint that kept it from going far enough to hurt as well as our father did.

On February 2, I wrote Thor: "Daddy and Mummy came home. Oh, joy! Everyone talks at once and it will take years to catch up on things." And the following day: "I got home and we talked a while and then Daddy asked me if I got the letters from that boy [Thor, of course], terrible handwriting, etc. I yelped and dove for them ... was I run around about all the things I've done in the last month. I really got it for having you here [before he went to Vancouver]. At supper we aired our grievances to a not too sympathetic committee, but it was fun." Lots of laughter at the end of a Sunday of church and various visitors when "a cute little brown mouse ran across the kitchen floor when Mother and Mary and I were sitting there. We all had fits and Daddy was awfully funny about it. Then Mary and I started rioting and fooling around and had a gay old time. Daddy tried to be stern, but he laughed so hard he could hardly stand up." He rarely did succeed in scolding very hard – it was too easy to make him laugh with us! The letters describe Roddy as "having four men here about the Natural Resources Conference at the end of February. He is going to Seattle to speak at the end of April."

Another of my letters to Thor makes passing mention of Roddy going to Vancouver to make two speeches that week and to Victoria the following week. Whenever he was away Ann took advantage of his absence to do jobs that created confusion, like redecorating. Keeping the house reasonably in order and having a decent dinner were part of what Ann did to provide a supportive atmosphere for Roddy's work. This time she was "painting white enamel on the frig and all the other things that are white in the kitchen including our lunch kits. We have a new cat... Two very nice Dutch men came collecting for flood relief tonight. They stayed and talked for a while. Mary is teasing Alan. Celie is fine and her eyes do still twinkle."

.10. Unfolding Horizons (1953 – 1956)

Over the next few years life in the house by the river changed, as it inevitably does in any family as the children start to make their way out into the world. In the fall of 1953, I went to Vancouver to study at the University of British Columbia, and the flow of letters full of family life was now from my mother and father to me. Mother's were often stained from being included in a package with a cake or, more often, a loaf of good brown bread. Celie was off to the first grade in the new school just down the road from us, Alan was struggling toward high school and Mary was in grade ten that fall. The letters are many and the details of home – family and visitors, writing and court, garden and very occasional fishing – were a delight to an often-homesick daughter, especially in the first year. There are gaps when news was exchanged either during my holidays in Campbell River or on Roddy's frequent trips to Vancouver – fortunately, or this story would stretch to several volumes. Even without *all* the details, it is obvious that the demands on Roddy's time were expanding enormously.

A mid-September letter of my first year away told of Edward Dunn and Glen Trimble having been for the annual grouse hunt and "the usual run of visitors ... I have had to go to court more than usual ... And I now have speaking engagements in Vancouver on Oct. 3 and 7 ... presenting the Crandall Conservation Award and the P.E.O. Convention of some 2000 women." The next letter took a page to list the visitors over just a week people from Chile, Toronto, Philadelphia, Montreal (a CBC International Service producer concerning a translation of a chapter from *Measure of the Year* for the Austrian section), Calgary, Victoria and California, to say nothing of local people. "Tomorrow I have to talk to the Ratepayers about the Stipendiary Magistrate and his job in the community. [Stipendiary Magistrate – meaning he got paid something – was Roddy's official title.] Last night Mother went to a Recreation Association meeting. New York sold a Chilean trout story to *Field and Stream* for me for $500, which is nice and is why your monthly allowance check arrives so promptly. Yesterday Mother did a heavy pruning job in the driveway ... She has canned loads of pears and is getting a terrific total stock – freezer full, every jar full, eventually she thinks every jam jar full. The dogs are tied out under the trees to keep the coons away."

In mid-October Roddy gave an address titled "Divine Discontent" to the Annual Assembly of Victoria College in which he urged the students to be "discontent with things as they are, discontent with yourselves. But let it be a constructive and informed discontent ..." This address was later printed in pamphlet form.

At the end of October there was a report of "a wonderful dinner party in Victoria with the Stu Keates. Quite literary. Dr. Trueman of the National Film Board, Bruce and Mrs. Hutchinson, Art Mayse and his wife and a Mr. and Mrs. Lee of the *Times* [Keate was editor]." The same letter continued: "We were both a little horrified at your report of drinking something or other. I wouldn't for the world tell you not to, but I think you are a little young for spirits in any form – which includes all whisky, gin and brandy, and so most cocktails. Preferably limit yourself to wine and maybe an occasional beer if you happen to like the stuff. And one cocktail before dinner if it seems indicated; but not two, and not highballs and don't drink after dinner, and never drink the damn stuff straight out of a bottle. All this in the nature of advice, of course, not prohibitions. But it's a ruinous habit and an insidious one, and there's too much of the damn stuff around. Do a maximum of observing and a minimum of participating." Sound advice, which I generally followed.

Mid-November reported the river in flood "though less than in 1939 or 1935. It has dug a big hole in the cribbing near the well and caved in the bottom of the border." Our grandmother had come to spend most of the winter. There is a long series of exchanges between my father and mother and me about the three of us going to the Christmas debutante ball in Seattle at the invitation of Aunt Glen (Kerry Trimble) – which we did and a very glamorous event it was. It probably still ranks among the top half-dozen elegant occasions in my life, though I was aware even then that it was outside the real course of our lives.

At the end of November Roddy had been "correcting proofs of *Mounted Police Patrol* [a juvenile novel about a tough orphan boy from Toronto sent to live with an uncle in Alberta who is an RCMP constable] ... and am now getting going on the new book [about fishing and people in Chile], though I spent most of today, which was fine, cleaning out gutters and fixing odd weak spots in the roof." A new electric hot water heater was going into the basement to replace the system involving coils running through the burner of the oil stove in the kitchen. "The next step, sometime next year, I hope, will be to put in an oil furnace and perhaps follow that with an electric stove." He had taken Alan along when he went to speak at a Medical Society banquet in Victoria – Alan went to a movie.

In early February of 1954, mixed with the domestic news in a letter to me, was the report that "Mother said, for the first time since I have known her: 'I'm bored.' And I guess I just don't know what to say, but I'm not bored." In the same letter, "I got the first sixteen chapters of *Fisherman's Winter* off to New York late last week and then did the short piece for the Standard Oil people ... As soon as [the book] is done I hope to burst away on short stuff and make some money, though I'm rather scared already about these two Ottawa speeches in April. One is 'A National Policy for Wildlife and Recreation,' the other is 'Wildlife and Recreation Objectives.' The affair is a sort of Resources Conference for the whole of Canada." And, as almost always, the letter concludes with the farm and garden news. "The chickens are laying 6 or 7 eggs a day, the sheep are still bunked under the balsam tree [to protect them from dogs] and, I think, a little bored too; and the birds are still coming to the feeding table. Nothing as spectacular as the evening grosbeak you saw, but today I saw a tree creeper in the acacia. Very much love, old thing. Have a good time and work pretty hard ..."

A week later Roddy wrote me, "Your suggestion and invitation for my birthday is stupendous, and I will certainly take you up on it, at least as far as the tickets to Marian Anderson are concerned." I knew my father, who liked music but wasn't ever as dedicated a listener and concert goer as my mother, did care particularly for the voices of Marian Anderson and Kathleen Ferrier. I enjoyed that concert in an old hockey arena – the best Vancouver could provide at the time – as much for his company as the music. I rarely hear Marian Anderson without remembering that evening.

By March *Fisherman's Winter* was finished, Roddy had been to the B.C. Natural Resources Conference and dealt with the lambing at considerable cost – his back was troubling him again. Grandmother went back to Aunt Mary in Seattle until preparations were finished for her to live in a small house near Uncle Bucky, now in California. She could no longer be much on her own, and Aunt Mary could not care for her and manage her landscaping business at the same time. "We are fighting Buttle Lake hard again. I got after the Minister of Lands at the Resources Conference ... wrote the Premier the same thing ... then the Affiliated Fish and Game Clubs put through a resolution ... Most of this is based on the B.C. Electric cable [from the mainland to Vancouver Island, which it was hoped would make more power generation in the Campbell watershed unnecessary]."

Alan had a route for the local paper and was very busy with Boy Scouts, Mary was seeing lots of movies, Celie had finally begun to recover from tracheal laryngitis and Roddy was to be on a panel at the school on their promotional policies. Ann was tutoring friends' children in English, math or French as she had done for many years. Roddy complained about Mary's choice of courses: "Mother and I are all for more Latin and less Home Ec ... We are also for continued Latin for you next year and wait to hear again, with gestures, what stands in the way of that. Whatever it is is not enough." (Oh, yes, it was.)

On the serious side: "Thayer Hobson seems very happy with *Fisherman's Winter* and I believe it will come out safely this fall. I am now working on a thing for CBC Wednesday night on Izaak Walton ... We are still struggling about Buttle Lake – but I am not too optimistic ... The most interesting visitor we have had since you were here is John Gray, head of MacMillan's Canada, who stayed weekend before last. He wants me to do a short child's story on Captain Vancouver.

"Mother has just come back from a trip to Courtenay with the Catholics ... Celie has a popcorn mania, which reduces her to tears of frustration over a smoke-blackened face every night, but we've just managed to complete a batch after sending the previous batch up in flames [over the study fire]. Alan ... is reading. Mary is reading ... Mother is also reading. Lin is standing by the door, wants to go out. I'd better stop."

The response to an exam time letter was: "We are desolated that you are having to work so hard and forbear to point out that that is what you went down there for." I survived the ordeal and came home for the summer, to work at a local lodge, with Mother who had been to Seattle to collect some family things from her mother's house.

In September, a letter pauses after Roddy stated: "I'm going up to the Islands [Pool in the Campbell] this afternoon." And resumes: "Later. Went up and caught a 10 lb. coho on the dry fly – the first mature Pacific salmon I have ever taken or heard of anyone taking on a floating fly."

Later that fall Roddy wrote: "Mother is out at a P.T.A. meeting ... All the organizations have started up with a bang – on Saturday she had a Catholic Women's League cake sale, a Scout executive meeting and a Campbell River Recreational Association meeting." Mary was to play basketball on the Recreational Association team and also instruct for them. Mother was away the day Celie had her class picture taken, "so there she is for posterity, looking like a tramp with hair ragged and T-shirt on backwards. She still looks cute."

At the end of October Ann and Roddy went to Nanaimo where he spoke to the Chamber of Commerce. "Don't believe a word of what the *Province* newspaper says I said ... I didn't say anything like that. Mother is busily making Celie a tweed coat out of an old coat of hers ... Alan carried the cross at some recent processional ceremony at the church and made quite a hit with the priests involved. They told him he'd make a likely priest and he said not at all, he intended to be a cougar hunter. They didn't know what that was so he explained at length.

"I got a good review of *Fisherman's Winter* from the *N.Y. Times* this morning, and a request from Longmans, Green to do a child's book on Simon Fraser. Do you know anything about the guy? I can't see a book on him selling well outside Canada ... I'm still enjoying Capt. Vancouver, but have a lot of reading to do yet." Haydn Pearson wrote in the *Times*: "I recommend *Fisherman's Winter* without reservation to fishermen and to all readers who are interested in our neighbor countries to the south ... He discusses the people, living conditions and the countryside. He evaluates social, cultural and economic conditions honestly and kindly." *Mounted Police Patrol* also came out in 1954, to mixed reviews.

A month later, after a trip to Victoria for a Book Week appearance, Roddy was "making the living room table [a new one designed to fit the bay of the window there], planning the study bookshelves [the collection grew as ever] ... I should really be writing away at Vancouver." He also "planted 100 tulip bulbs under the lilacs and a dozen regal lilies in the border" and harrowed most of the vegetable garden.

A letter to Edward Dunn in early January of 1955 thanked him for a Christmas present of *Birds of Prey* "a fine book" and went on to describe watching two Cooper's hawks chase blue jays with the book open on his desk. The weather had been particularly bad and Roddy inquired after Edward's prize rhododendrons, gave news of the children and, in conclusion, wrote: "Father has his land for the church across the road, and I expect to see the first steps towards building any time." Roddy and Ann had given the corner of the barn field so the first Catholic church building in Campbell River could be erected. Until then Catholic services had been held in the chapel of Lourdes Hospital on St. Anne's Road. The nuns were leaving the hospital and new arrangements were necessary.

The Captain Vancouver book was finished by the end of January 1955, and Ann was typing it a second time because the publisher wanted a copy for the illustrator – neither Roddy nor she thought it needed illustrations. The work was interrupted by a quick trip to Seattle to speak to the Press Club there. Fishing was lousy. "– no fish. I even took the canoe up to the Line Fence Pool yesterday, but still couldn't get one."

At the end of February Roddy wrote: "I found my resources paper [for the annual B.C. Natural Resources Conference] a struggle to write – the old, old story and I'm sick to death of talking it to so little real effect." He spent his birthday in court and "came home to find that Mother had arranged a wonderful birthday party with the Simmons and the Nichiporuks [neighbors up the river] –Dimitri's birthday is the day after mine and we are the same age." The sheep were still being lost to marauding dogs, in spite of being penned at night: " –just the ram, one ewe and two lambs left now. We lost three more the first night I was in Vancouver."

By April the Vancouver book was back for a rewrite, slowed, as ever, by a steady stream of visitors, both business, especially court, and social. Other projects never came to fruition, although in at least one case Roddy still got paid for work done. These included the text to go with pictures of wildfowl migration for *Collier's* magazine, and a script for a salmon film for the National Film Board.

That summer Roddy took Alan on a trip to his old haunts on the Nimpkish River. They went with Ed Lansdowne and his boys. Both men relived some of the wild days of long ago for the benefit of their sons. It was Roddy's first trip back since he left twenty-two years earlier.

In August, Roddy wrote a long plea for the preservation of Strathcona Park in a five-part series for *The Victoria Daily Colonist.* It had been decided not to build the dam at Buttle Lake, partly because, as the defenders of Strathcona had argued, the soil beneath the proposed site was too porous. But tenders had been let to build a dam on Upper Campbell, the lake below Buttle, in two stages. The second stage would be high enough to flood Buttle as well so that the heart of Strathcona Park would still be ruined. The level of Buttle was to be raised only ten or fifteen feet, but for such a steep-sided lake it would be enough to drown all the creek mouths and narrow beaches and most of the spawning water, to say nothing of creating a need to log the virgin timber along the shore so coveted by friends of the government of the day.

In the fall of 1955, Gretchen Harlow came to live with us for a year. Her father, Robert, was the producer for the radio talk series Roddy continued to do for CBC. When Roddy arrived one day to record, he found his producer most upset because his wife had left and he had no idea how he would care for his young daughter. The solution that evolved was for her to come and live in Campbell River. So the first September letter told of "the old routines gradually taking shape ... Mary seems happy in Grade XII, with some reservations of course. Alan, rather to his surprise, is quite happy with Mr. Jantzen in Grade VIII. Celie is easily making a stick of it in Grade IV, having caught up in arithmetic [she had skipped a grade]. And Gretchen is doing comfortably in Grade I with Mrs. Taylor. Cousin Celia arrived on Monday. She leaves tomorrow and Dr. Higgins, our cousin from Victoria, arrives Saturday evening for a short weekend. On Monday Ada Hartman comes briefly. And later in the week Bob Harlow...

"Apparently the judges picked me for the Crandall Conservation Trophy and the Canadian Tourist Association offered to send me a TransCanada Airlines pass to Montreal ... to receive it. But I felt I had to say no, because the Buttle Lake situation is so tight. It would be silly to be off getting a conservation award if we were losing the battle here. It is fast getting to a stage beyond me anyway; all this injunction stuff is highly involved ..." In the end Roddy did make a quick trip to spend a day at Ste. Adele, Quebec, to receive the award "after a hard day of long distance telephoning, mainly about Buttle Lake." There were frequent speaking engagements concerning the dam question. "The fight goes on at full pressure and gets more difficult all the time. There is masses of mail and someone is always asking me to speak. I am tired of it all, but can't possibly stop because I am far more certain than ever that we are right. Shall be talking to the Victoria Chamber of Commerce and the CCF convention in Nanaimo." (The dam finally went ahead, but on an ironic note, Bill Reid, the California oilman who had helped so much with the long battle, died soon after, and heavy winter snow collapsed the main cabin of his little camp on the lake before it could be flooded.) Added to the schedule was a one-day trip to Vancouver to shop for a rug for the study and home the next day via Victoria to have lunch with Lady Baden-Powell, touring Canada again as world head of the Guides.

The rewrite of *Captain of the Discovery* was finished and Roddy was working on short pieces for *Maclean's*, *Saturday Night* and "a fishing article to catch the start of the trout season." It appeared the following spring in *Outdoor Life*. A revised Criminal Code came into effect in 1955 and added to the responsibilities of magistrates, but not their earnings.

Christmas came and went, and in early January of 1956, Alan sprained his wrist "learning to jive with some other male character and the jiving turned into a wrestling match during the course of which the character sat on the hand and did the damage. Today Mr. Jantzen, plugging the cause of education before the class, said to him: 'I'm sure your father understands the value of a good education, Alan. I expect he went to a Canadian university after he came to this country.' 'Oh no, sir,' said Alan. 'He was kicked out of school when he was 17.' Oh dear." The same letter continued with a gruelling schedule for a four-day trip to Vancouver – banquet speeches to a medical gathering and a writers' conference, talks to two UBC student groups, at least two high schools and attending the writers' conference in between. "... a pretty full schedule and a confusing one so far as I'm concerned. I'll probably end up by giving the wrong speeches to the wrong people."

There was a B.C. centennial coming up in 1958 and Roddy was involved in the planning of an anthology for the occasion as well as writing a piece for the collection called "Diplomat's Fish." He was reading proofs of *Captain of the Discovery*, which had already had an annoyingly negative pre-publication review, which said it was "not too bad, but fairly dull reading for children, I should think." Publisher John Gray had said it was over-researched – Roddy got so engrossed in the subject that it was hard for him to leave anything out.

Several trees had fallen or been heavily trimmed over the winter and the spring cleanup took a week of hearty outdoor work. "Had fires going Saturday and Sunday, and everybody helping Sunday – Mary, Alan, Keith, Celie and Gretchen – which pretty well cleaned it up" and made lots of wonderful wood for the fireplaces. He was also clearing Scotch broom so Ann could move her vegetable garden from down by the river to behind the perennial border.

The previous Saturday Ann and Roddy had been "to watch Mrs. Ferry and her pupils at Indian dances in the old school on the Spit – really a very good show, with Sam Henderson on the drum, singing the songs, a Henderson boy of about 17 dancing many of the principal parts." The native bands of the B.C. coast were beginning to bring their culture back into the open after the long years during which their ceremonies and dances had been ruled illegal.

By early April, Roddy had finished "my swan story and quite like it." The story did not sell at the time, but was published as "Place des Cygnes" in *Writings and Reflections* and has since been anthologized elsewhere. "Got a good royalty report from Wm. Morrow, with *Mounted Police Patrol* still selling well."

A later April letter reported that Roddy would be in Vancouver "next Friday to record a broadcast at 3 p.m. and appear on a television show Saturday 1 p.m. to 5 p.m. with Roy Daniells, J.B. Priestly and George Woodcock." Daniells was head of English at the University of B.C.; Priestly, the noted English writer; and Woodcock, a leading literary critic, historian and writer – illustrious and stimulating company. Roddy would have been looking forward to a public appearance for once. He would also be going out to Shaughnessy Hospital to see Tommy Brayshaw who was there for minor surgery. Ann's brother Bucky had been up to confer about their mother who was still managing to live on her own near the Elmores in California, but becoming increasingly absent-minded.

In late April, senior CBC producer J. Frank Willis "a charming guy, but drinking far too much" had been up. "I seem to have agreed to go to work on a radio history of B.C. for him, to be ready for 1958, anything up to 13 one-hour broadcasts. A good fee per b'cast ... should be sound financially for the next 18 months, though other jobs have to be fitted in." The Chamber of Commerce presented him with a life membership "for winning the Crandall Trophy – somewhat to my embarrassment. On Saturday the Woodcocks came ... and we are preparing for the arrival of Ron Kelly of the CBC. He is scouting the ground for a television profile. Mary and Alan are going to wash the study windows this afternoon, we hope."

I stayed in Vancouver that summer, partly to be near my serious boyfriend, Joe Cvetkovich, and began by taking typing and shorthand as my father had done so many years before in London. He certainly didn't acquire any skills in those areas and neither did I, especially since I got a job after a month or so.

In May Roddy reported that Ron Kelly had been up "plotting out the television profile ... Same old stuff, of course, but it was interesting to get to know someone else in the business and watch him at work." The garden was beautiful, but too dry; the girls had good report cards, Alan's, "discouraging"; and he had caught a 3-pound rainbow in the Islands Pool. Alan was taking up his summer occupation of snorkeling up and down the river collecting spinners off the bottom and selling them along the riverbank. "He got 56 in one afternoon in the Quinsam pool and has already sold quite a bunch of them." Mary was finishing high school and had a summer job at the hospital.

In July, Roddy went to Banff to receive the University of Alberta's National Award for Service to Canadian Letters. "I'm probably a fool to go, but both Mother and I think it is common courtesy to do so. Actually one accomplishes nothing and gives nothing at these affairs, and I have an uneasy feeling that they are slightly immoral – an easy trap for an old man's vanity." He was forty-eight years old.

In September, a letter from Roddy to Margaret Andrew (she and her husband, Geoff, a UBC and fishing friend, were close friends of my parents by this time and they often wrote) thanks her for her kind words about the CBC television profile that Roddy had not seen. He continued: "It felt fairly good at the time and of course George [Woodcock] is a wonderful interviewer – all that skill and knowledge in drawing me out, and so completely self-effacing. Both Ann and I are very fond of him and Inge ... I have spent a confused summer trying to get in shape to write those historical broadcasts for the CBC ... Alan and I had a wonderful trip through the Interior, with a little good fishing thrown in, but I'm not sure I'm much wiser about it all ... Gretchen Harlow has gone off to be with her father and Ann's mother has come up from California [to live with us permanently]." Mary was now in first year at UBC.

Roddy's work in October included "an essay on Thomas Hardy for George Woodcock and Bob Weaver and the new little Canadian magazine [*Tamarack Review*]," more of "the damned B.C. History" and outlining "a fly fishing course for Victoria College adult education." Court was "busy as usual these days" – a Victoria lawyer "defending a case of misappropriated funds ... various assaults and thefts that will be defended, and a leading game case." A new (to us) yellow Buick "has created quite a sensation, especially with Alan." Grandmother was settling in and "is a great favorite with Alan and Celie."

A rare comment on world news concerned the recent events in Hungary. "I am terribly depressed ... yet I suppose it was too much to expect anything else ... After coming in in the first place and killing numbers of civilians, it was impossible for the Russian army to pull out without admitting a gigantic error of behavior and policy. Now, of course, the Russians have damned themselves forever with all those people, as they already had in Poland and the Ukraine ... Sooner or later they will be thrown out, just as surely as the white people will be thrown out of South Africa. But now it will be later rather than sooner. It is an immense tragedy."

In November, Joe Cvetkovich and I were married, several months sooner than we might otherwise have done because I was pregnant. In early December, Roddy wrote: "With allowance for adjustment to the surprise [and embarrassment, no doubt], I find I am increasingly satisfied about you and Joe, and so is mother. My first feeling was that you had bought yourselves a very difficult two years [Joe was in his final year of law school and had another year as an articled student beyond that], instead of a bright and easy start with no visible problems. Many people who should know tell me that this is not the case ... a year or two of shared problems are good, not bad ... One would always like to see ones children float easily and happily into a carefree world; but fortunately the children have better ideas and anyway that isn't what the world is all about." This passage is followed by advice about articling for Joe and then the family news. They were considering boarding school for Alan – reluctantly. Grandmother liked the woman who came to stay when Ann and Roddy were away, "fortunately," and "this is the night Kay Armstrong [a Vancouver ballet teacher who came once a week to give classes that Celie took] and her piano woman come to stay."

So the first of the children was really gone (if children ever are gone – I certainly didn't consider myself so), and external demands were beginning to take a larger and larger part in Roddy's life as his reputation as a writer and conservationist continued to grow.

.11. B.C. History and the Library (1957 — 1962)

Roddy's career had already spread well beyond the household which Ann had kept running so smoothly and well for over twenty years. But with the children becoming slightly less demanding, Ann, too, was now able to consider a move beyond her work with church and school organizations. It was about to be her turn to make a mark in the larger community.

In mid-January of 1957 my father wrote me of my mother's positive report on the Vancouver apartment Joe and I were now in. At home there was a little snow so "Celie and I put on snowshoes and made a few little trips about the fields. Everything looks very beautiful and with a warm house one can't ask much more than that."

After Christmas Alan had been sent to the Christian Brothers' Vancouver College in hopes that his school work would improve. The stern father, who was undoubtedly having some qualms over the decision, wrote me: "He is there for better or worse, and he can't talk himself out of it ... By all means give him sympathy within reason, but no more than he absolutely needs ... we have not the slightest intention of taking him out of the school or compromising in any way." A letter to me from my mother, signed "Ann," as her letters often were, summed up the situation thus: "Alan is now sort of mad at us, which I *think* is a healthy second stage, better than bleak despair." The rest of the letter is reminiscent of *her* correspondence with her mother when she was first married — details of wedding presents, household furnishings and other matters domestic.

By the following week, Roddy had spent three days in Victoria doing research at the Provincial Archives for the B.C. history broadcasts for the CBC, and Alan had been home for the weekend. One Sunday afternoon, Roddy, Ann and Grandmother had driven the thirty miles south to Courtenay to hear the touring Vancouver Symphony "and enjoyed it very much. Celie spent the time skating at the Perkins and enjoyed *herself*, though she was mad because we didn't pick her up as soon as she was through." (He would have been amused by her fury.) His letter and Ann's of the same day both thank for an addition to the collection of blue Wedgwood jasperware we were giving our parents as anniversary presents, in anticipation of the day they would be on their own: "seems all too close, too, now that we are already so gravely reduced."

A letter from my mother at the end of January told of her decorating plans for both our households, talks Roddy gave in Qualicum [eighty miles south on Vancouver Island] and Campbell River and her work on a book on the Catholic liturgy – she was acting as editor for the Rev. H. A. Reinhold of New York, whom she had met when he was in Campbell River. "I'm helping him, believe it or not, to make a new book for Lenten services." The book was never finished because Father Reinhold fell ill.

In February Roddy was about halfway through Script #4 of the B.C. history for the CBC (of a planned thirteen to be completed at the rate of one a month). "I haven't dared take the time to go out, but badly want to go up and look for my swans and perhaps try for a steelhead sometime. Alan ... keeps the pressure on us here, with constant wails about the school and its conditions and his own misery." Alan told me many times over the years that he only survived the ordeal because the school gave the boys considerable freedom on the weekends. He spent much of his time wandering the deep woods of Vancouver's Stanley Park when he wasn't with me or Mary. He disliked both the group dormitory and the emphasis on team sports and, although he read copiously, hadn't yet got to like studying, so he was seen as a non-participant and a rather hopeless student.

A month later a letter chronicles the steady stream of demands on Roddy's time. "I periodically sweat to think of how to fit in all the other things [besides the writing]. Seem to waste a lot of time, but never have time to waste ... a juvenile court hearing to remove a child from welfare custody. A call about a woman drinking again, necessitating several other phone calls. Fed the animals and hauled several loads of peat moss to the lawn while Mother went to town ... Fr. Bullock from Qualicum turned up, with Sister Superior, his mother and so on. Left peat moss to find him key to look at new church. Wondered about asking them to tea. Mother came back at right moment, did so. All the while Girl Guides cooking dinner in kitchen [probably to qualify for a merit badge under Ann's supervision]." And that is just part of one day. In one week there were fish and game meetings, *three* talks to PTAs and Ann went to CWL and her French lesson.

Mary and Alan came home for a weekend, picked up from the Vancouver ferry in Nanaimo by Ann (a hundred miles each way, but a rather lovely drive with the Strait of Georgia in sight most of the way, which she did "at the drop of a hat," as she would say, for many, many years. It also gave her a chance to be alone). While Ann was gone, "Grandmother, Celie and I," wrote my father, "went over to the 'amateur show' at Campbellton School – a successful affair in which Celie and Sandra Wood and Ratsey [yet another Labrador retriever offspring] achieved a third prize for a rendering of the 'Mad Dog of Islington.'" In that same week "Campbell River Magistrate's Court [Roddy] heard its first murder charge – just a reading and remand, of course. I am glad to say I shall probably be away for the preliminary, but it will be a depressing affair."

The schedule for the rest of the spring was heavy with travel and speaking engagements. On the way to Toronto and New York for three weeks in April, Roddy spoke to union members at Fishermen's Hall on East Cordova in Vancouver. The trip to Toronto was to work with J. Frank Willis at the CBC on the scripts. In both cities Roddy met with publishers, and with his agent as well in New York. He also fished a little in New York State's famous trout waters. After only a week at home Roddy was off to the annual Magistrate's Conference at Harrison Hot Springs up the Fraser Valley.

In late April came a check for my twenty-first birthday and a query about the dates of Convocation at UBC. Joe and I were both graduating – he in law and I in English literature. Convocation turned out to coincide with a trip to Saskatchewan, to my eternal disappointment. In among all this Roddy was working on pieces for *Sports Illustrated* on Pacific salmon and fishing the Beaverkill River in New York, and continuing the B.C. history scripts. A conference with Brother Bates at Vancouver College yielded the information that Alan was "o.k. in every way, except he is not a good student." Alan had been overheard saying "it was no good for him to study, because if he did well he would be sent back next fall. I told Br. Bates he would be back anyway."

The Saskatchewan trip, on which Ann went too, was for Forest Conservation Week. In an interview with the *Regina Leader-Post*, Ann described their life together. "'I type, he writes in longhand and I offer no suggestions whatsoever.' She enthusiastically added that she had a brand new pink electric typewriter. 'Rod has his own ideas; he is just full of any subject under the sun. You know, one can start by talking about fishing and it leads to many subjects. It is a basic topic that moves on to the discussion of many things.' ... her main introduction to fishing was listening to many famous fishermen talking about it. They would say 'so I took off the black one and put on a red one, and it goes on and on,' she said laughing."

Roddy gave talks to ten different service clubs and schools around Saskatchewan in eight days, as well as visiting museums and wildlife sites. The reward was three days of fishing in northern Saskatchewan. Ann fell in love with the province – "it's remarkable a hundred ways and beautiful in a thousand" – she wrote in a note to me during the trip.

Once Ann was back from the trip, her letters are full of plans for my baby. Mary was home from university and working in the laboratory at Lourdes Hospital. Celie, now ten, was looking forward to the arrival of her horse, for which she had been saving pennies for five years, with the promise of having an equal amount given her when she had saved half the cost. She wrote me a sad note in July: "Everything has gone wrong. Cooper was killed by something. We think it was distemper. We're getting another kitten ... but it won't take the place of Cooper."

On July 17, my daughter was born. She was the first grandchild on both sides of the family; we named her Ann after both her grandmothers. In August I took Ann Luja up to Campbell River and joined in the summer confusion of visitors and gardening and canning and freezing. In early September, my father wrote: "Having finished Script 7, made out my half-yearly statistical returns [for his court work] and my monthly court record returns, I am indulging in a little correspondence on a pleasant Sunday afternoon – after mowing and edging the lawn, of course. Everything is fairly normal here. Fruit is ripening and the dogs bark at coons or bears every night. Last night was especially good at 3.15 and again at 7.15. Then the Knowles' black and white cow [pastured in our field] wandered on to the lawn. A lovely dewy morning. Mother went out in my dressing gown, so I pulled on a shirt over my underwear and was out in the road trying to shoo the cow through the gate wondering if I might get pinched for indecent exposure. Only one car passed and the police haven't called yet."

Alan had worked the summer on a local wharf taking care of the salmon sportfishermen and their boats. And he must have done a fine job of persuading because he did not go back to school in Vancouver. Deep down Roddy probably sympathized with Alan's miseries over boarding school, and it clearly made Alan so unhappy that the school could hardly have been construed any longer as being the solution to his problems. He was in grade ten at the Campbell River high school and had committed to two hours of daily study with Ann. "His latest clothing theory is a vest; everyone has expressed appropriate horror and we hope the theory will not be pursued. But you know Alan."

Later that month Roddy spent a week on the Quinault River on the Olympic Peninsula in Washington for a fishing story for *Sports Illustrated.* "Lovely Indians, lovely canoes, lovely river, lovely weather, stupid fish all hiding in the dark holes," he wrote. "A most refreshing change from the broadcasts." The outside of the house was being painted. In October there is a long letter describing a hearing on a plan to develop the Campbell River waterfront by filling in the beach the main street curved around, in conjunction with building a terminal for a car ferry to Quadra Island. The town and council were opposed, but the developer, who had the ear of the provincial government which was building the terminal, had his way, and Campbell River lost its beachfront.

By late November, Script #10 was underway, Roddy was proofreading an article on B.C. for the *World Book* encyclopedia, he was turned down as a blood donor because of his wartime jaundice and Christmas planning was proceeding well. Ann and Roddy were going to Victoria the next week for more B.C. history research.

In mid-January of 1958 after the usual big family Christmas and a later, intellectually stimulating evening with Dr. Wallace Wilson and novelist Ethel Wilson, Ann wrote me: "Daddy, instead of being full of them, started prowling aimlessly around the house and when questioned said: 'I miss my baby [the new granddaughter],' and that he'd love to go out, which shows how undone he was." They had had a large New Year's party which Grandmother so enjoyed that "she came down dressed for a party and wished us Happy New Year every day until Sunday." Alan read *Island in the Sun* "because he's so interested in the Negro question, then read *Cry, the Beloved Country* and then got sick – as he slowly realised, then we did, from emotion." Ann despaired over the untidiness of the house: "It seems as if I were sweeping one way and Alan and Grandmother and Daddy and Celie were all sweeping the other way – to say *nothing* of those five animals [cats, dog and puppies]."

The history scripts dragged on with little response from the CBC about when, or even if, they would be produced. Court was busy, with twenty-eight cases of breaking and entering, mostly juvenile, by mid-month. Alan and his friend Robin Woodward had bought a "shocking wreck of a Model A Ford for $20 and aim to put it in running condition."

Celie had her eyes examined and was "just entitled to glasses, which she insists on having. That makes all four of you. What a myopic outfit, if I may say so." Roddy was growing a beard for B.C.'s Centennial year and not much liking it, "but Mother and Alan are highly in favor of it ... Celie has the good taste not to approve." The house got a new shake roof in April.

The boys "bought a '32 Graham-Paige car in senile condition" and Roddy towed it home from south of Campbell River in May on the way back from picking up Mary and friend Judy Harker, who were finished their university year. Mary got a job at the new pulp mill that summer because the old Lourdes Hospital, which was no longer large enough to serve the rapidly growing postwar town, had closed. The broadcasts were going to air and Roddy was quite pleased with the result. Several Toronto publishers were interested in a book based on the broadcasts. Longmans, Green of Toronto eventually published *The Farthest Shores,* about the early exploration of B.C., and *Fur and Gold*, the story of James Douglas, the first governor of the colony. These were based on parts of the thirteen one-hour CBC scripts and there was material for others, but Roddy never did get around to any more. A CWL convention in June included a lunch on the lawn for 120 guests – Roddy and Mary shampooed the rugs in honor of the occasion. It was most unusual for Roddy to do domestic chores, but he liked things "tolerable tidy," would have been intrigued by the shampooing machine and couldn't have done much work with it buzzing around him anyway.

Roddy's immediate plans included a fishing trip to the B.C. Interior with UBC friends and "getting some sort of start on the Pacific Salmon profile. As soon as that is done I shall start on *Fisherman's Summer. Sports Illustrated* also wants a northern pike profile for 1959 and no doubt there will be other commissioned jobs, but it is really quite important to get some books done.

"Tomorrow Mother goes to see Bill Reid, the school inspector, about a 'proposition' he has for her. She's not at all sure what it is, but expects to take him up on it." The meeting led to Ann's first school job – running the high school library for three months that fall until a qualified librarian could be hired. She also taught English to grade eight and nine classes.

The summer was, as usual, filled with comings and goings of friends, as much friends of the children as of Ann's and Roddy's now. My husband, Joe, had been called to the bar in the spring and was working for a small Vancouver firm, and our second daughter, Charlotte Marta, was born in late September. A letter of congratulations on the new daughter went on to say that Roddy thought of me often because he had been working in the garden and could see lots of plants that would go well around our new house. He had transplanted a row of Port Orford cedars to the field east of the house, and was beginning a major changeover of the perennial border to rhododendrons and azaleas. He was also trying to get in as much fishing as possible as research for *Fisherman's Summer*, but got out less often than he would have liked.

In November, Celie's horse finally arrived. "The Bouldings' Simon, and a nice little animal too. Celie is fit to be tied ... There are plenty of complications, including the stabling, but it will probably work out now that the creature is here." (The barn got a new roof.)

Ann and Roddy spent a week in Vancouver in early December. Roddy spoke to the Capilano Rod and Gun Club, a high school and a creative writing class at UBC, as well as recording a review of Dr. Margaret Ormsby's history of B.C. for the CBC, attending an Old Carthusian dinner (Charterhouse alumni) and our dinner for Joe's boss, Monty Caple.

Roddy left the day after Christmas for the east. Writing from New York in mid-January of 1959, he told me: "I think the most exciting thing was the summons [via Brooke Claxton, then chairman of The Canada Council, who had come to visit in Campbell River the summer before] to an hour's interview with the Governor General in Ottawa – completely unexpected. Delightful talk. Sherry. Completely alone in the library. I wouldn't have missed it for anything, though it scared me more than a little and I didn't do awfully well. It is rather much for an immigrant boy to compete with, even though he is our own man and remarkably easy to talk with." (The governor general of the day was Vincent Massey, the first Canadian-born governor general.) Roddy went on from there to Montreal, New England and New York where he did the round of publishers and spoke to fishing clubs. He described the Anglers' Club in New York as "a fine evening, lots of good friends, all in a good mood: Charlie de Feo, Meade Schaeffer, Ed Zern, Lee Wulff, Ezra Bowen, to name a few."

A sour note crept into my letter from New York when Roddy said: "My leg holds me up barely." He flew back to Victoria, where Ann met him, and went to see the army medical examiner there. The leg trouble was because of a pinched nerve in his back which was attributed to an injury in a jeep accident during the war and, therefore, came under the aegis of the army. The Victoria doctor wanted him in traction right away, but Roddy insisted on going home to catch up on the mail and court. He then went to the new Campbell River Hospital where he spent ten days in traction. He read Joyce Carey's *To Be a Pilgrim* and Robertson Davies' *A Mixture of Frailties* and tried to work.

Home again, undergoing a course of rest and physiotherapy in hopes of avoiding an operation on his spine, Roddy was finishing up both the first juvenile based on part of the B.C. history radio script, *The Farthest Shores*, and *Fisherman's Summer*. He was planning to start work on the B.C. section of *The Face of Canada* to be published by Clarke Irwin in Toronto. George Silk was due to photograph him for a *Life* magazine story on anglers, but Roddy was hoping Silk would be delayed because of the difficulties with his back. Ann was getting work as a substitute teacher and that soon turned into a regular job every Wednesday at the school on Quadra Island, relieving the principal so he could do his administrative work. Roddy spoke to a Vancouver Island school principals' conference in Nanaimo, and then Ann drove home in haste while there was still light because the car's generator was failing and the headlights could not be relied on. Once home, they rushed out again to a Fish and Game banquet where Roddy was presented with a life membership and "a very fine marble desk set with two Parker 51 pens ... Couldn't have surprised me more or pleased me more, though it was really a moment of confusion and I couldn't think of anything good to say."

By April Roddy was in Shaughnessy Hospital in Vancouver again, reading Proust and waiting to have his back operated on. Two damaged discs were removed and three vertebrae fused, which ultimately solved the problem, although the recovery was slow. It was discovered that Roddy's bones were very brittle and after a complicated series of diagnostic tests it was decided that he had a congenital condition that prevented his system from properly absorbing calcium. Daily doses of potassium citrate were prescribed, along with plenty of milk. Joe and I, and Mary, usually with Bernie Bowker, her "young man," visited often.

Once Roddy was home again he began work on a book on the natural resources of British Columbia which was intended as a companion to an atlas of B.C. resources. Both books had grown out of the annual B.C. Natural Resources Conference – an early attempt at having industry, government and conservationists gather at the same table. He also wrote "The Writer in Isolation" for the first issue of a new quarterly called *Canadian Literature*, edited by George Woodcock. Ann's brother Bucky came from California to visit and confer about their mother, who was becoming increasingly more difficult to care for as her memory deteriorated. She often wandered around at night waking the household and no longer knew most people.

In August Alan went with Roddy on a trip to Saskatchewan to research pike fishing for a *Sports Illustrated* story. Alan went partly so he could do the lifting and carrying and spare Roddy's still-healing back. *Sports Illustrated* was not exactly Roddy's style, but they paid well and promptly, so it was hard to turn down their requests. The fishing included grayling in the Fond du Lac River, which was no doubt a high spot for Roddy – I'm not sure the pike appealed much. The morning of the day they returned Celie fell off Simon and broke her arm. "We went straight up to the hospital and found her, right forearm in a cast, looking somewhat small and frail in a great big bed, but quite cheerful. She came home next morning."

A few days later, a call came that Roddy's Aunt Elspeth was nearby, aboard Bertha Boeing's yacht from Seattle. Ann and Roddy joined them for lunch. "Elspeth was wonderful as always and much less sharp than formerly," wrote Ann to me. "Full of talk about Joan and Val and Decie (she sees him more than ever, though they are divorced). To Roddy's horror, all the Pope family talk sounded *exactly* like the kind of thing he walked out on thirty years ago – needless to say, made him gladder than ever that he had done it. Elspeth came back with us for tea and loved the house. I adore Mrs. Boeing, as you know, and am thrown into something of a trance by her."

In a summer letter to Edward Dunn, Roddy reported that he and Ann would be in Seattle in late September when he would speak at a psychiatrists' convention, and then he would be going back to Shaughnessy yet again for further checks on how his back was healing and whether the calcium treatments were working. Mary had spent the summer working in a genetics lab at UBC and was now engaged to Bernie Bowker. Bernie had his B.A. in English and was beginning work on an M.A., and Mary had another year to go for her B.A. "Alan is growing in strength and grace, though I daresay one has to be his father or mother to notice it. He failed Grade Eleven fairly dismally, but is actually working a bit better (again, you have to be a parent to notice it) ... Celie has her horse, a strong-willed character. She manages him and all her other manifold affairs and still is an honor student at school. If she only learns to keep her room tidy we shan't be able to live up to her at all."

The September checkup at Shaughnessy was very satisfactory and by October the routine was back in place. "Mother busy harvesting, but at least as busy with teaching (Wed. and Friday and Wednesday night New Canadian English), selling Overture concert series tickets and writing the minutes of the community hall [board, of which she was secretary]. Alan has been getting some quite good marks. A present distraction is Vickie Assu, a great-granddaughter of the old chief [of the Kwagul'th] at Cape Mudge. Celie's school work is fine and she has enough to keep her busy. My book is going very slowly – I became badly stuck in geology." Early reviews of *Fisherman's Summer* were good. "But the reviews are always much better than the sales." *The New Yorker* said: "Mr. Haig-Brown is a talented fly-fisherman who is also gifted with uncommon sense and sensibility ... his purpose is to demonstrate that 'there is more to fishing than fish and more to sport than filling a bag.' He succeeds, once again, most amiably."

In November, Ann, Alan and Joe went to Seattle to pick up a load of furniture from Ann's mother's house, which was being sold following Ann's sister Mary's death in a car accident in California. Ann was asked to take over the librarian's job at the high school again after Christmas – of course, she did. In January of 1960, Grandmother went back to Bucky and Gar in California for six months. A great worry over that winter was a poor man who had decided that people like Roddy and the police should be gotten rid of. A friend "came up with an anonymous letter he'd had from the man – a snapshot of a sign he has in his front yard vilifying Daddy and a note on the back saying responsible citizens should get rid of rats like Daddy and Cpl. Gray." The threats gradually got worse and more frightening over the next four years. Eventually the police went to arrest the man and, apparently, when the man came out of his house they fired at his rifle which went off and killed him. Roddy said, in a letter to Alan in 1964, "It is a sad business and I don't feel at all good about it."

In a January 1960 letter, my father wrote: "Mary and Bernie [who were to be married in May] left this afternoon ... I was very sad to see her go. It seems like the last time she will be just Mary – yet I don't know why such an idea should come up. You seem to be still Valerie, even with two children, and no doubt she will be still Mary, maybe more so again when the waiting's over. Parents always have to fret about it, though I don't know where's the sense of fretting." His work on the resources book went on slowly as he struggled with statistics of one kind and another. But there was time for some fishing now and then, and his back was improving steadily.

In April Alan and Vickie Assu were married. "It was a case of have to," as Roddy put it in a letter to Edward Dunn, "and they are both much too young, but otherwise we are well-satisfied. Vickie herself is shy, very quiet, very pretty and I think exactly what Alan needs. We are already very fond of her and are rapidly getting to know her very large and attractive family." Alan remembers being very formally introduced by our father to Vickie's great-grandfather, Chief Billy Assu, on the street in Campbell River when he was about five. He says he knew, even at that age, that this was a man whom his father honored and respected. Vickie's father, Herb, was a seine boat skipper legendary on the B.C. coast for his ability to read the tides, and Alan went to work for him that summer in the commercial salmon fishery. They lived in the cottage at Above Tide which had been refurbished. "A new roof on, garage removed, carport built [behind the house], bathroom addition on the cottage," wrote my father to me. In September, after a long labor for Vickie, their baby died, which was very hard for both of them.

That winter Alan was asked to fish for herring with Vickie's father, a hard and dangerous job in the cold winter water off the northern coast of B.C. Alan wrote, many years later, in his book, *Fishing for a Living*, "I learned a lot that winter. Among other things, I learned about learning, so that eventually I went to school to finish grade twelve and then went on to train as a teacher. Fishing paid the way and the people with whom I fished kept me focused. They told me about the residential schools and about the Japanese Canadians who had built and lost the boats which now carried me safely through southeasters off Cape Mudge."

The work on the cottage contributed to a general cleanup around the place that was going on in preparation for Mary's wedding which was to be held in the Catholic church across the road – as Alan's had been –with a reception in the garden afterwards. I remember the realization dawning on us as the day neared that *many* people had accepted their invitations, even from far away, and, in spite of a new pergola over the terrace to hold an awning, where would they all go if it rained? But it didn't rain and all the planning did come together. The wedding party walked across a path mowed in the field and greeted the guests as they arrived on the sunny lawn for a gathering that celebrated the glory of years of work in the garden at the same time as it celebrated the beginning of Mary and Bernie's life together. It *was* a lovely day.

Just after the wedding *Life* called and, as Ann put it, "wants Daddy to write a thousand words to conclude the picture series on angling, which makes him again a writer more than a fisherman and will pay him well, which solves What will we eat next winter after two weddings?" The pictures of Roddy fishing had been managed earlier that spring in spite of Roddy's still-tender spinal fusion.

After a "normal" summer, Ann went back to what now seemed to be her job as the librarian at the school. She investigated getting the "proper" qualifications at either the University of Washington or UBC – she had a B.A., but neither a teaching nor a library science degree which the job officially required. But such formalities seemed less necessary as time went on, and Ann taught happily for many years on letters of permission – certainly a case of doing good work being recognized as more important than formal qualifications. We still meet people regularly who remember her with great pleasure from their high school years in Campbell River, both for the love of books that she communicated and for her concern for her students. Alan tells of visiting a Vancouver nightclub to interview the lead singer and having to show the bouncer his card to get in. He settled to watch the show and, after a while, the bouncer came over to ask if his mother taught school in Campbell River. Alan said she did and the big man reminisced happily of his time in her classes.

Roddy finished the B.C. resources survey, *The Living Land*, and was writing a speech for a Toronto gathering. Celie was now at boarding school in Vancouver – the Convent of the Sacred Heart – a sister school to the one Ann had gone to in Seattle at the same age. Ann said she would have sent Mary and me, too, only there wasn't the money at the time. Her teaching salary made the difference now. Ann's Catholicism was strong, if questioning, and she felt her children should have a proper religious education. Celie stood the separation from home better than Alan had done, but in the end she only stayed two years. Roddy supervised the little girls who voluntarily saw to her horse's needs while she was away – probably more trouble than if he'd done it himself.

The best part of a Toronto trip that fall to make yet another speech was bird-watching along the shore of Lake Ontario "with most enthusiastic and erudite bird watchers, from the president of the Ontario Audubon Society on down, and not very far down." Roddy didn't mention in the letters who he spoke to that time. He found his publishers very much wanting "another juvenile, so perhaps the Nootka whaling book." He was also trying to get in some fishing research for *Fisherman's Fall*. The letters were shorter and life obviously quieter with only Grandmother, who had returned from California that summer, left in the house. Vickie was there as well from time to time when Alan was fishing and she wasn't with some part of her family.

Christmas came and went with lots of parties, including one at Above Tide – a rare event. So many people came to the house for one reason or another anyway that a planned party was unusual. "It really went very well, though we ran out of glasses, ice and whisky owing to my miscalculations and a certain proportion of unexpected guests. No one notices such things particularly except the host, anyway." Ann didn't think much of one party they went to "– no school teachers she said." The next "was just the opposite and they all took their hair down a bit towards the end – most unprofessionally, as they all agreed."

The family car, a big yellow Buick, was hit from behind on New Year's Eve on Quadra Island in a complicated chain reaction started by a guy using canned milk for brake fluid. Alan was driving, but it was in no way his fault, and the upshot was that there was no car for several weeks. The first of the baby lambs arrived in late January in 1961 – there were only three ewes left now, and the last cow had gone some time ago. Ann and Roddy celebrated their twenty-seventh anniversary on January 20 "with just Vickie here, dinner in the study, curried shrimp and white wine." A month and a day later, Vickie made a banana chiffon cake for Roddy's birthday. Work went on with the Nootka book.

In March, publisher John Gray of Macmillan's gave a party at the Vancouver Hotel to celebrate *The Living Land*, after having given a similar one in Victoria at the annual Natural Resources Conference. The B.C. government did not buy the book for its use, as had been expected, stating that: "Both the Conference and the author have frequently been critical of the government." By May, Roddy wrote me: "... my book is going badly and I never seem to have time to get it straightened out before I have to dash off somewhere else. Tomorrow it's the Salmon River with the Hawthorne Foundation [annual spring trip with UBC people]. Next week Shaughnessy [to monitor his calcium retention], Vancouver School of Art [speech] and on Saturday the Librarians' banquet at Qualicum."

In the same letter there was news from the kitchen – an electric stove had replaced the old oil one. "Mother is ... learning the hard way about the new stove. There are so many wrong buttons to push. I hope the controls for the famous push button war are somewhat simpler. Last night a tongue was atomised while we had a drink before dinner." This stove led to the family legend about "MAX." Even when she got the controls under control, Ann was always in a hurry and frequently set things on maximum heat, causing parts of many dinners and even some pots to be MAXed.

In June, my father wrote me, "Mary and Bernie and I had a wonderful trip to the West Coast [of Vancouver Island to look over the setting of the book Roddy was writing about the native people and the whaling culture of that coast] and I was hardly back from that before it was time to take off for Portland and Seattle ... a surprising interest in *The Living Land*." The Massachusetts Audubon Society review described the book as "a lively, interesting non-technical account of the natural resources of British Columbia." The summer months were, as usual, crowded – added to which, in those years, were trips to events at the Vancouver International Festival. Tickets Ann bought with her teaching salary kept us all rushing about madly to opera, ballet, concerts and plays.

In August, my father wrote: "Celie has decided to become a fisherman, so we have had some practice on the lawn and today she came to the Pumphouse Pool with me. Fell in, caught two little fish, had a whale of a time, casting and casting with the utmost determination and independence, much as you used to do." We all learned something of casting on the lawn and, occasionally, in the river – there was usually a rod lying in wait along the shelf below the books in the study. Fishing talk with friends and admirers often drifted out on to the lawn to try out a rod or just show off a little, and we were welcome to join in. But none of us have become avid flyfishers.

That September Mary and Bernie went to the Queen Charlotte Islands, where Bernie, who had received his B.Ed. that spring, had a job teaching at Masset on the northern edge of Graham Island. Alan started to work on finishing high school in Vancouver, and he and Vickie rented a little house. Grandmother was "feeling her oats a bit – bust up the gate at the top of the stairs tonight; said she couldn't see the sense of it." Of course it was to keep her from falling when she wandered about at night, sometimes in the dark. Ann's theory had been that her mother should stay with us until she didn't recognize any of us any longer. She continued to know Roddy and Ann for a long time, but that too was fading, so in October Ann, after consultation with her brothers, took her to live at St. Mary's Priory in Colwood near Victoria. The nuns there ran a home for older women who needed more care than their families could give them.

In a rare "one letter to all," Ann wrote: "I miss Grandmother very, very much – much more than I expected ... her reactions to St. Mary's Priory – very charming to the nuns – to me in asides: 'Did you ever see such a ghastly place? If this isn't the damnedest bunch of old women. What the hell are we doing here?' I couldn't help but agree; though, of course, I didn't." A friend saw Grandmother a few days later and reported to Ann via his wife, "Tell her her Mother is getting along very well, and we'll leave it at that. Not very consoling. I wonder whether the nuns were getting a full load of the profanity, or whether she was very upset or what. She was to have been put in with the very old and infirm; but when they saw her, they decided on the part for the most active ones, and it was they that got the benefit of her observations. This week I finally realized that there isn't a right decision and a wrong one about things like that, so neither answer is going to be fully satisfactory."

That same month Roddy went to Montreal to be chair of the first day of the first federal natural resources conference. In November Edward Dunn came for a weekend of grouse shooting, and Ann and Roddy went to Vancouver for a conference and to visit the Vancouver Aquarium, whose director, Murray Newman, wanted Roddy as a consultant for a major exhibit on Pacific salmon. In December Roddy finished *The Whale People*, and was about to start work on the B.C. section of a book for Doubleday, to be called *The Pacific Northwest*. At Christmas Ann gave Roddy an aquarium because he had expressed interest in a kit in a newspaper advertisement. Roddy said, "But I didn't mean I *wanted* it." The aquarium led to hours of observation of the little creatures that lived in the river, and several chapters of *Fisherman's Fall*.

By February of 1962, Roddy was finishing his section of the Doubleday book and then would be in Vancouver to speak at several schools. I gave a dinner party in his honor. Bursitis in Roddy's shoulder was a problem —cortisone made no difference. "Am planning next a primer of fly-fishing for which Morrow already wants to sign a contract. Should be a snap ... Have taken to running (jogging would be a better word) around the fields every morning before breakfast. Feels fine and the waist line needs it. But how little spring is in the ancient legs." (He was fifty-four that month.) Our old friend Mary Weiler, who still lived on Cortes Island, was to illustrate *The Whale People*. Roddy particularly wanted the illustrations done by someone who would have an understanding of West Coast Indian art — there were not yet any Nootka people that he was aware of who might be able to do drawings —and he knew he did not want a New York or Toronto artist chosen by his publishers.

In March there were no lambs for the first time in some fifteen years —"practical, but sad," wrote Ann. The publishers liked Mary Weiler's illustrations. An April letter from Roddy told of an inquiry into development on the Puntledge River at Courtenay at which he delivered a brief, getting the living room painted and the back porch fixed. Roddy and Ann made a quick trip to Vancouver to have lunch with Lady Baden-Powell, who had asked to see them. Most letters brought news of the little aquarium —in April a coho fry from Coal Creek "settled in beautifully, seemed on quite good terms with the bullhead, chewed the little mayflies very successfully ... Unhappily he jumped out while I was at court on Saturday morning. I ... have now sent for a proper aquarium canopy to prevent such tragedies in the future.

"The running ... isn't going too well ... swelling in my left ankle ... and the left knee which also became sore. I strongly suspect the [varicose] veins." Sure enough, and on May 8, I arrived in his Shaughnessy Hospital room to find a note saying, "I expect to get back here about 3.30 or 4 p.m. ... I should be pretty conscious by then." He was much longer than that —he had put off the surgery so long that it took quite a while to get all the bits and pieces of deteriorated veins removed. By the time the surgery finished, the recovery room staff had gone home, so he came back far from conscious and I remember being quite shocked to see my father so still. I sat with him and listened to incomprehensible talk well into the evening, as he worked his way out of the anesthetic.

.12.

Demanding Years (1962 – 1969)

In June of 1962, Roddy spoke to the Duke of Edinburgh's Commonwealth Study Conference in Vancouver. The subject was the natural resources of British Columbia, and he delivered his speech from a bridge across a huge relief map of B.C. This was only one of the growing number of talks Roddy gave in these and succeeding years. There are certainly far too many to write of them all. He spoke as a writer, magistrate or conservationist to gatherings that ranged from national and international conventions and symposia to the grade six class at the school just down the road from the house. Fish and game clubs often appear on the list – they were probably the main conservation groups in the fifties and sixties. He spoke to high school graduation classes whenever he could possibly fit them in, but sometimes the pressure of other work led him to turn down such prestigious items as, for example, a Canadian Club gathering at which soon-to-be Canadian prime minister Lester Pearson and the U.S. ambassador were to be among the guests. The letters often tell whom he was speaking to, but rarely mention the topic, although that is generally evident from the organization involved. The speeches were usually made from notes on 3" x 5" file cards kept in the inside pocket of his gray flannel suit or navy blue blazer. Many of the card sets are among the collection of his papers at the University of B.C. library.

That fall Celie did not go back to the Convent, and Bernie took a teaching job at Manson's Landing on Cortes Island, east of Campbell

River beyond Quadra Island, so one child was at home and one closer to home – although transportation to and from Cortes was unreliable, being by private boat or chartered floatplane, and very subject to weather conditions. Mary was expecting a baby in late February. Alan was in Vancouver at school – he and Vickie were living aboard an old boat at a wharf under the Granville Street bridge. They later moved to a small cabin at the top of the wharf there.

Celie now had a second horse, Sundancer, and divided her time between school and horses. One night the horses got out and trampled the lawn rather badly, but in a letter to Alan, Roddy reported: "We have rolled the lawn to get rid of the worst of the hoof marks and I don't think it will be too bad next summer." The perfection of the lawn was very important to Roddy and over the years he spent a lot of time and energy on it, as well as money on water pumps, sprinkler systems and lawnmowers.

In November, Roddy travelled by plane and bus as far as Winnipeg as patron of Young Canada Book Week. He was asked partly because *The Whale People* had just been published. He particularly enjoyed the large audiences of young children who came to hear him speak. *The Whale People* was awarded the Canadian Library Association's medal for the best children's book of that year. At the end of the tour he came back through Vancouver and took all of us who were living there out to dinner to celebrate Alan's twenty-first birthday.

A letter to me from Ann after Roddy's visit said I had "sent him home in much better shape than I expected." She went on to say: "It sounds appalling – but isn't too – the big fir blew down Friday night. [The big fir had warranted a chapter in *Measure of the Year* in which Roddy had assumed it would outlive him.] It broke off about ten feet above the ground, so the trees on this side of it are quite all right, and we'd always been afraid that however it came down, they'd be damaged. It didn't reach very far on the ground – 150 feet ..."

Ann and Roddy made a trip to Parksville on Vancouver Island "to speak to the Fish and Game Club – and drove slowly home to look over the salmon creeks." This was background for *Fisherman's Fall*. Roddy went back to Parksville a couple of weeks later to look over the creeks again and pick up a trailer he had bought to haul around with a small tractor he now had. The trailer "follows along behind the Jaguar at 70." The car was one of a series of used, but treasured and troublesome Jags – all part of Roddy's love of a little luxury in his life. Seventy miles an hour was a little above the speed limit for the Island Highway, but then, what's a Jaguar for? The first job the new trailer was used for was to begin cleaning up the big fir for firewood. In the same letter Roddy wrote of a trip to Gold River with Skate Hames and Maxine Egan, where he got "a nice 14-pound steelhead." The local bookstore was out of *The Whale People*, "in fact all my books." They were ordering more and a Victoria store reported the new book selling "like mad." The B.C. Department of Education did not order the book for the schools, claiming there was no demand, despite sales of 4000 copies in Canada within five weeks of publication, to Roddy's annoyance.

In January of 1963, Ann and Roddy went to Victoria overnight to meet Uncle Edward and Aunt Glen at the Empress Hotel for dinner. Roddy also went back to the Gold River with friend and neighbor Van Egan and caught one nice fish in spite of a low river. He "wrote a piece on Commercial Fishing for the London *Times*, but haven't yet made much more progress with *Fisherman's Fall*." Celie "arrived back from school with two Stevenson girls from Quadra – their mother died recently and they are going to stay with an aunt somewhere soon, so Mother invited them over here." The girls were twins, aged sixteen, and they ended up staying with us. Roddy wrote me after a late January visit, "The twins were with us when I got back and are here until June, boy problems, bad grammar and all. They keep things lively and (who knows) we may be able to help with their problems, semantic and romantic." One sister, Isabel, left soon, but Mary stayed and has said her time at our house meant a great deal to her. He went on: "This letter is being written at the usual intervals of listening to a drunk woman screaming over the phone, sending the police to do something about it, going up to Van Egan's for a small meeting on Parks, and so forth. In other words, everything is just about normal."

In February, daughter Mary came to stay and wait for the baby, just as Mary Weiler also used to come from Cortes to wait for hers. Ann wrote to me: "She's awfully good to have around. Daddy and Celie and I have had pretty bad colds and Mary keeps things sweetly calm. Mary S. does all the washing and ironing; Isabel, the cleaning and Celie and I, food and dishes ... Needless to say there are quite a few little conflicts and without Mary, our gentle referee, I don't know what we'll do. In a letter to Alan, Roddy reported: "[Local native carver] Sam Henderson has made me the killer whale – a little larger than the other one – and the two look very fine over the study fireplace together." The second whale had been commissioned to celebrate the publication of *The Whale People*.

The "gentle referee" was around until March 6, when Celia Gwenith was born. Roddy wrote me on March 18: "Mary's baby is a fine little creature and has been putting on weight at about twice the normal rate so far. We brought her home from the hospital last Tuesday and they took her over to Cortes on Sunday, after the christening. She hollered all through that, but seemed pretty well settled down by the time we put Mother and child on the plane at 2 p.m." Roddy was able to get in some more fishing, this time with Ted Weeks, the editor of *The Atlantic Monthly*. (*The Atlantic* had bought the first chapter of *Fisherman's Fall* which Roddy said was Ann's idea.) Celie was in a performance of *The Egg and I* at school, "A huge success and more particularly a hell of a lot of fun for all concerned. I doubt if Celie has the makings of a great actress, but her ability to whistle through her fingers was hugely appreciated by both audience and cast." (Celie can still whistle down a cab or an errant child from a major distance, and does.)

In early May Roddy wrote me: "Tomorrow morning the water-line people are going to blow the big stump by the barn – another landmark gone, but I don't think we shall miss it much if that's all they do." At the end of the month he wrote, "Our big excitement of the past week has been the 20" pipeline [for the town water supply] going through. They took out the whole barn field fence and put it back in good shape, blew out the big stump by the gate and part of the barn roof with it, but they were a nice bunch of fellows and I kind of enjoyed it all."

In mid-July, Roddy wrote me: "I did my first skin-diving last night and it was above my expectations in every way – one sees beautifully, everything, bottom, bubbles, fish, weeds and so forth; it is warm and comfortable; the flippers make swimming very easy and effective; the various breathing tricks take a bit of getting on to, but it is simply a matter of practice." The diving was an enormous pleasure and became the stuff of several chapters in *Fisherman's Fall*. Roddy says in that book that "curiosity ... love of the fish and love of the water" led him to take up the very new sport with Campbell River friends. Ann, on the other hand, used to say she stood at the bottom of the lawn by the river and worried a lot.

By fall Mary and Bernie had moved to West Vancouver; Bernie was teaching at a North Vancouver high school; Alan was at the University of B.C. working on a B.Ed.; and Celie was still happily at home. Ann used to say that she and Celie had such good rapport because they "went to high school together in the sixties." Roddy was delighting in watching the salmon come back to the Campbell River to spawn from under the water – "skin-diving the salmon home" as he put it in a letter to Edward Dunn.

The walnut tree on the lawn had a huge crop that fall – "I should judge not less than 16 buckets." The walnuts were an essential part of the fruitcakes we always had for Christmas. Celie was deep in the world of horses, with much "excitement over the formation of a Campbell River

Riding Club. She went to a [church] retreat over the weekend of the initial meeting ... but seems to have been nominated for all the various offices and seems pretty determined to be president and run the show if she can. Fortunately she has a sense of humor about herself and it."

In mid-November Glen and Edward came for the grouse hunting weekend: "... luxurious – lousy hunting, beautiful weather, excellent wining and dining. Court has been very busy and seems to be going to hold up that way. I now seem to sit [as magistrate] most of the day on Mondays, Tuesdays and Fridays, and somewhat still on Saturdays."

By February of 1964, Roddy was attempting scuba diving. He bought tanks of his own a few months later, which he justified to himself as being affordable because *Sports Illustrated* bought the diving chapters of *Fisherman's Fall*. The endless procession of meetings and talks went on with the annual gathering of the B.C. Natural Resources Conference in Victoria, and a meeting of the Fisheries Council on the new Fraser River plan in Vancouver and, next day, talks to both Teacher-Librarians and the Capilano Rod and Gun Club. The B.C. parks were under threat from the right-wing Social Credit government's development schemes and there was a great demand for statements for the papers, talks to stir the troops and meetings with anyone and everyone. "The parks business has been a fearful disturbance and looks like going on for a while. Frankly I feel desperate about it."

In mid-March, "The Bishop came to breakfast after Mass on Sunday with considerable ceremony. Mother and Celie served from the kitchen while the Bishop, Father, Ray Carpenter, Al Malo and I breakfasted in state in the living room ... the Bishop is a charming guy and was most interesting about Rome." The bishop was Remi De Roo, recently named head of the diocese, who became a good friend of both my parents. He is a very liberal Catholic and a fly fisherman, thus he and Ann and Roddy had common ground in at least two areas. On March 24, Ann's mother died quietly at St. Mary's Priory and was buried in Colwood Cemetery nearby. She was ninety-one.

In June, Celie finished high school and graduated with due ceremony. "She ... looked beautiful. Everybody, but everybody commented that evening and next day." Roddy "flew up to Sointula [near Alert Bay] and spoke to the six graduates of Malcolm Island school ... I stayed overnight with the Art Lansdownes [part of the Lansdowne family from Nimpkish days], which was a lot of fun – much visiting and talk till 4 a.m." Roddy reported to Alan: "Celie is driving the car and takes her test next week. Poor old Jag. It's running well though and may survive. It had better. I've been working so badly that I'm not making much money and I haven't managed to talk the attorney general out of any more salary [as magistrate] so far."

In July, Roddy's sister Joan came from England to spend the summer, joined later by their cousin Agatha Leas. We all made a point of visiting in their honor – not that we wouldn't have been there anyway – and showing off the great-nieces. A Pacific Northwest Writer's Conference interrupted the summer in August and Ann fitted in a couple of Vancouver Festival cultural events as well.

In the fall Celie stayed in Campbell River for grade thirteen (first year of university). Mary and Bernie and Celia II or G., as she was often called then, had gone to England to spend two years travelling and teaching. Alan was at UBC and Vickie was also going to school. She went on to UBC and completed her B.Ed.

In September, Roddy went to a major environmental conference in Aspen, Colorado, sponsored by Trout Unlimited and attended by such national figures as Stewart Udall, then Secretary of the Interior. He was picked up in Denver by old friends Martin and Hopi Bovey and driven into the mountains after seeing a conservation center being developed by the Public Library there. The conference was impressive, and Roddy was thoroughly enjoying himself when his back, which had been bothering him before he left, went completely. He was put in traction in the Aspen Hospital, which was, of course, well-supplied with bone specialists who got lots of experience on the skiers. It was thought that a screw in the fusion had come loose. After a few days, a friend of the Boveys flew him to Livingston, Montana, where he hoped to join the post-conference fishing, but instead he had to go straight on to Shaughnessy Hospital in Vancouver where they sorted out the trouble fairly quickly. By the end of September he was home and swimming in his wet suit again.

Household improvements that fall included an electric baseboard heater in Roddy's study, new carpet and lamps for the living room and Spode "India Tree" pattern china for the dinner table. The lamps were made from two ornate bronze vases complete with cherubs inherited from Roddy's Aunt Katie. Things were getting quite elegant!

A Primer of Fly Fishing was finally published after much annoying stalling by Morrow, as well as *Fisherman's Fall.* Doubly annoying to have two books come out at once, since it was bound to affect sales. In retrospect, the saddest aspect of this double event is that these were the last two books Roddy wrote, other than a couple of commissioned ones for the federal fisheries department. He had plans for others, especially on birds and on being a magistrate, and considered an autobiography, but the pressure of the other aspects of his life kept him from getting started on them. Roddy summed it up only too well in a letter to me in November, in which he first gave the details of his next Vancouver-Victoria trip. "I am still going very slowly with my work, and there has been no time at all to go swimming or anything. All this going off speech making is the worst trouble, plus refusing other requests to speak and generally dealing with the mail. As soon as I get that done I'm back in court for a couple of full days, then there's mail and stuff again. I've got to stop it somehow." It can be argued that, if Roddy had wanted to, he would have made time to write more. But he did have an enormous sense of obligation about the kind of public service represented by his work on the bench and in the conservation movement. There was also the changing nature of publishing. Roddy had originally formed a close relationship with the people at Morrow in New York, but there were new people there now and the era of the blockbuster bestseller was taking over. Books on fly-fishing were no longer likely to be the big thing on the list – and Roddy felt, anyway, that he had written all he wanted to on that subject. He also felt some annoyance at not being noticed by the wider literary community, in spite of his often-praised ability, but neither the essay form that came naturally to him nor the subject of fishing were particularly valued in those circles.

Another interruption was Roddy's appointment to the Federal Electoral Boundaries Commission. The boundaries of the ridings had to be redrawn according to population shifts. The three appointed commissioners were required to hold public hearings all over B.C. Roddy was often in Vancouver for hearings, or on his way to or from other parts of B.C., so we heard much of the deliberations. He enjoyed the process and spent a great deal of time poring over maps and statistics to arrive at logical boundaries according to population, natural geographical divisions and traditional corridors of travel and commerce. Roddy served on the Commission again in 1972-73 and finally in 1975-76, by which time he was growing a little weary of the job.

In February of 1965, Roddy went on another marathon trip east, beginning with a talk in Minneapolis to flyfishers at the Country Club. He continued east via Toronto to Boston and New York, where he both entertained and was entertained lavishly by friends old and new. He spoke to the Flycasters in Boston and the Anglers Club in New York. He wrote Ann four letters during a week-long stay at the Algonquin Hotel in New York, wishing very much that she were with him. On February 14, he started a letter: "Here I am at last, and just at the moment I find myself wondering exactly why I bothered. Bumbling around the countryside without you doesn't seem to make very much sense and I don't think I'm going to do it any more." (He always regretted that, by the time Ann's responsibilities at home eased off enough so that she might have travelled with him, she was deeply involved in her librarian's job most of the year and could not.) When not meeting with publishers or friends and acquaintances, Roddy saw as much as he could of museums, especially Impressionist paintings.

In a letter to Alan in May Roddy said: "I have my deputy magistrate now and my court clerk has been made a Justice of the Peace, so things should be easier. I have my regrets though, because it will take things further away from people and red tape will creep in." The court clerk being a J.P. meant there would be fewer people requiring Roddy's signature to court and other documents, to say nothing of the police themselves. It had become an almost daily occurrence for a police car to swing up the driveway, and an officer get out and walk around to the study door with a handful of official blue papers to be signed. When I was little the policeman was the father of a friend, but by this time he was often a young, very polite man rather in awe of the judge.

Later that same month, Roddy wrote Edward Dunn about a visit Edward was planning in June to look at land on Quadra Island. The letter went on to say: "We've just had a merry gymkhana day [competitive events on horseback, but gentler than rodeoing] here that everyone greatly enjoyed, thanks to the ideal weather. Between that and track triumphs, Celie's room is so beribboned that little wall-space is left. I have been diving occasionally and now have an underwater camera, though I haven't yet solved the matter of underwater exposures. Alan has been up here for his practice teaching and now has a job relieving the principal [Ann's old job at Quadra Island] three days a week. Vickie has gone back to Vancouver to finish her school year."

In an effort to improve a crumbling marriage by a change of scene, and in pursuit of an idea that had been around for some time anyway, Joe and I moved to Campbell River in the summer of 1965 and Joe opened an office. The town had grown so much that there was room for a third law office in addition to the two small firms already there. This, of course, meant no more letters to me, but there were others, as the family continued to spread out. Celie joined Alan at the University of B.C. in the fall, and Mary and Bernie were still in Europe.

But the major event that fall was Ann's new job as librarian at the Senior Secondary School. She was still working on an annual letter of permission and had worried, when the high school was split into junior and senior sections, that she would be unlikely to get the senior library. The principal of the new school was John Young and he had some rather revolutionary ideas about education. The students were expected to take considerable responsibility for themselves and often did individually tailored courses arrived at by negotiating with their teachers. This made the job both challenging and stimulating for Ann. The library was to be the core of the school and she settled in with some 10,000 volumes and proceeded to make it just that, through all the political ups and downs of the next few years.

At the end of the first term John Young wrote Ann a memo that read, in part: "I have already expressed to you, orally, my pleasure and satisfaction at the exceptional manner in which you have approached the formidable task of setting up the new library. I am very much aware of the great amount of extra time, and effort – and love – that you have devoted to the library. You have done it all with competence and efficiency. As a result of your labours, the library is quite clearly our pride and joy."

In January of 1966, Ann wrote Celie of a dinner party in Victoria that included Ted Weeks, editor of *The Atlantic*, and Bruce Hutchison, editorial director of *The Vancouver Sun* – "six people who all knew what the others were talking about." Ann had admired the freesias on that dinner table, saying they reminded her of elegant Seattle parties, so Roddy got some for their anniversary a few days later, to her great delight. At the end of the letter, Ann reports: "Daddy is sadly sawing off broken branches from almost every tree." Heavy, wet coastal snowfalls frequently damaged the many exotic trees on the place.

In February Paul St. Pierre, best-known for his books on the people of B.C.'s Chilcotin Plateau, in his column in *The Vancouver Sun* nominated Roddy as "The Average Canadian," who was bound to be sought with the Canadian Centennial just a year away. St. Pierre dealt with the rather un-average fact that Roddy had written twenty-two books by this time, by saying, "We all have to make a living somehow." After a brief rundown of the "ordinary" details of Roddy's life, such as: "He still keeps a few sheep on the place, together with a 3.8 Jaguar," and "His most notable display of business acumen was when he bought Giant Mascot mining stock at a dollar, just before it dropped to 10 cents," St. Pierre went on:

> *He remains thin, a condition his mother long attributed to his habit of reading gloomy Russian novels. He has a face which would serve as a model for an Indian head on an American nickel.*
>
> *He dresses neatly, almost nattily. In his court he uses words such as 'sure' and 'okay' and often when there is something worth smiling about, he smiles ...*

He has had less money than some people and more sport than others. But is there anything so typically Canadian about him, except perhaps the reverse typicality of failing to fit any pigeonhole of anybody's desk?

There is one other feature: He is, above all, a natural man, with quiet manners. If we're going to have candidates for Average Canadians let's not, for heaven's sake, pick noisy ones.

In an unusually long letter to Alan in March, Roddy wrote in detail of the cleanup and fencing he was doing around the place with the help of the tractor. In answer to Alan's suggestion that he quit, after listening to his complaints about the time court took, Roddy wrote: "Because I don't think it would be right to – though I am certainly tempted. When one has put in this much time gaining experience, one wants to pass it on to someone who will carry it on reasonably well – not just leave it all to chance ... I wish, though, they would appoint a deputy [the previous one had been taken ill] and also start paying me in a semi-reasonable way."

Alan was finishing his degree and looking for a job – he hoped to go to the Interior of B.C. to work with the native people. Ann was papering the newly remodelled kitchen; "one way or another we are keeping the old place together, but where we'll get to in the end I'm damned if I know – I think the taxes will be up this year." A crew from the National Film Board was coming to see about making a film on fly-fishing. The cat had three kittens and Roddy had kept all of them – I had been in that morning with the granddaughters who were "packing the kittens all over."

To Edward Dunn Roddy wrote of "Alan getting some very good marks indeed and Vickie is happy with her kindergarten courses." Alan still relishes the story of the day he was in a group reading class marks posted on a professor's door and heard someone say, "Who's this guy Haig-Brown who gets all the high marks?" Sweet revenge for the kid who was the despair of his parents all through high school.

In early June the annual Magistrate's Conference was held in Campbell River. "We had a tremendously busy week, people here every night and sometimes twice, but it all went very smoothly indeed and we got some useful business done, perhaps even some final and useful settlement on salaries." By mid-June Celie was taking census statistics on horseback and starting work at the local paper. In July Roddy's sister Valerie came to visit and so did Ann's brother Bucky. Mary and Bernie got back from Europe and returned to West Vancouver where Bernie was head of English at Carson Graham High School. In the fall they adopted Desmond Alan, a Haida boy who was only a few weeks old. Alan and

Vickie settled into their little cottage on the place for the winter, as they both had teaching jobs on Quadra Island.

In January of 1967, I gave up on my marriage after trying to come to grips with the problems of a manic-depressive (only we didn't know it at the time) husband, and went to Toronto. The children stayed with their father for three months and then went to live with Mary and Bernie until they came to me in Toronto in early December. I had found editorial work through a connection from my university newspaper days, and we lived in Toronto for the next ten years or so.

It fell on the family to deal with a lot of chaos from my departure. The first concern was the children and, although I wanted them to come to me, it was decided they should go to Mary and Bernie at first. It soon became evident that Joe could not carry on his law practice either. My father and mother spent many hours supporting him emotionally or trying to calm his manic phase – neither was easy, or even possible – and the burden of worry added considerably to the stress of that year, to say nothing of the time it took to sort out the details of winding up his law practice and selling our house.

Even in the midst of our agonized correspondence over the consequences of my leaving, there were still reports on the progress of the season. In April, my father wrote: "The camellia is blooming and very beautiful. A lot of daffodils are out and the flowering trees won't be long – in fact the quince on the study has already started a little. I have three loads of fresh gravel on the driveway, which looks nice and the car has just been waxed, which also looks nice. The grass has not started to grow over the new septic tank and drainfield, but at least I have seeded it." It was always clear that a day working around outdoors in the garden and the fields was an antidote to the pressures of the rest of life. Roddy spoke in Portland (the Flyfishers Club of Oregon); Alberni, on the west side of Vancouver Island (Education Week); and Spokane, Washington, that spring. The Spokane talk was to "the Pacific Northwest Trade Association, presumably a group hostile to any respectable conservation ideas." The flight to Spokane was through Seattle so Roddy and Ann stopped overnight and went to the opera with Glen and Edward.

The National Film Board fly-fishing film made the previous year was to be called *Fisherman's Fall*; Roddy went to Vancouver to do the narration in June. A new film on Babine Lake in northern B.C. was being planned. Celie went to Expo67 in Montreal (as did Alan and Vickie later in the summer) before going to summer school in Vancouver in order to get the jump on her final year at UBC. In mid-summer Roddy went north and Ann went to California to visit Bucky and Gar, her Aunt

Mai and two cousins. Roddy "got most of my material for the Babine Lake film script and spent a week up around the Spatsizi Plateau, at the headwaters of the Stikine, Nass, Spatsizi and Finlay, making a [CBC] TV film for their Telescope series. Exciting country, good fishing, but very far north – we woke up to find frost on our gear the last two mornings."

At the end of August, Roddy, Ann and Celie went to the third annual Conclave of the Federation of Fly Fishers in Jackson, Wyoming, where Roddy was one of the main speakers. They made a leisurely trip down and the conclave was "all good fun and very instructive." Ann flew back to be in time for the opening of school, and Roddy and Celie went on to visit with the Bovey family and fish around Montana. Possibly the longest lasting result of the trip was that, while they were in Nevada City, they "picked up a stray border collie that had become mysteriously locked in the old brewery. Very cute and smart. Named her Montana, Tana for short." Tana worked her way into Roddy's heart as no other dog had done, and there are probably more references to her in the letters than any other dog.

Alan had finally reached his goal of working with native people by getting a job teaching at the residential school in Williams Lake, B.C., that fall. The school was in its final year, and Alan went from there to teach in the small native villages of the Chilcotin Plateau for several years. The now-empty spaces in the main house and Alan's cottage soon filled up with more of the succession of, in those years, teenagers needing room to grow. Sometimes they were children of friends, sometimes kids attracted to Campbell River by the growing reputation of John Young's school for freedom to study in one's own way or slightly older people who wanted to know Roddy better because of his writing and ideas, especially about conservation.

In October, Roddy was working on the Babine script. Next was to be "a long piece for a new quarterly called *The American Sportsman*. It isn't too easy to write these days, or at least I don't find it so. My renovated court set up is a great improvement over the old ... but it seems to keep me down there longer hours and on the whole I seem to get more exhausted." Tommy Brayshaw died and Roddy went to Vancouver for the funeral. Then he and Ann went again in a few days – she for a librarians' conference and he to see the finished salmon exhibit in the Vancouver Aquarium for which he had been a consultant and written the text.

In early December *The American Sportsman* piece, "In Search of Trout," was finished, Roddy talked to "the NDP caucus at the Discovery Inn [in Campbell River]. Court is busy. I go to Gold River [to hold court there, a weekly event] again this Wednesday. Next weekend we have some musicians from California coming to stay and, they hope, catch a steelhead. I also have to go to Vancouver to speak to the John Howard Society banquet. Sounds like a roughish time to me." Roddy reported on that trip to Gold River, a new pulp mill town on the other side of Vancouver Island, fifty miles west of Campbell River, in a letter to Alan a few days later: "I went to Gold River in a snowstorm and a howling gale. Took four hours to come home. Loaded logging truck jack-knifed across the road, trees down, everything you could want. I had an axe." He made these trips in a Volkswagen beetle they had bought as a second car – far more practical for rough travel than the patrician Jaguar of the day.

Year end letters told that Mary was expecting another baby in June; my children were settling in happily in Toronto; and Celie was dealing with her final year of university. Roddy spent a night at the jail sitting with one of the resident kids who had been picked up while high on an asthma remedy with friends – "Watching them in the high state is a rather shocking experience ... there have been many discussions and meetings of school counsellors and probation officers and social workers since then. The kids are reasonably scared and I don't think they'll experiment again for a few weeks or months."

To Alan in February Roddy wrote: "I have been running scared, trying to catch a deadline with a piece about Pacific salmon for *The American Sportsman*, and writing very few letters ... Very busy evenings last week. Had to speak at a panel at the school – Love and Marriage ... Thursday night Mother took me off to see *Georgy Girl* at the local movie palace. It was good, and few people there. Some popcorn, but no crawling brats. Friday night was the Fish and Game Smoker. Quite good fun. Tonight the Parish Committee had dinner here and a brief meeting and have now gone off to a bigger meeting ... I offered Mother a beer in the Quinsam after the movie, but she didn't think so." (I doubt either Ann or Roddy ever set foot in the local beer parlor in their lives.)

In March, Roddy and Ann spent a few days in New York with a brief stop in Toronto. The New York trip was to speak to the Theodore Gordon Flyfishers. "Mother managed the ballet, the Philharmonic, the Metropolitan, the Frick museum, the Public Library and St. Patrick's Cathedral on St. Patrick's Day. We had a wonderful dinner with the Ruddicks – the Lionel Trillings and the Frank Russells – a dinner with the Theodore Gordon people at Luchow's, the banquet ... and gave ourselves an expensive dinner at the Rainbow Room. I had successful meetings with various editors – *Life, Sports Illustrated, The American Sportsman.* A much less satisfactory lunch with the Wm. Morrow people. I am still not sure what exactly was wrong with it, but plenty was." The fact is that Morrow did not publish Roddy's books again, and the lunch was probably bought only out of a sense of duty by people who weren't terribly interested. But the fishing titles were all picked up by Nick Lyons when he was an editor at Doubleday and he has kept most of them in print ever since, either with Doubleday's Crown imprint or, later, with his own firm.

In May, Roddy made a trip to the west coast of Vancouver Island with a Vancouver Aquarium collecting expedition which he much enjoyed. Robin Taylor, his publisher at Collins Canada, came to discuss their reprints of the books; and Ann had arranged for an ex-teacher friend, Jenny Tweed, to come in occasionally to type and organize for Roddy.

The previous fall Mary and Bernie, in view of the much larger family they suddenly had – they had expected my children to stay longer – had a new house started in West Vancouver. It was completed that spring and Roddy described it to me: "It really is a spectacular place, all glass and unpainted cedar and different levels that make big spaces and quiet crannies. No doors or walls except on the ground floor [children's bedrooms]. No garden except woods tight around the house. It scares us silly to see the youngest, Dabby [for his initials D.A.B.], climbing up and down the open stairways, but he just grins and Mary says it's o.k., not to fuss."

In May of 1968, Celie got her B.A. Ann and Roddy went to Vancouver for the occasion and to "a small dinner given by the Koerner's afterwards." Among the guests was honorary degree recipient, writer Hugh MacLennan, whom Roddy and Ann admired immensely. Celie had a job that summer with Montana State Fish and Game "looking at deer guts." She planned to go on for an M.A. in biological sciences later.

In mid-June Mary and Roddy were both in hospital. Mary gave birth to Elizabeth Ann, who got off to a worrisome start for a few days, but has been going strong ever since. Roddy had a lump removed. Ann described it all to me: "Daddy had a lump on his cheek which had been bothering me like mad and him moderately all winter. It was removed ... and to my incredible joy and amazement it wasn't cancer, but a sort of infection in his salivary gland. He believed all the doctors that told him it wasn't malignant; but I didn't for a minute ... Two crises at once at least dulled the edge of each other and make now incredibly beautiful."

In July Roddy went to Iceland with Bill Gregory from Minneapolis to write on the fishing for *The American Sportsman*. "I enjoyed [Iceland] immensely and had probably the finest fishing of my life. Very beautiful country, lots of arctic birds and flowers, splendid Atlantic salmon taking beautifully in a lovely little river. *The American Sportsman* sent a very hot New York photographer ..." I remember particularly my father talking often of how much he enjoyed being with the guides who told the sagas (oral history) as if the events they record had happened yesterday.

In August Ann and Roddy went to California via the Oregon coast to view Trout Unlimited's Hat Creek fisheries enhancement project in the Sierras near Fall River Mills. Their host, Joe Paul, then took them down to San Francisco where they spent four days "pretty busy, with two private dinners, a very large reception, a fund raising lunch at the Bohemian Club and so on. But we had some time to ourselves, too." On the way back they visited Ann's brother and sister-in-law, Bucky and Gar, briefly, and then went on to spend three days on the beach at Otter Rock, Oregon, where they had picked out the perfect place to stay on the way down.

In Victoria on the way home they refurbished Roddy's study. In an anecdotal list of some household items she did years later for her children Ann described the day. "... the Jaguar coughed up trouble just as we got off the ferry. The garage was by the Hudson's Bay so in we went and I showed Roddy the wool rug sample I had thought of to replace the worn-out turquoise one in the study. He borrowed it, went down the line of drapery samples and picked the curtains. Then I found him sitting happily on this gold couch (on sale for $400) with the curtain sample thrown over the back of it and the carpet sample at his feet. All set."

Nothing slowed down in September, either in Roddy's travels or the decorating. Celie was off to Mexico for the fall with an artist friend, with her father grumbling that she should have got going on graduate school. Roddy went to a Sportsmen's Show and a Magistrate's Conference in Vancouver; their bedroom had huge new windows and lots of fresh white paint. "Mother is doing her 10 a.m. to 6 p.m. stuff in the library and liking it rather well. She also has the place filled with waifs and strays – one in the house and three in the cottage. The rumor around town is that the place is a front for drugs. Oh well." That was to Alan and a little later he wrote to me describing the same scene and said: "I guess the only real way out is to burn down the cottage and tear the top floor off the house. I growl at them like an old lion and don't give them any lee-way, but Mother's care and sympathy more than make up for that."

In October one week: "I had to go to Powell River [on the B.C. mainland] to hear a case, which made five solid days in court [this says nothing of the time spent out of court on paper work or studying the law] this week, and on Saturday the Cape Mudge councillors were here to discuss how to change the Indian Act. It isn't just that easy to decide even what is desirable, much less how to get at it." Increasing population up and down the coast meant more cases in the courts and more serious crimes. Judges covered for each other when one was away or ill, or when there was a conflict of interest – always possible in small towns. Thus there was yet another increasing demand on Roddy to travel.

The weather over Christmas was particularly cold. Alan and Vickie and Celie were all there for the day, and Mary and Bernie and their three children came the day after for a few days. Celie went back with Alan and Vickie to work in Williams Lake in the B.C. Interior as a teacher aide.

In January of 1969, Roddy was still overwhelmed with court business. "At the moment there is no district magistrate and I seem to be filling in for one – at least I have to go to Alert Bay next month for two preliminary inquiries, a murder and a manslaughter. My own court is busy with trials most days of the week ... We had a CBC crew here for a couple of intensive days finishing off the Babine Lake film for 'Telescope.' I was also cleaning up some short pieces for various fishing magazines, but I hope I am free now to settle down to a book. It has been a long time and I am not really happy without one going." Ann wrote that "our overall school atmosphere is not very good. The new board is determined to pick on every detail, so the happy atmosphere which was really all we ever had is kind of gone."

In February Roddy was still overburdened with court work. "Everything is to be changed soon anyway; most of us are to become judges of the provincial court ... I wish I had more time to go fishing, and lots more time to write, but both will come to me in time I imagine."

In March the very heavy snow of that winter was still around in the trees and the frost still in the ground. Roddy had two packed showings of the newly released NFB *Fisherman's Fall* film in the local school, which he showed again in April to the Boston Flycasters when he and Ann went there. They also stopped in Toronto for two days to visit with me and their granddaughters. Shortly after Roddy wrote: "Home in good time – looking at Pacific brant geese on the way, having looked for Atlantic brant off Cape Cod the day before."

In May Roddy's back laid him low for a week, but he recovered in time to go to Vancouver for a Fisheries Advisory Council meeting and then drive up the Fraser River to visit Alan in the Chilcotin. Afterwards he wrote: "It was a wonderful visit, with more interests and excitements than I had possibly imagined. Stoney is a wonderful place and its people are beautiful." In the same letter, "Mother has gone off to a Voice of Women [peace activists] meeting, to the distress of some of her Catholic pals who came last night to warn her not to get mixed up with those communists. Mother said: 'You had better not say any more or I will go and get myself elected president.' I told them to stop, too, because I was afraid she might."

In June, the annual Magistrate's Conference had Roddy back in the Cariboo region at Prince George, a pulp mill town at the confluence of the Fraser and Nechako rivers. Later in the month, Roddy went with UBC friends to fish at Penask Lake, west of Lake Okanagan, also an annual event. The summer seemed quiet "except that Mother has a thing about immense gatherings. She had thirty teachers here for dinner on graduation night. On the weekend following, the Palo Alto string orchestra, with an open house for their trio on Sunday. Today about 10 assorted Catechism teachers to lunch, and next weekend a reception after the concert to be given by a Vancouver string quartet. I have to admit that at least some of it sort of 'happens' to us, but it sure raises the tone of the old establishment."

The summer ended with Ann and Roddy travelling to Sun Valley for the Federation of Fly Fishers Conclave (Roddy was a senior adviser) where they "stayed with the Jack Hemingways —pleasant and very interesting, as Jack talks quite freely of Ernest. I had some good fishing in ... Stoker Creek." Jack was Ernest's son and, as an avid flyfisher and fan, had visited Roddy in Campbell River years before. Roddy's prose is sometimes compared with Hemingway's, so he may have been interested on that account in the son's perception of the father.

After spending "most of her summer working in a meat packing plant and going around to every rodeo and stampede in the country riding wild cows and anything else that's handy," Celie was taking teacher training at UBC. Roddy was speaking to the Totem Fly Fishers in Vancouver, the National Parks Association in Calgary, writing a fourth piece for *The American Sportsman* (on steelhead) and wanting to get on with "a good solid book." The letter ends, "Tell the children the animals are fine, the Gravensteins are ripe and the beaver cut down the larger of my two willow trees at the foot of the lawn. I have put galvanized sheathing around the other, but I'm pretty mad. The one he cut was just getting to an important size. He seems to live up along the Line Fence Pool."

At the end of September Roddy wrote: "Mary has her new [adopted] baby, part Negro and straight out of the hospital at 4 days old." The first of the literary papers —eleven boxes —were sent off to the UBC Library Special Collections that fall. The cottage, still very much Alan's house, was being upgraded with heaters, a new counter, and a new sink. Later, after his first visit with Mary and Bernie's new baby, Benjamin Edward, Roddy wrote, "He is just fine, very dark eyes, pleasantly placid, yet very alert and strong. Mary is very well and extremely happy with them all."

.13. Fisherman's Fall (1969 – 1976)

The children really were all on their own by now, but any decrease in family demands was more than offset by the much greater demands made on Roddy, particularly by increased responsibilities in the wider world. His seemingly innate sense of public service continued to keep him from his writer's desk. An event of major impact on Roddy's life (and his time) in the fall of 1969 was his election as chancellor of the University of Victoria. He ran at the request of the faculty who were involved in a controversy over tenure, and, while he was quite aware that the position was honorary, he felt that he could probably make a difference. To congratulatory friends from the academic community he wrote, "I am probably the unlikeliest Chancellor that ever tipped a mortar board, but they – and I – will have to make what we can of that."

Within a couple of months Roddy was appointed to an even larger job. He was named one of the six commissioners on the International Pacific Salmon Fisheries Commission, a position that required a great deal of hard work and was far from ceremonial in any way. There were three commissioners from the U.S. and three from Canada, and their job was to regulate the catch of salmon from the Fraser River and its tributaries, as well as to coordinate enhancement and conservation activities in the Fraser. A Seattle paper wrote at the time: "Commercial fishermen and sports fishermen on both sides of the border are thoroughly familiar with the name and fame of the new commissioner. For the information of others, it may be fairly stated that Roderick Haig-Brown is possessed of the most informed eloquence on the subject of fishery conservation of anyone in this part of the world ... His appointment to the Salmon Commission is no mere political plum. It was made on the recommendation of Fisheries Minister Jack Davis, whose parliamentary constituency has a long frontage on the Strait of Georgia. Mr. Davis has demonstrated on other occasions his courageous devotion to the cause of fishery conservation ... Haig-Brown's eloquent voice, never long silent, will henceforth have the added weight of official authority."

By March of 1970, Roddy was deep in both jobs with no let up of other demands either. "Last weekend I went to Edmonton to make the keynote address for the Alberta Wildlife Federation Convention. This weekend we drove to Victoria in a violent snowstorm to spend the whole of Saturday at an Environment Teach-in at the University ... In some ways it's quite a different way of living. Essentially we do the same things – live at home, go to the library, go to court, clean up outside, feed the animals and so on, but practically all the time we are fitting and planning other things into it – or vice versa, I'm not sure which. It is stimulating, often pleasant and quite exhausting.

"Next week is a bit easier. I do have to go to Gold River for a full day of court and probably to a Salmon Commission meeting on Friday. The next week is bad again. Monday is a University Board of Governors' meeting. Tuesday I am visiting the colleges for lunch and dinner, I have a seminar in the p.m. and a lecture in the evening. Home the next 3 days (in court) then we both go down to Victoria to the AMS [student society] awards banquet Saturday night. I describe all this to give some picture of what has happened to what seemed busy before but now seems to have been fairly peaceful." Much of this work meant travel by car – a four-hour drive to get to Victoria, or flying to Vancouver and changing planes, or catching a ferry instead after a two-hour drive. Salmon Commission meetings were often in Bellingham – midway between Seattle and Vancouver. In winter weather travel any way could be unpredictable at best and dangerous at times.

To Alan, Roddy wrote: "The Salmon Commission is also interesting and complex. The international implications are formidable, and not simply vis-a-vis the U.S. I am really much more looking forward to the possibilities of more development and improvement work on the watershed ... I get a little writing time, but speeches and letters keep it to short things." To Edward Dunn, he said: "... I'm afraid the terms of reference [of the Salmon Commission] are a bit restrictive. I don't think I will let them muzzle me though, and am already looking for ways to get at the

Lower Fraser pollution." Roddy's correspondence with Alan also talked of plans to set up Native Studies courses at the University of Victoria. It was hoped to eventually have a transitional setup to perhaps make it easier for native students to succeed in the campus setting.

In the summer of 1970, my children came out from Toronto to spend part of the summer with their grandparents, and I came home toward the end of August to gather them up in time for school. "Home" wasn't much changed and the children spent their time much as I had in the summers – and as they had before they moved to Toronto. The house was a constant and a center even as we all spread out. Celie had finished her teacher training and had a job in the high school at Kamloops.

At the end of September, Roddy wrote: "My life seems to be an endless round of speeches and meetings. My main crusade now is for the Fraser salmon – clean up pollution, block the Moran dam which has come up again, get money for development [of salmon enhancement structures such as spawning channels]. But then we have the U. Vic. bit, too. Board of Governors meetings, social events, and philosophical musings on the function of education. Tomorrow Mother and I are going off to a Judges' meeting in Duncan [south of Nanaimo] and on to Victoria the next day to a president's reception for newly promoted professors. In between times I get back here, answer my mail, sit in court and refuse further speaking engagements." Ann was feeling stressed, too, as the political pendulum in the community swung to the conservative side, and John Young's school began to be seen as too progressive and free. Ann's library was never under attack, but the atmosphere in the school was no longer as congenial as it had been.

In October, after going to Kamloops and the Thompson River tributary, the Adams, home of one of the Fraser River's most spectacular sockeye salmon runs, for the "Salute to the Sockeye," Roddy wrote Alan: "... the salmon were beautiful, a full spawning of, we think, about ¼ million. The right channel of the river has been greatly improved and should produce a much higher survival rate than the last few cycles. The Minister [of Fisheries] and the U.S. Ambassador were there ... We had a drink with Celie and her cowboy friend, Ted, but he said he wasn't going to talk, and by God he didn't ... Uncle Edward and Aunt Glen were here the weekend just past for the grouse." The chancellor's job had Roddy in the midst of controversy "over this damned fool provincial edict about firing teachers who express support for the FLQ [violent Quebec separatists], as you have probably noticed."

In January of 1971, Roddy wrote Alan: "Things here are hectic as usual. I am depressed tonight [a rare admission], because court seems to be getting very hopeless. There are the everlasting drugs, and trafficking means jail sentences. Now I am starting to get heroin cases ... I could go on, but won't. U. Vic. is also acting up. We had a students' protest meeting ... I kind of enjoyed most of it and learned a lot. They were perfectly nice to me, but essentially it was a sour business and there will be more trouble ... On the brighter side of things, Mother and I spent a happy weekend in Vancouver ..."

By March, "Celie is more and more interested in Ted, so maybe we'll have someone in the family who can fix fences at last. We've been fixing fences some ... Mother and Celia are still planning to go to Italy and I guess I'm going to Iceland sometime in July ..."

Ann wrote Edward Dunn about the U. Vic. situation: "... first the pres. calls Roddy and worries for half an hour – then a radical student comes up and explains it all his way – then the chairman of the board gets him on the phone before he's up – then the faculty sends him a most reasonable petition. And poor Roddy, who's accustomed to hearing *two* (only) sides of a question and then deciding in his wisdom, hasn't got a legal right to knock any two heads together." As for herself, she said, "Mr. Young, principal, told me yesterday he hadn't heard me when I last resigned; and I, feeling fine, told him I hadn't said it – so here we go again. Our school, having been attacked, triumphed last month, so it's feeling very good."

In April, Roddy wrote me about U. Vic.: "I shall be glad to get out [he still had a year to go] with honour not too much tarnished." A year or two later, in a note titled "UVic Board of Governors," he said: "On the whole we were a compatible group, though with diverse political and philosophical convictions, and used to making hard decisions. Yet time and again we sweated blood, straining intelligence, conscience and convictions to arrive at sound decisions. It was a healthy experience, generating respect for the complexity of dissent and the integrity of one's fellow man even when in deep-rooted opposition."

The letter continued: "The Salmon Commission is much more practical and more satisfying, though it too has its complications ... and now Hugh Keenlyside [former diplomat, then chairman of B.C. Hydro, great dam builders] has asked me to join the advisory committee on fisheries to the B.C. Energy Board, which is sort of awkward ... In spite of living in the same house Mother and I don't really see much of each other – always off at work in the daytime and now I have to make all these damn trips and she can't get away very often." This lament may be common now, but by comparison with the way Ann and Roddy had lived for the first three decades of their marriage, it was an enormous contrast. Then they both went about their lives under the same roof all day every day, and they travelled very little. In spite of the demands of four children and many friends, they had a great deal of choice over when they did things, at least. And quite a lot of time for the very important garden and the place in general.

Still, it was possible now and then to take a break. That summer, Roddy, Ann and Celie, who was to be married in August – "not a big bash" she had said – went to Europe for the month of July. For the first couple of weeks Roddy went back to Iceland to fish some more of the country he had been so taken with a few years before. Ann and Celie went to Italy. This was Ann's first of many trips to Italy, most of them centered on Florence. She had decided that, now that she could afford to travel, it was too late to see the whole world, so she would concentrate on the center of her greatest interest, Renaissance art and architecture. She set to work to learn Italian also, and became fluent in time. In mid-July everyone met in England and visited many of Roddy's copious family. Although Roddy had seen some relatives during the war, he had not gone back to Dorset and his maternal grandfather's house at Wrackleford (now owned by a Pope cousin). This visit was his first in forty years. They also went to a Charterhouse celebration of the 100th anniversary of his Haig-Brown grandfather's moving the school from London to Godalming.

In August Celie married Ted Vayro, as planned, in a relatively small and casual wedding – the ceremony in the church across the road and the reception in the study. They lived in Kamloops where Ted, who had been a champion bareback rider, had a business contracting to supply stock for rodeos. Celie continued to teach English and biology at the high school there.

Roddy managed a second break in the fall when he and Edward Dunn spent a week in the Chilcotin visiting Alan. But Ann was stressed again – the school had lost its accreditation (meaning it no longer met provincial standards properly), and John Young was battling the education bureaucrats with support from the Teachers' Federation.

Roddy enjoyed a visit from Tom McGuane. "He's quite a guy. Tall, good-looking, medium long hair, western outfit. He's published two novels and much short stuff ..., has read just about everything Mother and I ever heard of. A good fisherman and, I suspect, a pretty good horseman."

Life continued at the same peak pace it had for the previous couple of years. In January of 1972, Roddy "managed to get a long piece written on the Moran Dam and the salmon runs." This was part of the ongoing campaign to keep the Fraser free of dams. But the demands on his time continued. "Art Laing [a federal cabinet minister] called me from Ottawa a couple of days ago and asked me to go on the 2nd Century Committee [forerunner of The Nature Trust]. I tried to say no, but couldn't make it stick. More interestingly, I took the occasion to talk to him about Moran." The committee administered the Second Century Fund, the purpose of which was to buy up land for the protection of important habitat and ecosystems. The land would then be turned over to the appropriate authority, usually government, to manage. One place they bought was along the banks of the Adams River to protect the sockeye spawning beds. After Roddy died the area was named for him, in spite of fierce opposition from some members of the provincial cabinet of the day.

By spring John Young had been asked for his resignation, refused, and was ultimately fired. Roddy's comment in March was: "The faculty stays pretty faithful, but it is wearing on them and hard on the school. Mother doesn't like it at all, though I don't think they will bother her library much. It works too well." On the family side, in the same letter to Alan, Roddy reported: "Mother has just come in with the news that Mary and Bernie have bought a ten-acre farm on the Saanich peninsula just north of Victoria, and will be moving over there at the end of the school year." The Bowker family moved to Vancouver Island as planned, and over time have created a beautiful house and garden from the small cottage in the midst of a tangle of blackberry vines that was on the place when they arrived. But the letter goes back to the larger worries. "We seem to have beaten the Moran thing again this time, but I am afraid they still have it in mind and am scared stiff of a flood from this year's [heavy] snowpack." (A flood would stir the public demand for the dam, although the main purpose for which it was intended was hydroelectric power.) Twenty-five years later the dam has still not been built, though it rears its ugly head again and again.

In June Ann wrote: "Daddy is working a lot with Indian court aides and thinks they are great. He's resolved not to repeat the U. Vic. three years which end in December, but has many other commitments – Electoral Boundary Commission again, a Federal Government Water Board for the West Coast oceans, 2nd Century Fund which buys parkland in the province, and the most important, Salmon Commission." Summer brought the usual flood of visitors, including grandchildren from Toronto, and the peak of the Salmon Commission work as almost-daily decisions had to be made about when commercial fishing would be open around the mouth of the Fraser River as the various runs made their way in from the ocean.

In September Roddy managed a trip to the Queen Charlotte Islands off the north coast of British Columbia to fish for coho salmon with a fly as part of a film being made by a Toronto crew. The film, called *Flashing*

Silver, was never widely distributed, but has some good footage of Roddy fly-fishing, releasing silver cohos and wading among the spawning salmon in a rain-flooded creek.

Alan and Vickie had returned to Campbell River and their little house on the place with a foster child, Nora, who was with them for many years. Alan was substitute teaching at local schools after fishing for salmon in the summer and Vickie was pregnant. Their son, William Edward, was born on Celie's birthday, October 7.

That winter, Roddy's term as U. Vic. chancellor ended, but with another round of hearings and meetings to redefine the federal electoral boundaries brought on by Roddy's second appointment to that Commission, he was away from his desk in the study as much as ever. In February of 1973, Roddy turned sixty-five and Ann reached the same age on May 3. She had had quite enough of the school library by this time, and so retired on that day and headed for Italy a few days later. On this trip she was taking an extension course for a month, and then Roddy was to join her for three weeks in July.

During the time Ann was in Italy on her own, Roddy wrote her lengthy letters filled with details of the household, and much about the garden and the birds in it. Letters to absent children always had some of this, but not nearly as much as he wrote to Ann about their shared pleasures. He reported to her that Alan was hard at work in all the fields with a brush cutter (when he wasn't teaching) taking out the broom that had grown up now that the sheep were no longer around to keep it down. There were horses —Alan and Vickie had a couple and, any time there was room, various little girls would come begging to pasture theirs at Above Tide. Roddy wrote a long list of trees he planned to plant once the broom was gone. Not all of that list got put in, but there were always new trees of one sort or another going in, often seedlings from existing trees that needed more room. The cut broom was burned on rainy days and one day Roddy "used the big fire to help with a massive cleanup around my desk. I've even written a few long-delayed letters, I have it in mind to try a cleanup of the tool bench in the basement." Much of Roddy's correspondence was done now with the help of Rosalie (Teddy) Smith. He dictated either to her or on tape and, when he was away for any length of time, she would come in to deal with what mail she could to keep the pile down.

One bird report read: "The Swainson's thrushes were back yesterday and the pigeons were cooing down by the big cherry tree. The orange house finch was back for quite a while today on the kitchen windowsill. He is very aggressive and has himself a lady, so I guess he is a fully mature variant. Peg-leg [another finch] was also back, hopping around on the trellis. And the pink dogwood is out."

Roddy had ordered a "suitcase fly rod" (a Hardy "Smuggler") and thought to try the trout in the Arno at Florence. Court that week included the trial of "the logging truck that blocked the ferry [to Quadra Island], which should be good for an inward smile or two, if not a good laugh." In the end "a pompous and incompetent defence counsel endlessly and voluminously pursuing a line of argument that I'm sure is perverse" meant the whole thing had to be adjourned until he got back from Italy.

That weekend Roddy went to Victoria to stay with the Hugh Keenlysides and participate in the ceremonies of the Spring Convocation as Chancellor Emeritus. He rather enjoyed the ceremonies and the people who gathered for them, and perhaps it was some reward to be able to participate without having the worries of the tumultuous years as chancellor. He wrote afterwards to Ann in great detail about who was there, what they said and even what the women wore at the traditional Chancellor's dinner for honorary degree recipients.

In his last letter to Ann before he left, Roddy reported that he "spent a good part of the morning reviving the Kingfisher Creek diversion." This was an idea he had had for some time to divert the little creek that ran behind the barn and into culverts under the school yard, the roads and a lumber yard to the river. Roddy thought to restore it to daylight by putting it back into an old outlet channel that ran through our place to the river. The impetus this time was that the school was having problems with its culvert. Ultimately, Roddy himself decided it took too much precious time to sort out all the intricacies of the plan. After he died, a few dedicated friends did accomplish the diversion and continue to work hard to keep it in good shape for the cohos that return each year to spawn under the alders.

The letter ends with a note on the current state of affairs on some enhancement work the Canadians wanted to do on the Fraser. "... things are going rather well with the salmon talks and the U.S. seems about to agree that Canada can go it alone on the Fraser program and claim all the benefits. They don't want to prejudice this position by letting the U.S. in on even a small project such as this one, nor do they want to abrogate the treaty by going ahead Canada only; so they are hoping to get U.S. consent to that before re-negotiating the treaty." Just a small example of how complicated it was to get on with the actual work of caring for salmon that did not recognize the forty-ninth parallel.

After a day in Vancouver mixing Boundary and Salmon commission meetings, Roddy left for Italy. I can well imagine Ann's delight at showing Roddy around her beloved Tuscany. When they came back he used to say that Mother walked at such a leisurely pace that she could easily walk around the world. Being a wandering tourist wasn't exactly his style, but he would have been quietly interested in the art and architecture and paid equal attention to the trees and birds and rivers – and throughly enjoyed the wine. Ann often told one story of the time they spent together there. They ended the trip sitting on the terrace of a little hotel near Siena having lunch, so relaxed that it only slowly dawned on them that it was that night, not the next, that their plane left Rome for the return trip. They did get there in time.

In September, Alan and Vickie returned to the Chilcotin and a new job at Alkali Lake. Ann was able to concentrate her energy on the harvest as she hadn't done in her teaching years, and was thoroughly enjoying that and the gardening. The tone of Roddy's letters that winter is a little calmer than it had been for several years. Once the spawning season ended, the Salmon Commission meetings were fewer, he had more help in court and Ann was home to run interference much of the time. In a November letter to Alan – all our letters were less frequent since we were beginning to develop the telephone habit – Roddy talked of his book plans. "We have lots of birds around – juncos, towhees, song sparrows, chickadees, the odd swamp robin. There was a tree creeper in the acacia the other day. Mergansers in the river. I always hope some evening grosbeaks will stick around. I am planning a book about birds – just a friendly sort of book – not scientific or informative or useful in any way, just pleasurable."

Christmas was particularly lively that year, both Ann and Roddy mentioned it in their letters – Ted and Celie, and Alan and Vickie with Nora and William – "loud talk, eating and drinking," said Ann, and "good fun all the time, though we stayed up too late every night," said Roddy. Ann got Roddy "a wine rack partly filled with a good lot of French wines and he was thrilled. There was one bottle of French champagne for our fortieth, when I think we'll be in Vancouver."

In January of 1974, Roddy wrote: "It seems fairly clear that the authorities want to be rid of *all* lay judges as soon as possible. Under the right circumstances, I would be happy to quit and get back to writing – to say nothing of a little freedom – but I am not prepared to be pushed out as incompetent, and that is the present (collective) inference." On the cheerier side: "Six of my fishing books are being reprinted in New York by Crown Publishers and Collins will be sharing the editions for Canada. *Panther* [first published forty years before] was in a new Houghton Mifflin edition this year. So things do go on."

In February, Roddy "finished the salmon brochure for the Law of the Sea Conference." This was the text for Canada's presentation to heads of state, ministers and senior officials to encourage their support for the proposal to extend national boundaries to two hundred miles offshore in advance of the next meeting of the Conference. Dave Denbigh (artist and fine binder), Bob Reid (the typographer who had done *The Living Land*) and Bill Reid (Haida artist and leader of the renaissance of native art in B.C.) came to talk about the illustrations and design for the major presentation portfolio (18" x 24") that would contain the text Roddy had written and illustrations by several artists, including Denbigh and Bill Reid. The result was a most impressive gathering of text and art that celebrated the salmon of the Canadian coastal waters. Ann attended a church retreat led by Jean Vanier, famed for his work with disabled people.

A week or so later Roddy was "working on the diplomatic comments on the Law of the Sea brochure – not too much, but they want to have things two ways – propaganda, but not propaganda, salmon as a world resource, but not *really* a world resource, Canada's world resource. Well, one can always try, within limits. But committees can't write books. I've enjoyed it though and they really haven't interfered much." Ann and Roddy went to "Sam Henderson's big potlatch feast. It was a lot of fun, hundreds of people there, all kinds of dancing and masses of gifts [for everyone there, in the old coastal native tradition, banned by law between 1884 and 1951, but kept alive in secret and now reappearing]." Ann's winter project was rearranging "*all* the books, discarding a few, making new classifications, dusting, moving, vacuuming and Lexolling [oiling leather bindings], to dignify a sound product with a verb," and taking Italian and Art History courses.

In March there was a family gathering at Kamloops when Roddy went up to speak at Cariboo College and Celie's school. Ann went with him and Alan and Vickie came down from Alkali Lake. Mary and Bernie were leaving to spend a year travelling in Europe with their four children. It was a European year – I went for a couple of weeks to England and France, and my daughter Ann finished high school and spent several months there.

In Campbell River, Ann was now able to have people for dinner often and she did ("Daddy loves it"), both Campbell River people and the many people who came to visit – old Seattle friends, as always, and literary, legal, fishing and conservation people, who often already were, or soon became, good friends. And interspersed were the local children. ("'Can I show Paul the books. You're the only lady we know that has a study.' Most of them live in trailers.") She wrote more often, too. In response to my report of a concert she said, "All the time in the world isn't enough for music and museums – they yield and yield and never surfeit – especially of course when you live in C.R. and have to work for them." Triggered by a reference to Salvador Dali in the magazine I was working for, she said it "contained the remarks on Dali that I've always wanted to make. I never can because people who know I have what they consider a perverted taste for modern art sometimes try to be nice by talking about Dali – the bastard."

In the fall they finally bought a TV "because it seemed eccentric not to have one," said Ann. Roddy said, "We watch it occasionally, usually 'the National [news]' just before going to bed. I've been hoping for some baseball, but there doesn't seem to be much." He was ever a fan – we used to listen to the World Series on the radio together. Ann was doing the church bulletin "because there's no committee involved and it gives me a chance to push and pull with the power of selection up to a force of a milli-millilitre on the 'monolithic' Church of Rome."

A late September letter to me from Roddy began, "For the past year or so I have been making inquiries about the possibility of some deal with the government under the new Land legislation that would (a) protect this place from subdivision and development and (b) get us out from under taxes that are beginning to look as though they may eventually be too much to handle. Considerably to our surprise, it turned out that the government already had ideas of its own on the matter and suggested that we sell them the property, reserving lifetime right of use and occupancy. It was something of a surprise to learn that they were hoping to receive the house pretty much as is, with furniture, books, etc. ... Mother and I said we would have to think that over and discuss it with the children, and that a good many items, such as family silver, would not be included. The price they will be paying [$130,000] is roughly the appraised value at 1st January 1972 [Valuation Day]. Being able to live here tax free, pretty much as we would have done anyway with some assurance it won't all go under the bulldozer as soon as we die, is a considerable advantage." The taxes had reached $2000 a year and were threatening to double, and the area east of the house toward the town had gone from farm fields to light industry, so it seemed essential to act. The government plan was to make use of the house for a conference center and to keep it forever as Haig-Brown House, but the purpose of the purchase was to preserve the green space and its trees.

Roddy went on to tell me he had swum the whole river in his wet suit, and that his annual holiday from the bench was to be in October. He and Ann spent two weeks going first to the Provincial Judges' Conference in Victoria, and then on to visit Alan and Vickie (Ann's first trip to the Chilcotin) where they had Thanksgiving, then back with Ted and Celie to Kamloops and the Salute to the Sockeye celebrating the arrival of the salmon on the spawning beds of the Adams River. The Judges' Conference produced "absolutely no news on Daddy's future, although retirement on fairly unsatisfactory terms seems to be just around the corner."

Christmas was quieter than the year before but the pace of Roddy's life stayed pretty hectic. The Boundary Commission was to start again in March of 1975 with Roddy reluctantly serving for the third time to give continuity, as he was the only one of the three commissioners available from the last round. "Personally I am rather dreading going back to all those figures for the third time." Discussion was starting on the "Fisheries book," a study of sport fisheries management in Canada for the Federal Department of Fisheries and Oceans. And the ongoing Salmon Commission. The fisheries book would require travel and discussion all across Canada.

An article on Roddy by noted Canadian writer and poet Al Purdy in which he described the young man as a "gung-ho, cockadoodle-do kid" and the older Roddy as a "brown buddha" was published in *Weekend* magazine. Roddy wrote, "We enjoyed it and most other people like it, though some do not." Purdy later republished the piece in a limited edition, along with their correspondence at the time and a poem regretting the loss of the chance to develop their friendship, called "Dear Judge." The poem moved me so, I cried.

The end of Roddy's career on the bench was approaching when "legislation retiring all provincial judges who are 65 or more comes into effect on Feb. 1st, and provides for retirement in 30 days. During that time we are supposed to tidy everything up. It's an unsatisfactory deal in many ways, but I think I'm glad of it." Part of the reason Roddy considered it unsatisfactory was that he was given a lump sum instead of a pension because he was not considered to have been a full-time judge. But more important was that the new rule was seen as a ploy to get rid of all judges who did not have law degrees. Roddy felt most strongly that appointing only lawyers as judges took the law and the courts farther from the people they served. A lawyer judge would not fill the requirement that "a man be judged by his peers."

The deal on the house was settled. "This is highly satisfactory, so long as inflation doesn't become too drastic. Even then we should have a pleasant place to live tax free and would only have to dig up some grub somewhere."

April saw Roddy in Toronto for a Nature Conservancy meeting, meetings with publishers and Fisheries book people. But life was a little quieter and he was enjoying being home for as much as a couple of weeks at a time. In July I came from Toronto; my daughters, who were wandering about in a Volkswagen beetle, turned up; Alan and Vickie and theirs were in Campbell River, as were Ted and Celie. With Mary and Bernie back in Victoria again after their European year, it was quite a family collection that summer.

The Salmon Commission work was made more complicated by having to deal with the impact of the Boult decision in the State of Washington which opened up native fishing rights. This meant an unknown factor in the fishery and would require more negotiations and adjustments.

In September Ann went back to Italy for a month, accompanied for two weeks by Roddy's sister Valerie, a convert to Catholicism. Alan began a new job as Co-ordinator of Indian Education for the Williams Lake District, which included the schools he had taught in in the previous years. Much of the thrust of his work was to allow the local bands to take control of their schools on whatever basis suited them. Roddy drove north along the Fraser to Prince George for both Boundary and Salmon commission work. He then made his way gradually south, looking at rivers and salmon, visiting Alan and Vickie while the Boundary Commission sat in Williams Lake and then spending the weekend with Ted and Celie at the rodeo in Lillooet farther south on the Fraser, after Boundary hearings in Kamloops. The details of that weekend got a little muddled in rodeo dust or something, but we do know that there was a beer strike. It is probably the only time that Roddy was ever known to drink a sweet bubbly wine called Baby Duck —you have to wash the dust down somehow.

After spending Monday morning loading rodeo horses with Ted, Roddy and Celie "paid our respects" to the salmon at nearby Seton Creek and went on to look at the Bridge River Rapids. Home to Celie's and on to Oliver in the Okanagan next day, and then east to Nelson for more Boundary Commission hearings through the rest of the week. Through all this Roddy wrote letters to Ann in Italy almost daily. Even after there was no more chance of letters reaching Ann there, he kept notes for her. There was no diminishing of his aching need for her company; there is as much love and longing in these letters as there was in the ones he wrote when they were engaged in 1933. Even in the details of what the garden produced for his lunch, the work of cutting some dead willows for firewood, the particularly perfect weather that fall, there is a longing between the lines to share it all with Ann. One letter after he got home ended: "All my love to you. I miss you even more when I am here and very much in bed." And at the end of his notes after the fall rain had set in: "It worries me more to have you away in the bad weather than in good. I have a fire in the study and it seems you should be in out of the rain."

Teddy Smith came and went with correspondence; the outside of the house was being painted; Richard Brautigan, writer of *Trout Fishing in America* and other far out books, had called in twice while they were away; people were begging to rent Alan's cottage; to say nothing of writing, meetings and the steady stream of people wanting various kinds of help and advice. Roddy even noted the plots of the last two episodes of the television series "The Pallisers" – "good high society soap opera," he called it, but admitted he "wept practically all the way through" the last episode. "Pathos. Bathos. Something the critics despise."

The provincial election that fall "was a great disappointment, but has to be endured." Roddy had, for the first time ever, declared himself politically and supported Dave Barrett and his New Democratic Party government in their run for a second term. His reasoning was that it was the only hope for the environment. The alternative was a totally business-oriented, right-wing Social Credit government which B.C. had already endured for years before Barrett got in. But, in B.C.'s polarized politics there was no middle ground and Social Credit was back.

In January of 1976, Roddy was "answering endless correspondence, messing around with the Fisheries book and not getting much done, making arrangements about money and trying to fight off other assignments. Don't really know how I manage to waste so much time, but a lot of it goes in reading magazines and scientific papers. Mother has been going regularly to her Art History and Italian courses and has been knitting a hearth rug for the living room." Together they had what Ann described as "four good bonfire days, clearing out a little of the brush and dead willow from among the poplars – my idea of a beautiful time."

In February Ann and Roddy went together on the first of the travels for the Fisheries book. Quebec City, the Maritimes and Newfoundland made for chilly winter travel, but they had a good time. They were in Quebec City at the time of *Carnaval d'Hiver*, an annual festival celebrating winter, "which was fun in its way. New Brunswick and Nova Scotia were excitingly different ... I learned a fair bit about fish and land-holdings and various social complications as well as ichthyological ones." When they got back "Ernie Schwiebert and Dan Callaghan ... interviewed me almost constantly for 48 hours." Noted fishing writer Schwiebert was doing an article on Roddy, and their mutual friend Callaghan, an Oregon lawyer, was there to take photographs. There were meetings in Vancouver and Bellingham (just across the Canada-U.S. boundary in Washington and convenient for members of the bilateral Salmon Commission), and people staying for a retreat, but Roddy did get in a day of fishing on the Quinsam River. In March the Fisheries book travels took Ann and Roddy to the

Prairie provinces. In April a crew came to film Roddy about the Salmon Enhancement Program for the Law of the Sea Conference. "I varied things a little for them by putting on a wet suit and going in the river."

In May there was a Pacific Rim Children's Literature Conference in Vancouver. Ann went too, and "we went twice to the Joffrey Ballet and once to the touring Edmonton Symphony. I spent much of a day sitting in on the Berger hearings [on a proposed gas pipeline in the Mackenzie River Valley in the Yukon]. Lots of American Indian Movement types around, some impressive, some not so. Also managed to get to the Fisheries Association Conference and a Second Century Fund lunch." Summer brought the usual round of family and friends as well as Paul Grescoe doing an interview for a story in *International Wildlife*. This story also brought Christopher Springmann from California to take particularly good color photographs.

In July a Federal Recreational Fisheries Conference took Roddy to Toronto. He worked hard at the meetings – it was a conference of biologists and fisheries managers from across Canada. The book Roddy was working on was particularly relevant to them, so he was very much in demand. He also gave the keynote address at the official dinner. I spent a lot of time with him and thought he seemed rather tired. The visit ended on July 17, my daughter Ann's birthday, celebrated with an elegant brunch before his plane left.

Celie had started a new job as co-ordinator for the Native Indian Teacher Education Program in Kamloops. The job made her a visiting professor at the University of B.C., and she was to spend the next several years coordinating the studies of native people who were doing the first two years of a bachelor of education degree, which they would then complete at UBC. Her work and Alan's often connected directly, as Alan steered people interested in teaching to the Kamloops courses, and some of the people Celie taught became teachers in schools in Alan's area. That same fall my Ann started at Reed College in Portland, Oregon, visiting her grandparents on the way.

On October 3, Roddy wrote: "I have been engaged in a monomaniac frenzy to finish my book and get it out of the way. It is finished now and on its way to Ottawa. Now we wait to see what they think of it, but I am not losing any sleep over that. Celie phoned this morning to say that she is seven weeks pregnant and very happy about it all. We have to go to Vancouver on Wednesday and, by fortunate coincidence, so does she, so we shall see her there. Mother has been very busy with the organization of a retreat down in Duncan next week. This week it has been Women's Place and we have seven of them boarding here for a conference ... Young, lively, amusing, generally somewhat unkempt and very busy with a strange world of grants, groups, proposals and semi-thoughts, rather painstakingly differentiated from standard middle (or any other) class values. Fun, but one wonders where it is all going to end up. Mother knows just what to do with them all.

"Since finishing the book I have been getting out a good deal and enjoying it very much." There follows a long list of garden chores accomplished in the last while, including getting two trailer loads of wood for the fireplaces, building a new cement bulkhead at the foot of the border and a ten-foot gate, and "planting three hundred or more daffodils in the birches, mainly big King Alfreds."

The Vancouver meetings were Second Century Fund and Salmon Commission, and Ann and Roddy also had a birthday dinner with Celie. They came home late Friday night and, on Saturday morning, Ann went grocery shopping. When she came home at noon, she stepped out on the back porch to call Roddy for lunch from where he was just putting away the tractor after mowing the lawn. He turned toward her, collapsed, and died there almost instantly of a heart attack. It was October 9, 1976. Thanksgiving weekend has never been the same again.

A simple funeral was held four days later in St. Patrick's Church across the field, even though Roddy was not a Catholic. (The great monolithic church had eased the rules a little in some places from the time when Ann and Roddy had had to be married in the church vestry.) The church was filled mainly with people from Campbell River and the rest of the Island. Because of the holiday weekend traffic on the ferries it was nearly impossible to get to Campbell River from anywhere else. But Edward Dunn and Glen Trimble, so important to all of us, did come from Seattle; and the people of the Salmon Commission chartered a small plane. I asked the choir to sing "All Things Bright and Beautiful" because I thought he would like it. (They had to borrow a hymn book from the Anglicans because it wasn't in their repertoire.) As Alan drove down the Fraser River filled with spawning salmon on his way to the funeral, he knew he wanted the first part of "The Death of the Salmon" from *Fisherman's Fall* read in the church, but he asked me to do it for him. "Do they all die ...," it starts, and ends: "I am still curious about the manner and meaning of it, but I do not question that it has manner and meaning." We knew the manner of our father's death, no matter how sudden and unexpected, but the meaning of such an early death when it seems he could still have accomplished so much still escapes me.

A few days afterwards Ann, alone in the garden, scattered Roddy's ashes over the daffodil bulbs he had planted a week or two earlier.

.14.

Ann Alone (1976 – 1990)

Any death is a shock, but often there is at least some warning, if only because of the health or age of the person involved. But there was no warning of Roddy's death and the shock to all of us, but particularly Ann, was overwhelming. She never thought she would be a widow at sixty-eight. The way of the modern world is such that people are expected to rush back to their lives a few days after a funeral, and we children and grandchildren did – to jobs or to school – taking our grief with us. People attempted to fill the awful space for Ann, often by just listening as she had done for so many others. Granddaughters, especially, came to stay, dozens of friends called and hundreds of letters of condolence arrived. Ann filled some of those first weeks alone answering every letter. A woman I met not long ago told me that "everyone in Campbell River" was aware how devastated Ann was without her Roddy (perhaps they were also reflecting their own sense of loss). She sensed that what Ann needed was a wall to talk at and, she said, "I was that wall." So, probably, were others.

The family gathered again at Campbell River for a Christmas that seemed an empty ritual with a hollow center. But the "life goes on" cliche was borne out by Alan and Vickie completing arrangements to adopt a baby, James Robert William, the son of one of Celia's students at Kamloops, named after his Secwepemc birth mother's three brothers.

Ann said after a few months that her silent response to all the kind people who said, "You'll get over it," was, "No, I won't. I don't want to 'get over it' – I'll learn to live with it, maybe." She also said in later years that she found she remained so numbed that she could no longer act – only react. But react she did, in ways that made a great difference to a great many people.

In early February of 1977 she wrote for herself describing one weekday: "I didn't go to Mass because I was going to my friend Larry's for records. Larry called quite early that he couldn't make it so I decided to be lonely – but it was impossible. Ron came to borrow the wheelbarrow; I went to pick up firewood sticks and visited with the Kings who were doing the same thing across the fence, lent them a block and tackle, came back to find the man here to fix the record player ... Don Calimente called to thank me for a History of Rumania I'd sent him. Phyllis [Rossiter] called to say she hadn't been in because she was sick and I promised to go there tomorrow. I visited with Ann Graham on the phone about the dogs barking at the horses; Denis called about coming to wash the car; Ron promised to come Saturday about a clean-up. I arranged Marty's package and the Standeven wedding present for Saturday. Mavis [Hudson] is coming for dinner tomorrow. The Schoenfelder boy brought me a hot loaf of bread his mother had just made." Ron Tremblay lived in Alan's cottage in return for some help around the place; Mavis Hudson was Ann's oldest and dearest friend in all the Campbell River years; and Phyllis Rossiter, who lived just up the road, was probably the most constant of those who just "kept an eye out." Her husband, Len, had wired the house when we first got electricity in 1942, and they shared with Ann a love for rhododendrons.

Even without Roddy, Ann drove to Vancouver and Victoria often. She went to see her children – Alan and Celia were often in Victoria or Vancouver for meetings about their work; to attend meetings herself – she was on a provincial Universities Council and an Arts Council, and there were Church organizations and retreats as well; or to go to concerts. Music was a passion and a solace for Ann; she had season tickets to the Friends of Chamber Music series in Vancouver for several years. It became a tradition to go to these concerts with Mary's mother-in-law, Gwenith Bowker.

In April, Ann went also to Spokane, Washington, to stay with her niece Charlotte, her brother Buckie's daughter, while she had her first baby – her mother, Gar, had died not long before. Then on May 31, Celie's Sophie Ruth was born, and Ann went to be grandmother to her new, red-headed granddaughter for a couple of weeks. She followed this with a trip to Seattle to visit Glen Trimble and Joanna Eckstein. The sad family news was that Alan and Vickie had split up.

And, since she could not go again to Italy with Roddy, she decided that I would be next best, and had plans in the works for us to go to Perugia for a week-long music festival in September, and then to Florence, Pisa and Siena. Her summer letters are all crammed with the details of flights and hotels – all of which worked out admirably and we had a wonderful time. Three weeks of concerts, museums, churches, old streets, a little shopping and a lot of good food. People said to me sometimes after I got back, "You went to Italy with your *mother*!" as if such a trip would be utterly boring and a great waste. But I replied, "You don't know my mother." Fluent in Italian, so steeped in the art and architecture of the area and so enthusiastic about music, which she had long ago taught me to love (with the help of CBC radio), that it was a total pleasure – a short concentrated course in the Italian Renaissance.

Ann celebrated Christmas at Celie's in Kamloops with Alan and Mary's families joining in, and my Ann coming from her studies in Portland, Oregon. The festivities were squeezed into the little house near town where Celie and Ted were living because, in the way of all new houses, their log house on a quarter section in the hills was not yet finished.

In the spring Ann went to Victoria to attend U. Vic. functions – a residence there was to be named after Roddy; and to receive the National and Provincial Parks Association's Harkin Award in Roddy's honor. At home she was as busy as ever. A birthday note to me in April, after reporting on a young man working on a bibliography of Roddy's published works, said: "Today has been good – ministering at church which I always find moving, breakfast with a good Italian pal, nature walk on Quadra with adored friends ... Tomorrow museum curator has a travelling curator who simply must come to see me; next day lunch out, a man to tell me how mad he is they won't name a park after Roddy, dinner meeting of parish council on which I'm new; Wednesday, garden boy, Indian Studies committee, open an arts and craft show; Thursday, wedding and overnight Japanese calligrapher and her interpreter; Sat., Anglican church garden sale to which I must contribute the many plants I can't resist raising for which I have neither time nor room; Saturday night, read and minister again – I love it. The following week there's a juvenile prison meeting ..., a young biologist who worships Daddy for overnight and then to Mary's with Mavis for my birthday." Stay as busy as you can and there is no time to brood on your sorrows.

A later week included Farrell Boyce, who did a wonderful woodcut of three salmon swimming upstream with Roddy's now-famous poem about the life of the salmon swirling along their sides, Robert Fish who was to do the beautiful drawings of fish for Roddy's study of Canadian fisheries management and Mia Hartman, the daughter of Harry Hartman of Ann's long ago Seattle bookstore days. In July, Alan and his new partner Maria Meyers, from Stoney in the Chilcotin, had a daughter who was named Helen Haig-Brown.

One of Ann's major concerns was what to do with the literary part of Roddy's estate. Because I had done a lot of editorial work already and was less tied to job and family than my siblings, it gradually evolved that I would take charge. I came from Toronto at Easter, looked over the situation and then took a leave of absence from my job in the fall of 1978 to get to work on a collection of stories and articles that were either previously published only in magazines or were unpublished. This became, with the encouragement of Jack McClelland and Linda McKnight, a set of three books called, collectively, "The World of Roderick Haig-Brown" published by McClelland and Stewart of Toronto in the early 1980s. Two volumes, *The Master and His Fish* and *Writings and Reflections*, were also published by the University of Washington Press in Seattle.

That fall of 1978 most of the family went to Celie's new house at Kamloops for a weekend celebration to dedicate the provincial conservation area along the Adams River to Roddy. It was a year in which there was a major sockeye run and the river was filled to brimming with the beautiful red fish. Roddy's friends and admirers in the conservation movement had had to press the B.C. cabinet very hard to get government approval for the honor, which was intended to mark his enormous contribution to the work of protecting the Fraser River salmon runs. The dedication was marked by the unveiling of a plaque with Roddy's poem to the salmon on it which took place under golden leaves with splashing red salmon in the river beyond. A large and illustrious group of friends and dignitaries, mostly from B.C., came, but the presence of Edward Dunn and Glen Trimble from Seattle was probably most touching to us.

In the summer of 1979, I left my Toronto job and returned to Campbell River to work on the McClelland and Stewart project – Ann was now paying the royalties from the literary estate over to me – and mind the house and garden while she went once more to Italy. This time she registered for a UBC course in Italian and was based at the hilltop Castello di Gargonza near Arezzo. She made weekend trips to the now-familiar Tuscan towns. The summer was hot and dry, and, although I had to work to keep the garden watered, I revelled in the what seemed almost like playing house while the grown-ups were away. The raspberry crop was particularly lush that July, and I picked and ate and froze daily, it seemed. Ann's regular callers called on me, too, as did some of the many people who were dependent on her for help – a sympathetic ear, a ride to the doctor, early apples from the orchard. The fans came too, as always, especially in summer, to get a glimpse of how the man they so admired had lived.

That fall I returned to Toronto to wind up my affairs there and see my younger daughter Charlotte off to Europe and a job as an *au pair*. I moved to Vancouver in October which meant, among other things, that Ann and I talked on the phone and saw each other more often. Most of the letters from this time concerned business matters between us – both literary and financial – or confirming of dates for family comings and goings. Alan and Celie came to meetings on things educational, so I saw them fairly often, and Ann came to see them or for concerts. Ann often explained her general financial affairs in letters, too. She took great pleasure in managing her money very carefully and delighted in explaining how it all worked whenever I visited. She watched interest rates like a hawk, knew the due dates of her credit cards, carried the minimum amount of cash to keep from spending impulsively and, consequently, could afford concerts, trips and help in the house and the garden. She actually managed to increase her capital at times.

The good news for 1980 was that the Fisheries book was to be published at last. It had been tangled in a mass of bureaucratic red tape, but the contract had finally been awarded to Douglas & McIntyre of Vancouver. The book was to be called *Bright Waters, Bright Fish* and was the first link in a continuing chain of D. & M. publication of Haig-Brown books. In the fall I made a major cross-country tour to promote the book – both stimulating and exhausting, as any touring writer can tell you. I got from it a personal taste of the admiration for my father all across Canada.

In May, after celebrating her birthday with me and Celia in Vancouver, Ann went on a tour of gardens in the U.S. southeast – it was azalea and rhododendron season – and to visit her brother Danny in Virginia. She came back from there in time to go to my daughter Charlotte's wedding in Toronto at the end of May, but missed my daughter Ann's commencement from Reed College the weekend before (but nearby Mt. St. Helen's blew its top in celebration instead). Charlotte had come back from Europe to marry Jim Livingston of Toronto and they were to live there.

Celie, who was expecting another baby in December, and her Sophie came to Portland with me for the commencement ceremonies, and Mary went with Ann to Charlotte's wedding – the sort of connecting of daughters and granddaughters that always gave Ann particular pleasure. I rushed to both events, of course. In June Ann wrote of a week of birthday parties, including June Painter's, wedding showers, a retirement dinner for a school colleague and meetings of the John Howard Society and the Strathcona Lodge Outdoor Education Centre – she was on the boards of both. Ted and Celie's Josie Valerie arrived as expected in December, another dark-haired and soon to be dark-eyed member of the family.

After Christmas Ann wrote Edward Dunn to thank him for a present of a book. "... books are the essence of H.B. Christmases and *Malaspina* was a high point." She described the round of book-giving that year and then talked of one from the previous summer called *The Dove in Harness*. "It answers – or tries to – more as you would than as I would – the question of *why* don't we 'sell all we have and give to the poor'? The subtitle is How can an ordinary man who is far indeed from being a saint live his life in the world and yet profess a faith that is meant for saints? English. I'll send it to you if you like." She went on to describe the garden under fresh snow, the chickadees in Roddy's coconut feeders, and said, "You know what snow on evergreens and on black branches looks like as the sun turns them gold at the top and then lights them all the way down, but I ache to tell you about it." Mavis Hudson had come to spend New Year's Eve night "which is our custom."

The year 1982 was a year of babies in the family. Charlotte had Ann's first great-grandson, James Bennett Joseph, in March; Celia had Roderick Edwin in June; and Maria had Linda Ann in October – the last two of thirteen grandchildren. I, with new partner John Russell, was moving to his family ranch in the Rocky Mountains of southwestern Alberta, where we built a house to serve as a base for his travels as a caribou biologist and mine to keep up with family and literary business. Ann's rushing about to keep up with the growing family had got her so many speeding tickets that she was required to take a Defensive Driving course.

In the spring of 1983 Ann went to England to visit with Roddy's sisters and cousins. She stayed mainly with Philip and Joyce Pope, who had come to visit her the year before, in their house with its beautiful garden near Dorchester. Ann and Joyce had found a strong rapport based, Ann felt, on being the in-laws in a large and complicated family and on their intense love of gardening. When she returned Ann wrote me: "This garden is as beautiful as all England – in the rain still the magnolia, pink – and white rhododendron and little blue one – pink, pink cherry and crabapple and now all around bluebells in green – so intense. I'm still exhausted – eye pain, jet lag, codeine, PiC visitors – I don't know but it will be enough to keep me sensibly slow for a few days. I've done a stint at NDP [New Democratic Party] headquarters, another this afternoon, then scrutineering."

PiC was Parents in Crisis, an organization for mothers, often single, who could call each other for help when they felt they were about to take out their despair on their kids. They also met regularly with Ann at her house to talk together. Some of these women became almost surrogate daughters to Ann – a case of giving freely of oneself and receiving unexpected benefits. Their children called her Granny Ann (the family children never called her anything but "Grandmother"), and their cards and drawings decorated the kitchen wall, along with more formal or elegant greetings from other loving friends and family. As well, Ann had volunteered to have women who needed temporary shelter for one reason or another for a few days until alternate arrangements could be made through social services. These women sometimes arrived in the middle of the night and often were in considerable distress. She rarely mentions them in her letters at all and never by name, although sometimes they came when we were visiting and we listened to them, too. Listening was one of Ann's most effective ways of helping troubled people.

In May Ann wrote, as so often, rather cryptically, "As to the B.C. election [won by the right-wing Social Credit party], I'm now into being upset about the U.S. bishops modifying their anti-nuclear message – it isn't a very satisfactory world ... My happy life is alternately gardening and rheumatism." This bout of rheumatism was the first sign of a severe case of polymyalgia (which translates loosely as "pain everywhere"). This lasted several years and was followed by other forms of arthritis or rheumatism, with all the attendant aches, pains, and treatments of one kind or another that usually brought their own disadvantageous side effects, were only effective for a time and never a cure. But Ann always continued to do as much as she possibly could, especially in the garden. In June she "gardened every day because, like a fool, I backed into a truck in my own driveway and was happily without the car for two weeks." In July she went "especially to Vancouver to have lunch with Joe [my ex-husband], which was nice. He fixed it himself and gave it to me in his garden."

In August she wrote Edward Dunn to tell him her delight at the arrival of an Edward Dunn rhododendron, a present from Mary who had been trying to get one from the nursery since Ann's birthday the previous year. She described her troubles with the polymyalgia, the cortisone treatment "*and* what the list of side effects calls 'disruptive behaviour'. But then I had a bit of that, didn't I?, before cortisone was invented." In spite of the aches, Ann went again to Italy in September, this time on a fairly luxurious tour in a small bus, that featured a lot of very good food along with the culture. She was home in time to join Celia and Alan and their families in Kamloops to celebrate Thanksgiving and Celia and William's birthday. In November she spent three days in Vancouver with Glen and Edward, and Vancouver friend Geoff Andrew (whose wife Margaret had died) going to museums and galleries and eating Italian dinners.

Ann's November letter was written while she was doing "her stint in the Birthright office – the only pro-life activity I approve of." Birthright counselled pregnant girls who wished to keep their babies or put them up for adoption. The house was at last getting a new roof after much negotiating with the Heritage Properties Branch of the B.C. government. The original sale of the property had been to the Lands Branch, but after Roddy died, friends had the house itself approved as a Heritage Property, so that department was now responsible for major repairs and upkeep – the informal figure was set at all repairs over $500, although Ann often did not submit bills.

Ann spent Christmas of 1983 at Mary's in Victoria, a pattern now quite set. In early January the Kingfisher Creek people (who took care of the creek and the area that was not immediately around the house and cottage) had an Open House: "... lovely; about 90 people and the whole Kingfisher Creek committee helped so much before and during that it wasn't hard at all." Pneumonia, followed by a pinched back nerve, struck in February and took a very long time to really go away. Ann travelled less and had more garden and household help – Murna Tracey, who had originally come to clean, gradually took on much more than that, as Ann's need increased. She ran errands, painted, did minor repairs – at times almost everything but cleaning. Pat Haines and her husband, Wendell, did a lot of garden work that was impossible for Ann – digging, moving heavy pots, getting barrow loads of soil and compost. Wendell did a major job of protecting the shrubbery while the house was painted. "The painting, as I knew it would be, is a comedy act." We went to help, too, when we could.

By June Ann was feeling much stronger. She had found a very good furniture refinisher in Campbell River and was having several occasional tables, mainly ones that had come from her mother's house, beautifully restored. The Totem Flyfishers from Vancouver came to make a "really elegant" presentation. "One of their members, head of the faculty association at Simon Fraser [university], had come two days before with a bottle of Harvey's Shooting Sherry, so refreshments were no problem." But a few days later she wrote: "Yesterday was one of those unavoidable too-much ones. Five sets of visitors, only one invited; so today I'm doing little – only wrapping the little Roddy's 2nd birthday present – admirable, eh?"

On another June weekend there was "a meeting of Catholic Indians from Church House and the west coast but living in C.R. because one of their priests was visiting. They came about 4:30 Fri, Sat. and Sunday and had a picnic supper and a Mass. It was absolutely perfect. I did nothing, the many children did not pick flowers, but played on the lawn while the elders watched them. In fact, Saturday night when I went out for dinner they even washed the stuff I had left." But in response to a request that she videotape some local historical items, Ann said (to me): "I will, but I'm rather sick of being Exhibit A." She had been tying up blue delphiniums in the garden after a windy, rainy night and, "I can't get out of my head the smarty saying of my college years: Nietzsche said: The three most beautiful things are love's first kiss, the color blue and the chord of the minor seventh. I've probably told you before; I suppose it lasts for me because I have no idea what the chord of the minor seventh sounds like." Nor do I, and she hadn't given me this little gem before.

Mary was considering a master's degree so she could teach properly in the school system, where she had been a volunteer and a teacher aide, now that she and Bernie had sold the print and framing shop she had run for years after Bernie went back to teaching. Celie was already taking courses toward a master's at the community college in Kamloops. She had taken a year off after Roddy was born, but was back at her old NITEP job. Alan had cut his job to three days a week and was working on a book about commercial fishing on the coast of B.C. (published most successfully in 1993 as *Fishing for a Living*) and articles for commercial fishing magazines. He also wrote a book for children about a seine boat called *The Suzie A*, which was published in 1991. Maria was working on a project to teach her Chilcotin language as part of the school curriculum and was in Vancouver at summer school. Alan spent his summer on the docks researching for his writing. My daughter Ann was by this time at Cornell University in Ithaca, N.Y., working on a Ph.D. in English literature.

Ann wrote a long letter to me in August with details of family visits – she had especially enjoyed a day with "the little Roddy" all to herself, plans to make the garden simple so it wouldn't get out of hand as she got older and her money. "Because of going to town on the furniture refinishing, etc., etc. I got rather overdrawn and saw myself going my mother's route. But it's all square now – all I have to do is scare myself and I stop spending."

In September, Joyce and Philip Pope came again from England to stay with Ann. In October, she drove to Williams Lake, for a happy visit with Alan and Maria, and then back for a couple of days with Mary in Victoria. Alan wrote me of her visit: "It was a fine success. The leaves were still on the trees and the Cariboo was looking its best, the children were properly deferential (in their own way), and Maria thought Mother was wonderful for getting me to clean out the cupboards in the guest room."

Later that month Ann went to the dedication of John Daly Park at Garden Bay on the Sechelt Peninsula. John Daly was the husband of Edith Iglauer, a writer friend whose lively company Ann particularly enjoyed. "... the chums were spawning thick in the stream – I planted a birch from here. The principal speaker, head of the Salmon Enhancement programme had Daddy everywhere in his talk and so did several others ..." Ann made a gift of a red rhododendron to the town – it was getting too big and Fred Coupal, who often helped in the garden, filled the hole with "my good compost." (Fred's grandmother, Mary Blaney, used to stay with Ann and Roddy when she came over from Church House on the Indian Reserve on Stuart Island northeast of Quadra, and his mother, Mavis, looked after my children when I first went to Toronto and was a devoted friend of Ann's.)

The University Women's Club was meeting at the house that week. "Mavis [Hudson] is coming for lunch and then I'm going downtown. I'm having little quavers of guilt about not having more private guests because I hate cooking so. I have my church group Monday nights [adults studying the Catholic catechism prior to joining the church]." A few days later Ann was "taking a C.W.L.er [Catholic Women's League] and the Women's Centre Secretary to lunch so they can amalgamate their work for a Transition House (without me)." The arthritis/rheumatism kept Ann alternating between good and bad days all through that winter.

In the spring of 1985 came news via Edith Iglauer Daly that the B.C. Book Award Society was naming their new award for the "best book of the year" after Roddy. This award, called the Roderick Haig-Brown Regional Prize, continues and is given annually to the book that contributes most to the understanding of British Columbia.

The other new arrival that spring was Christopher Haig Ross, Ann's second great-grandchild, born to granddaughter Charlotte Livingston on May 26. In a letter accompanying Robert Louis Stevenson's *A Child's Garden of Verses* for me to take to Christopher, Ann said: "The garden now has matured as Daddy planned and has had a sensational season for flowers ... A terrible lot of work and money, but so incredibly beautiful. The richness of my life is chiefly people with the garden as base. Last week started with a dinner for staff and board of John Howard at Gourmet-by-the-Sea; many former teachers at John Young's and other 'bleeding hearts' that I love dearly. They put us out at 12:15. Next day I had Mary Roberts for lunch. Next Phyllis R. came for coffee and I went to June P.'s evening birthday. Next morning at 9 – too early for me, I went to an estuary symposium that David Brown organized. Joe Painter was great. And that afternoon the monthly native gathering was a sports day and Mass for the Bishop's anniversary because he chose to spend it with us. Sunday I had Anthony Netboy, his daughter and Van Egan for lunch, the garden club in the afternoon and a lovely Italian Lorenzi family birthday party in the evening." Another page of such news, and "STOP IT," wrote Ann, "she doesn't want to hear any more." Actually I did, but it was sometimes hard to absorb it all, there was so much. A postscript on the next letter told of a John Steinbeck disciple coming "with a list of Roddy's books that Steinbeck had."

At the end of August Ann wrote of visits from the family through the summer – John and I had been in June. At the end of September Christopher Pope came with his wife, Sylvia, and Ann gave a dinner party. Christopher was one of Roddy's cousins and, as the eldest great-grandson of Alfred Pope, chairman of the board of the family brewery in England.

The fall of 1985 was a University of British Columbia year for the family. Mary was taking a Certificate in Special Education. Celie, who had already spent the summer at UBC, settled in with her children to complete her M.A. Vickie was also at UBC completing her degree in education, and William and James were with her. Alan was keeping his job in Williams Lake part-time and commuting to Kamloops where Maria was in the teacher education program Celie had coordinated for seven years. Their daughters, Helen and Linda, were with her – Helen at school and Linda sometimes spending the week in Williams Lake with Alan. Mary's elder daughter Celia was at Queen's University in Ontario where she took a B.A. in American History and, later, an M.A. as well, after getting a degree in education from the University of Toronto. Her son Desmond was at Camosun College in Victoria starting a B.A. which he later completed at Malaspina College in Nanaimo.

In a quiet moment that winter my mother wrote me on the subject of reading, so much a part of all our lives in the family: "I don't quite like to hear you say you've been reading more than you should. I still hear my mother say: 'How you can sit here and read when this room looks like this.' But she did it herself and, if I hadn't, I could never have been a librarian or have known about many things that have come in handy. But I needn't worry – if we're like that we'll do it – but we might as well enjoy it."

In the spring of 1986 Ann hired "Campbell River's best gardener," Marcy Prior, to help her. In the same letter Ann said: "Holy Week is rich and full for me. We even have a seder supper; I love it and feel released and exalted by Easter which now seems to be coming at the end of a long emotional journey." In June both my daughters and my two grandsons were with me in Alberta, which made enough of a critical mass to get Ann to finally visit. She told me later that she thought the house we had built ourselves would be "adequate," but was pleasantly surprised to find it much more than that.

After the summer cycle of visits from family, including Tom Elmore with his wife and children – he was Ann's brother Bucky's younger son – Ann settled into the fall routine of Campbell River friends and organizations, with the University Women's Club and Kingfisher Creek to start, mixed with visits to her children. Mary was back in Victoria teaching; Celie had finished her M.A., was starting a Ph.D. and looking for a publisher for her thesis (which appeared in 1988, titled *Resistance and Renewal: Surviving the Indian Residential School*); and Maria was working on her B.Ed. at UBC, so Alan and the children were in Vancouver, too. Alan's freelance work led him to a job as founding editor of a magazine for commercial fishers called *Westcoast Fisherman*. The magazine was a success and, over the next few years, Alan also developed *Westcoast Logger* and *Westcoast Mariner* for the same company.

In January of 1987, Ann wrote of brief visits from Mary and her daughter Elizabeth, Victoria friends for dinner and "a committee of University women – all fun, I love January. That elusive order in the world seems so close at hand. I've tidied and listed the Safety Deposit box, put away 1986 files, straightened, rearranged, washed and ironed all the table linen, owe only two or three letters – neat ... I've been asked to be on the committee for a dinner in Vancouver for John Fraser [former federal Minister of the Environment] in February, etc." Celie's weakening marriage was ending. By March Ann was deep in the gardening again – the garden was, if possible, a greater pleasure than ever. Ann had arthritis "that knee especially. I go to physio a lot – it helps some but is an awful waste of time, especially since my car [a Volvo bought before Roddy died] is being very temperamental. Mavis took me to a symphony concert yesterday. I went to the movie *The Mission* with the Roberts ... I think the azaleas will be perfect for the Open House ... I've just talked to Glen; somehow losing Geoff [Andrew] made me fear I'd suddenly lose everyone. But she and Ed are fine – just like me – wonderful gardens, no energy. Phyl Rossiter is being wonderful to me.

"I am fascinated by the summary of Ann's dissertation. [My daughter was just finishing her Ph.D.] One should read all those books. I should think being a Marxist would be logical in this consumer age. It's being a Christian that's tough. Last Sunday I had the Unitarian minister from Victoria for tea – he loves Daddy's books – gave me a copy of a sermon he had just preached on them in Courtenay."

Ann bought a new car in May – so frugal that she didn't even have a radio put in, but practical, too, in that she bought a Toyota Camry, considered a very good buy at the time. In a May letter to me she commented on a *New Yorker* article about a Catholic cardinal that I had sent her just after her seventy-ninth birthday and said: "A funny by-product was the aside that cardinals over 80 can't vote for the Pope. When they put that in I thought, 'Oh good that they should get rid of those old mossbacks.' Now I think: 'What do you mean, I couldn't vote for the Pope? Why – why, I'm fine.' Although at times I think I couldn't lift my arm to drop a black ball – or a white one – into the urn."

Mavis Hudson was "very, very ill ... I go daily." Mavis died in just a few weeks and Ann was now without that great comfort of old age, the person you have known forever with whom you can be completely relaxed and comfortable.

In July, when the announcement was finally made that there would be a national park in the Queen Charlotte Islands, my old boyfriend Thor Peterson hired a helicopter and flew Ann and John Fraser to Windy Bay to join such friends as environmentalists Colleen McCrory and David Suzuki in a small celebration. Suzuki told me later that one of his images of the day was the sight of his father and my mother deep in conversation strolling among the trees and moss. Mother was so excited by the trip that she called just to tell me about it.

In a letter shortly afterwards she wrote of garden problems. "Fred is cutting the lawn after an upsetting overgrowth – trying to make fertilizer, help, weather come together – an inevitable phase of Above Tide. In spite of deer attacks, the roses are rather great ... I'm also awaiting the arrival of a young battered woman who's at the hospital. (Rumour that they may name the transition house after me.) And I'm getting gold shots which much help my arthritis." They did name the transition house Ann Elmore House for all Ann's years of work with women in crises of one sort or another, and for the haven she had provided in so many emergencies. She was particularly honored and pleased at the recognition.

Then in mid-August, at seventy-nine, Ann suddenly had to have a hysterectomy because of cancer. Her daughters took it in turn to be with her in Campbell River, and then to stay with her in Vancouver while she went through the obligatory three weeks of daily radiation treatments.

Ann continued to have checkups every three, and then four, months, which she actually enjoyed because it was an excuse to visit her Vancouver children. The stress of a major operation, followed by radiation, took a while to get over; theoretically Ann was taking things easier that winter of 1987-88. But in November she was going daily to a mission at church "that I like because I see everybody twice a day for five days and the priest and the married couple that are doing it are young and intelligent." And one day the previous week she "had lunch with June, tea with Sally, a bit of shopping and went to a school play – dandy." Not very slow! Finally, "Someone just came in to bring me a beautiful card about a seat named for me at the theatre." The old movie theater was being refurbished for stage presentations and friends had made a donation in Ann's name.

In January, while writing post-Christmas letters, Ann was "doing the Audubon bird count, based on my feeder. But after five days of very clear, very cold, I'm afraid the number is down from even a week ago." Ann went to the annual meeting of the local chapter of the Cystic Fibrosis Society near the end of January. "And bliss – Alan is doing something in Comox Monday and Tuesday and will spend the night here."

In March, Ann was back in the hospital because of a blood clot in her leg. She didn't tell us until afterwards and admitted that she had been glad of the necessary rest while they got her blood thinned with warfarin, which she always referred to as "rat poison." A few days later some fifty people, including Colleen McCrory and Leonora Towell, aged eighty-five, who stayed with Ann the night before, and Ann's wonderful gardener, Marcy Prior, went to Strathcona Park to be arrested in a protest against mining. Ann admitted to being relieved that her doctor, Bruce Wood, who was a prime mover of the Friends of Strathcona group, told her she couldn't go. "I have to remind myself that I've only been out of hospital six days – I'm tired." The group of about fifty protesters who were arrested at Strathcona were later acquitted – Ann was there in the courtroom with them that day and had supported them in any way she could in the intervening time.

On May 3, Ann's four children gathered for the weekend to celebrate her eightieth birthday. We knew that was the best present we could give her – just the four of us with no spouses or children and no teasing hard enough to make anyone cry (a bad habit that we seem to have outgrown, actually). The garden has one of its peak blooms in early May with magnolia, azaleas and apple blossom, as well as the pink rhododendrons and yellow primroses we brought in to wind among the silver candlesticks on the birthday dinner table. As I remember, ours was the fourth birthday cake of the week – the celebrations among Ann's friends had been copious.

In September the University Women's Club gave Ann their Woman of the Year Award. "Pleasant, a bit embarrassing." In the same letter Ann wrote: "We had an astonishment here. Friends of Strathcona were having an annual gathering a week ago Saturday and two days before the gov't. announced that there would be no new mining and no logging in the Park. Needless to say, it was a heavenly gathering even though it was held in one of the devastated parts of the Park." Ann was doing the prescribed exercises for arthritis "counting in Italian, which makes them a little less boring."

In October Ann went to the Cystic Fibrosis Society of B.C. annual meeting and dinner; then to a Friends of Schizophrenics meeting and found that a support group needed a place to meet, so the group was to come to her every second week. "I cease to be surprised that I know so many schizophrenics when I find that they're one out of 100 births, CF is one out 1200. I had the John Howard AGM about two weeks ago and it was a small but lovely party. The Kingfisher Creek AGM and Open House will be next Sunday." Ann was also gathering the few walnuts the crows had left, and listening to Italian broadcasts on a Vancouver radio station. And the people converting to Catholicism continued to have the weekly Monday meetings at Above Tide.

In early January of 1989, Ann found, finished and sent me a needlepoint cushion she had been making from a kit Roddy had got her from *The New Yorker*. Ann started doing needlepoint after she retired and gradually found that her eyes wouldn't stand up to all the reading she wanted to do. (She was reading Sophia Tolstoy's diaries that winter: "1042 pp. – those Russian temperaments!") She spent the quiet evenings at home listening to "Ideas" on CBC Radio and stitching in her comfortable chair in the warm kitchen. During a post-Christmas visit John and I made, John had drawn plans for a new back porch. In March Ann reported that it had been built and a Community Work Service man (people on parole, supervised by the John Howard Society, often did work around the place) fixed up the raspberries on one side of the porch and Ann did the herb garden on the other side.

In June Roddy's sister Valerie, with her friend Anne Vickery, came to stay for a few days. Roddy's sister Joan had died a couple of years earlier, and Valerie, who was now retired from her job as head of probation services at Holloway Prison in London, felt she could make a long-planned trip to see all the Canadian relatives. Ann marshalled all her various forms of help and entertained as she had always done, with good food, comfortable beds and a lovely garden.

Later in the summer, Ann was organizing the library at the Transition House: "Such a relief when they asked for a volunteer to do it in the paper because I always thought I should do something for them but couldn't think what." Along with news of the summer garden and friends, Ann wrote: "A Dr. Larson, a Japanese-American lawyer, a Spanish one, three fish technicians from Oregon have been among the Roddy pilgrims. And I have bridal parties for photographs about every other Saturday. They're like fresh crops of flowers." And granddaughter Ann came from Texas where she was now teaching English literature at the University of Texas at Austin: "Fabulous for me, she will have told you perhaps how it was for her."

After much urging, Ann flew to visit me in Alberta in November. At Christmas, Celie's children were with their father in Kamloops, so Celie came to Campbell River and then went with Ann to Mary's in Victoria. Ann went back to Campbell River for New Year's and then to Vancouver, where Celie and her children and Mary's Elizabeth met her and took her to tea at Alan's new house in New Westminster. "I found it perfect, just as he had described it. And Maria had done a wonderful job of pruning and cleaning up in the well-shrubbed and treed garden. Ever since, I see processions of grandchildren every time I shut my eyes." After a routine checkup at the Cancer Clinic, Ann came home accompanied by Gwenith Bowker, who stayed for a few days. About as much family as can be crammed into one Christmas season.

A Washington filmmaker was making a picture for German television based on Roddy's *A River Never Sleeps*. He came and went and Ann "really liked him and he had proper respect for Daddy." In March the town of Campbell River asked Ann to outline a tree policy. Alan came and drove her up and down the streets, and Ann listed all the best trees that were growing on public land so that they would not be casually cut down, as is so common in growing towns.

In May, Ann's brother Danny was to come from Washington, D.C., to make a long-delayed visit. This visit inspired Ann and Danny's eldest niece, Garby, to declare an Elmore family reunion. Most of their brother Bucky's family lived in Washington State so had not too far to come. It was decided to have the gathering in Victoria because both Mary and Garby's brother Bruce lived there and had large houses. Also, the annual B.C. Book Awards was to be there on that same weekend, and Ann was, as usual, presenting the Haig-Brown Prize. Danny and his wife, Myrtle, came first to Campbell River, where I joined them and with some Campbell River friends, we celebrated Ann's eighty-second birthday. Then we all drove to Victoria, taking a little ferry across Saanich Inlet to Brentwood Bay where Danny had come from Seattle to school so many years before. The weather was beautiful, the Elmores filled two large tables at the dinner, the Western Canada Wilderness Committee won the Haig-Brown Prize for their book on the great trees of the Carmanah Valley on the west coast of Vancouver Island and, after a huge Sunday brunch at Mary's, we all went off declaring the gathering a great success.

Several times during the reunion – our family had never done such a thing before – people said how nice it was that we were together and it wasn't even a wedding or a funeral. Little did we know then that many of us would be back together again a month later for Ann's funeral. Shortly after the reunion Ann developed another blood clot in her leg, which her doctor diagnosed as a possible sign of a cancer flare-up and sent her to the Cancer Clinic in Vancouver. There it was soon decided that it was not, but Ann was sent to the nearby Vancouver General Hospital until the clot cleared. She stayed there a couple of weeks, visited daily by one or another of the Vancouver part of the family. Mary and Bernie came from Victoria on the weekend. On May 31, Ann was told she could go home. Mary's daughter Elizabeth, now studying at UBC, and Celie's son Roddy, whom Elizabeth was babysitting (she often took care of her cousins), went with Ann at her request. When they got home, Ann went straight to bed, so fast, said Elizabeth, that she was settled before Elizabeth finished thanking the friend who had met them in Nanaimo. After a very uncomfortable night, Ann went to the Campbell River Hospital, and Elizabeth called Mary to come up from Victoria. Mary came right away and was with Ann when she died early next morning on Mary's birthday, June 2, 1990.

So we gathered again. Twenty-three of us spent most of a week in the house that had been the center of our lives for so long – a clearing house of family news, a place we all knew we could fall back on if for some reason the lives we were making out in the world should fall apart, a place of comfort and security and fun and relaxation and memories. We decided that since our mother had not been able to spend the last night of her life in her own bed, as she would have preferred, we would have her spend the night before her funeral at home. And so we did. Friends came during the evening and then her four children sat with her in the study in pairs through the night, with grandchildren coming and going, sometimes with their sleeping bags. Marcy Prior came and cut flowers from the garden in the morning rain, and the children carried them across the field to put on their Grandmother's and Great-grandmother's coffin at the church. Many friends of all ages spoke eloquently and movingly of all Ann meant to them during the service, and more than we could count filled the house after the funeral.

Ann's funeral was one of the last in St. Patrick's Church. The church across the road in the corner of the barn field was to close the following week. The growing Catholic community had built a much larger church in the center of town; Ann had not been looking forward to having to drive there. We couldn't help wondering if there had not been some choice in Ann's timing. We'd had the reunion, the church was moving – why not go now? At the end of the week we scattered Ann's ashes in the garden where she had scattered Roddy's – to follow his into the ground water and the river and down to the sea.

Epilogue

Above Tide, the family house at Campbell River, has been beautifully restored by the Heritage Properties of B.C. site manager Kevin Brown – wooden houses on the Pacific Coast sink relatively quickly into the ground and need a lot of upkeep. The spirit of Ann and Roddy's original intentions for the place is being realized in the variety of activities offered there. The steady stream of guests goes on, too; Haig-Brown House is also a bed and breakfast. Marcy Prior continues to keep the garden growing in the same spirit that evolved over the fifty years Ann and Roddy loved it.

Kingfisher Creek winds through the fields under the alders and carries a run of coho salmon, as will almost any small coastal stream left in peace (or restored). Development on its headwaters, which is being carefully orchestrated, will soon lead to more water in the creek and, we hope, more salmon.

Celia and Alan have both won the Roderick Haig-Brown Regional Prize – Celia for *Resistance and Renewal*, her book on the Indian residential school experience; and Alan for *The Fraser*, with photographer Rick Blacklaws, a journey down the mighty river that is so important to the salmon, and to Roddy and Alan – to name only two of all the people of British Columbia.

I am often asked what my father would think of whatever current or continuing ecological disaster we have brought upon ourselves. My first thought is a silent, "I'm glad he isn't here to see it." But my answer is that, if you read his books, you will know what he would think. He warned of the consequences of our rush toward "progress" from the age of sixteen when he wrote a letter to an English paper about the effect of the run-off from tarred roads on the streams of his native county. And he never stopped pointing out the hazards of our behavior.

Books by Roderick Haig-Brown
(with date of first publication)

Silver - 1931

Pool and Rapid - 1932

Panther (Ki-yu) - 1934

The Western Angler - 1939

Return to the River - 1941

Timber - 1942

Starbuck Valley Winter - 1943

A River Never Sleeps - 1946

Saltwater Summer - 1948

On the Highest Hill - 1949

Measure of the Year - 1950

Fisherman's Spring - 1951

Canada's Pacific Salmon - 1952

Divine Discontent - 1953

Fisherman's Winter - 1954

Mounted Police Patrol - 1954

Captain of the Discovery - 1956

Fisherman's Summer - 1959

The Farthest Shores - 1960

The Living Land - 1961

Fur and Gold - 1962

The Whale People - 1962

A Primer of Fly Fishing - 1964

Fisherman's Fall - 1964

The Salmon - 1974

Bright Waters, Bright Fish - 1980

Alison's Fishing Birds - 1980

Woods and River Tales (ed. VHB) - 1981

The Master and His Fish (ed. VHB) - 1981

Writings and Reflections (ed. VHB) - 1982

To Know a River (ed. VHB) - 1996